John Chartres: Mystery Man of the Treaty

John Chartres

Mystery Man of the Treaty

Brian P. Murphy

IRISH ACADEMIC PRESS

This book was set for
IRISH ACADEMIC PRESS
Kill Lane, Blackrock, Co. Dublin, Ireland
and in North America for
IRISH ACADEMIC PRESS
c/o ISBS, 5804 NE Hassalo Street, Portland, OR 97213.

© Brian P. Murphy 1995

A catalogue record for this title
is available from the British Library.

ISBN 0–7165–2543–7

Printed in Great Britain
by Cambridge University Press, Cambridge

To my confrères at Douai Abbey, England,
and Glenstal Abbey, Ireland, whose help at different times
and in diverse ways made this work possible

In view of the remarkable, if not prominent, part played by Mr Chartres from 1917 to 1927, one may hope that full justice will be done to his memory. Hence 'if it were done when 'tis done, then 'twere well it were done quickly'.

Henry Mangan, 1935

His [John Chartres] Sinn Féin sympathies had passed unnoticed, and his last-minute selection caused surprise. Even to the Irish Delegates, some of whom knew nothing of him personally, he remained something of a mystery man throughout.

Frank Pakenham, 1935

Contents

Acknowledgments

This life of John Chartres began as a footnote; developed into an article; and finally has taken shape as a book. The reason for writing the book is explained in the Introduction. Here it is both fitting and necessary to express thanks to those who made the book possible. The staff of all libraries, despite the tremendous pressures that they work under, was always unfailingly patient and helpful. For permission to publish original manuscripts and for their assistance I thank the following: the Franciscan Fathers and Brendan MacGiollachoille at Dún Mhuire, Killiney—the depository of the Eamon de Valera Papers and some of the papers of George Gavan Duffy; the House of Lords Records Office; the National Archives of Ireland where Aideen Ireland's expertise in the Foreign Affairs section was greatly appreciated; the National Library of Ireland; the Public Records Office in England; Trinity College Dublin; and University College Dublin Archives where the advice of Seamus Helferty was of great value. Grateful acknowledgement is tendered to the trustees of the Mulcahy collection, and to the families donating the Mary MacSwiney and Hugh Kennedy collections which have been placed in the UCD archive. The library staff of Mary Immaculate College, Limerick University, under the direction of John Power and John Eustace continued to provide invaluable assistance—not only with their microfilm collection of past newspapers and journals, but also in many other ways.

In tracing the early origins of John Chartres and other basic information I was greatly helped by many librarians and archivists. Among them I would like to thank Patricia McCarthy, Archivist of the Cork Archives Institute and Tim Cadogan, Reference Librarian of the Cork County Library; Captain P.H. Starling, archivist of the R.A.M.C. Historical Museum; Mary O'Doherty, archivist of the Royal College of Surgeons in Ireland; Dermot J.M. Sherlock, Recorder of the Alumni, University of Dublin; Jonathan N. Armstrong, Librarian of King's Inn Library; Bruce Bradley, S.J., Headmaster of Clongowes Wood College; J.C.C. Sworder, Old Wellingtonian Society; Fiona Butler, Special Collection of University of London Library; Melanie

Aspey, Group Records Manager of News International; Major R.W.M. Shaw of the Intelligence Corps Museum, Kent; and Mrs J.E. Edgell, Librarian and Keeper of the Records of The Honourable Society of The Middle Temple. The last named, in particular, spent a great deal of time unravelling some of the complexities of Chartres's time at the Middle Temple. The Italian Cultural Institute in Dublin and Michel Fuchs of the University of Nice helped me with information concerning Annie Vivanti, the wife of John Chartres. Gerry Cronin helped me by translating documents and books that were written in Irish. The help of Felix Larkin, Brian Spain and my brother, Peter Murphy, was also appreciated. Without the assistance of these people and these institutions it would have been impossible to tell the story of John Chartres in any detail.

Other people who either had a knowledge of the events surrounding John Chartres, or who had some papers relating to those events provided information that in no small way made the book possible. Mrs Caitlin O'Neill, a cousin of Nancy Wyse Power, allowed me to use a copy of Nancy Power's statement to the Bureau of Military History which included a lengthy account of her time in Berlin with John Chartres. This information was indispensable to my study. Sister Petra Mangan provided me with helpful material concerning her father, Henry Mangan, as did Colm Gavan Duffy concerning his father, George Gavan Duffy. The latter also allowed me to use some manuscript material still in private hands. In like manner the families of the late J.J. O'Kelly, Stephen O'Mara and Dr Patrick McCartan allowed me access to private papers which enabled me to broaden the scope of this work. Dr Julian J. Putkowski provided me with important information concerning John Chartres and the administration of the Ministry of Munitions. Similar detailed advice was received from Professor Keogh of University College Cork concerning John Chartres and his role in Foreign Affairs. In particular he allowed me to read a recently completed thesis on Ireland's diplomatic relationship with Germany by Mervyn O'Driscoll for which I am most grateful. Many members of my own Benedictine Community assisted me greatly: Mark Tierney continued to amaze me by producing from his collection of original papers material that was relevant to my work; and Paul Nash showed much patience and great competence in ensuring that any problem with my word processor was quickly resolved. Without his help the book may well not have reached the printed page. Late in the day I established contact with George Chartres, a descendant of John Chartres and the family genealogist, who clarified many matters and provided important extra details of the Chartres family. The help of all these people added an extra dimension to my study of John Chartres and, taken together with the wealth of unpublished manuscript material that was uncovered in official archives, largely explains how a footnote became a book!

Lastly in the writing of the book I was greatly helped by the advice and knowledge of Professor T.P. O'Neill and his wife Maire. They have both written on this period of history and they not only shared their deep understanding of the past with me, but also they made me aware of various sources of information that proved helpful. Their assistance was of great benefit to me and their encouragement at all times was deeply appreciated. Many others deserve my thanks and I apologize for not mentioning them by name.

Introduction

Most of the books that deal with the Anglo-Irish Treaty of December 1921 contain a photograph of the Irish delegates to the conference. Many of them identify the plenipotentiaries and the secretary: Arthur Griffith, the chairman of the delegation, Michael Collins, Eamon Duggan, Robert Barton, George Gavan Duffy and Erskine Childers, the secretary. There is a seventh man in the photograph and very few books name him. He stands on the extreme right of the photograph, upright, portly and middle aged: he was John Chartres, the second secretary to the conference. Frank Pakenham, in his masterly work on the Treaty, commented that Chartres 'remained something of a mystery man' throughout the Treaty negotiations.[1] He has remained a 'mystery man' to this day. Pakenham, indeed, did reveal more about Chartres than most other books published subsequently, but his efforts to appraise the particular contribution of Chartres have not been improved upon. Despite Pakenham's precision in clarifying the role of the secretaries on the Irish side, the common assumption is that there was only one, Erskine Childers. The memory of Chartres is kept alive mainly in anti-Treaty circles, as witnessed by the evidence contained in the book *Survivors*.[2] The contention of these republicans is that Chartres was in British Intelligence and may well have been acting in the British interest during the Treaty talks. Some may find this suggestion fanciful, but Pakenham accepted the fact that Chartres had, indeed, 'served during the War in the Intelligence Branch of the Ministry of Munitions.'[3] Strange as it may appear this aspect of Chartres' life was common knowledge at the time of the Treaty talks. The *Irish Independent* of 11 October 1921 reported that 'Mr Chartres was, in 1915, Chief of the Intelligence Section of the War Office Armaments Output Committee. He was transferred in the same year to the Ministry of Munitions.'[4] Many questions are raised by this revelation: had Chartres left British Intelligence when he assumed the role of secretary to the conference? and how did he come to assume such an important role on the Irish side?

An attempt was made to shed light on these questions by Henry Mangan in a series of articles in the *Irish Independent* of October 1935. Mangan had participated in one of the financial meetings that were part of the 1921 Treaty conferences and had met Chartres. His articles remain an invaluable source of information but they raise as many questions as answers. Mangan concluded his investigation into Chartres with the view that 'we have, however, heard too little, yet also too much, and what we have heard may, or may not, be too true. But if the Chartres problem be left where it is, to the tender mercies of callous historians, they will not be deterred from their grim inquests by scoffing catch cries of 'Fantastic!' 'Melodramatic!' 'Absurd!' The auditors of history are not content, like their commercial confreres, to be watchdogs only; they develop the instincts of the blood-hound, and will carry on their pursuits for years on end amid the dusty vouchers of forgotten events ... In view of the remarkable, if not prominent, part played by Mr Chartres from 1917 to 1927, one may hope that full justice will be done to his memory. Hence,

> If it were done when 'tis done, then 'twere well
> It were done quickly,

while people who know things may still live, for the documentary evidence may prove but scanty.'[5] This study of John Chartres was carried out with Mangan's injunction in mind. Fortunately some people were still alive who, at second hand, could talk of Chartres and his influence; and most surprisingly a vast amount of documentary evidence has survived from which it has been possible to trace a significant outline of his life and work. While mystery still surrounds some aspects of his career, and while gaps appear at certain stages of his life, the following story may be told.

1

Early Life: the British Connection

John Smith Chartres was born in England on 5 October 1862 of Irish parents, and his birth was registered at Birkenhead, Wirrall. His father, also John Smith Chartres, was employed as a staff surgeon in the British Army, and his mother was Margaret Henry, the daughter of Dr Henry of Clones, county Monaghan. Their marriage took place on 17 June 1858. His father was born in Dublin in 1828 and entered Trinity College in 1842 at the age of fourteen. He had been privately tutored and was a fee-paying student. His father, Richard (1794–1862), was described as 'Generosus,' which in the quaint official language of the time indicated that he was a gentleman. The Chartres family certainly had a good claim to be recognised as gentlemen.[1]

They came from a distinguished line of French Huguenots which had participated in the Crusades when Christendom was united. The most famous member of the family was Renaud de Chartres, Archbishop of Rheims and Chancellor of France, who crowned Charles VII King of France in the presence of Joan of Arc in 1429. From the early years of the Reformation the family had supported the Protestant Huguenots and their chateau at Cherville was burnt as a result. In consequence the Chartres family was dispersed throughout Ireland and Scotland in the seventeenth century.

The branch of the family to which John Chartres belonged had settled in Cork, near Bandon, in about 1650. In the nineteenth century some 226 acres of this land in county Cork was still in the possession of the family, but the family seat was at Granitefield, county Dublin. Two members of the family, William and Richard, the grandfather of our subject, described themselves in the early years of the century as having a residence at Granitefield, and it is possible that the estate had been divided between them.[2] The estate and the family pedigree fully merited the title 'gentleman', but the amount of land available did not enable the family to be gentlemen of leisure. John Smith Chartres, senior, had to work hard in order to make his way in the world. His path in the ranks of the Army Medical Corps was long and arduous.

While enrolled at Trinity John Smith Chartres, senior, received a licenti-
ate from the Royal College of Surgeons, Ireland, in 1850 which gave him a
qualification in medicine. Thus qualified, he secured employment in the
Medical Corps of the British Army in May 1852 as an Acting Assistant Surgeon. In that year he had a residence at 30 Great Charles Street, near
Mountjoy Square, in Dublin with his brother Archibald (1823–1904). He
had another older brother, Richard (1825–1905), who was a wine merchant,
and a younger brother and sister. Their father, Richard, the grandfather of
John Chartres, junior, is also listed as a resident at 30 Great Charles Street in
1854, and the house remained in the name of the Chartres family until 1860. [3]
In the summer of 1857 John Chartres, senior, received his BA and MA degrees from Dublin University, and in the same year he qualified as a member of the London Society of Apothecaries. On 18 December 1857 he was
appointed a Staff Surgeon in the British Army. He received various appointments as Staff Surgeon, one of which led to service in Abysinnia for part of
1867/1868, before he qualified as a doctor in Dublin in 1870, receiving the
degrees MB and MD. He was then appointed Surgeon Major with the 8th
Hussars on 9 May 1872. [4]

John Chartres, junior, spent some of his early years at the Curragh and
in Dundalk, where his father's regiment was based. When his father died in
London on 31 October 1875 at Clifton House, Hampstead, he left effects to
the value of £100. It would appear that not only were the connections of
John Chartres with Ireland broken by the sudden death of his father, but
also that the family encountered a period of financial hardship. [5]

He entered Wellington College, Berkshire, a school with a strong army
connection, in September 1876 as a boarder and left in 1879. He was assigned to Hardinge house and was listed in the Mathematical, rather than in
the Classical, School. [6] He left school at a relatively early age and continued
his studies while working at other assignments. He matriculated at London
University in June 1881 and began teaching at Glenside, Holywood, county
Down, soon afterwards.

He was admitted as a student of the King's Inn, Dublin, on 25 October
1884, and on 7 January 1885 he was admitted to membership of the Inn of
the Middle Temple, London. Law was his career option at that time and he
passed his Intermediate Laws at London University in 1885, preparing for
these exams by private study. [7] While a member of the Middle Temple he
paid fees, which would normally indicate residence in London, for the Hilary
term (the January term) of 1885; for some of 1891 and 1892; for most of
1902 and 1903, and Christmas of 1904; and for the Hilary term of 1908, in
which term he was called to the Bar of England and Wales on 27 January. [8]

During this time he is said to have studied in Germany, but his main
preoccupation was to find work. In 1891 he was living at 1 Upper Bedford

Place in Russell Square, London, and was looking for employment. Approaches for a position with *The Times* were unsuccessful. However, in 1902 he married Anna [Annie] Vivanti. She was a celebrated woman in her own right and of cosmopolitan background. Born in London in 1868 of an Italian father and a German mother, she had studied in Italy and had sung in the opera in New York. She had also travelled widely in Europe, America and Africa. From the early 1890s she had established a reputation as a writer of poetry, plays and novels.[9] In 1891, while still a young woman, she had written *Marion, artista di Caffe Conorto*, and in 1900 she published a play, *La Rosa Azzurra*. It is not known how Chartres and Vivanti met, but marriage to a woman with such a background introduced Chartres to a far broader experience of the world than most of his contemporaries. One daughter, Violet, was born into the Chartres family, but the marriage itself, certainly after the 1916 period for which some faint evidence exists, was lived out in an unconventional fashion. For the most part Chartres and Vivanti lived lives apart and came together only on rare occasions—occasions, however, that appeared amicable and agreeable.

At the time of his marriage Chartres secured regular employment. He was called for an interview for a vacancy on *The Times* in 1902. His address was then 3 Bedford Place, and he may possibly have received an appointment at that time. He certainly became the first head of the Intelligence Department of *The Times* in 1904, a job which was created in connection with providing information for the *Encyclopaedia Britannica*. At that time, it should be noted, the columns of *The Times* used the word Intelligence to denote News; for example, it was common to have such headings as 'Intelligence from abroad'. The project Chartres was appointed to was a new one, and the department was responsible for maintaining cuttings files, indexing and providing a reference library. Chartres worked on this project and for *The Times* itself until 1914. While working on *The Times* he occupied chambers, for professional or residential purposes, at 3 Middle Temple Lane in 1904 and at Fountain Court in the Middle Temple in 1909. He also lived for a time at Mardock Lodge, Hertfordshire. In 1915 he published a book on the legal requirements of the Workmen's Compensation Act. At about this time he was also on the staff of the *Daily Graphic*, making contributions as an economic correspondent. The story was told that he had devised a way of breaking the bank of Monte Carlo, and that his wife was enjoying some success in an effort to put the theory into practice. When Chartres intervened their luck changed and the gains were lost, forcing him to go to America 'to repair his ravaged fortunes.'[10] Whatever the truth of this story it was certainly a fact that the pattern of his life was suddenly and dramatically changed by the outbreak of war in 1914.

As soon as the Ministry of Munitions was set up on 9 June 1915 Chartres became one of the ten Secretary Assistants in the Intelligence and Record branch of G section which was concerned with Requirements and Statistics. The Director of the Section was W.T. Layton.[11] In 1917 an office of the Department of Munitions was opened up at 32 Nassau Street, Dublin, to co-ordinate Ireland's contribution to the war effort, notably that of the munitions factory at Arklow, but there were also questions concerning copper mining in Avoca and deposits of bauxite elsewhere in Ireland.[12] Chartres may well have been connected with this office as he was in Ireland at this time and his name does not appear on the list for British departments. By October 1918, however, he had become a Section Director in the Labour Intelligence and Statistics Section which was based in London.[13]

Weekly reports were made on the Labour situation in England with particular regard to subversive groups, and Chartres was personally responsible for some of them. A report on Soviet Organization and Republicanism made on 16 November 1920 carried his name. It detailed the attempts made to draw discharged soldiers into the Shop Stewards movement and was one of many reliable and well compiled reports. Other similar reports with which he was involved related to the Shop Stewards movement and the Labour situation in Great Britain.[14] After the war he joined the Ministry of Labour and became a Principal Officer of the Secretariat and General Branch, which was situated at 8 Richmond Terrace, London. That was for the years 1918 and 1919. In 1920 he was transferred to the Irish Department of the Ministry Labour, which was based in Lord Edward Street, Dublin, where he was one of the Section Chiefs. There was also a training and appointment office located in Merrion Square. Chartres also retained a house in London.[15] Despite the rather grand name of 'Section Chief', it should be noted that Chartres was not the senior man in his department.

There were three men above him in the Dublin office. The senior Secretary's salary was £1,500 per annum; the two under secretaries were on a salary scale of *c.*£700–900; and Chartres, therefore, must have been on a lower salary scale. Moreover, the intelligence work he was engaged in would appear to have centred around civilian loyalties rather than espionage in an international context. His namesake, or almost so, Brigadier John Charteris, with whom he should not be confused, was head of battle order intelligence (MI3); Brigadier General G.K. Cockerill, later to become involved in peace initiatives in Ireland in 1920, was director of Special Intelligence (MO5); Admiral 'Blinker' Hall was head of naval intelligence and code breaking (ID25); and several others headed more important intelligence agencies. However, although Chartres was not in such senior intelligence departments, he was in a position of influence and trust in a most sensitive Ministry during the war years. The question then remains as to how John Chartres managed to act in such a responsible position as a British civil servant in 1920 and the next year was able to act as secretary for the rebel Irish government in the Treaty negotiations.

The Sinn Féin Connection

Chartres has given his own version as to how and when he became involved in the Irish cause. Writing of Arthur Griffith, he said, 'personally I became acquainted with him first in 1917. Passing through Dublin to the West I called at the office of *Nationality*.'[1] He asked for an interview with Griffith but was not able to see him on that occasion. Griffith was too busy and three weeks later he was still reluctant to meet. Chartres explained that he was on his way back to London and simply wanted to talk to 'a real Irishman'. Two and a half hours later, after a long conversation in one of Griffith's favourite resorts, they parted in Grafton Street. They exchanged views on Irish aspirations and English characteristics, and Chartres expressed his desire 'to be of service in the conflict then thickening with England'. Griffith suggested that Chartres write for *Nationality*. 'These were the days,' Chartres recalled, 'when Ashe was dying slowly in the hands of the English and the first article I sent over was turned into the leader which appeared in *Nationality* on Thomas Ashe's death.' Chartres continued to send articles and notes every Sunday even after Griffith was arrested in May 1918.

The editorial on Ashe appeared on 6 October 1917. It was a trenchant and well argued attack on the policy of the English Government in Ireland. Chartres excused the minor officials responsible for the death of Ashe, and declared that the English Government

> is responsible for Thomas Ashe's death, just as that Government was responsible for the shooting of sixteen Irishmen after Easter Week ... Mr Lloyd George, the bountiful dispenser of breakfasts and patronage to Messrs Redmond, Dillon and Devlin, is, with his Government, the cause of Thomas Ashe's death.[2]

Chartres made the point that Ashe was charged with 'hypothetical treason'—that under certain circumstances he would call out the Volunteers as he had done in 1916. Exactly the same charge, Chartres maintained, that could have been made four years ago against Sir Edward Carson, Bonar Law and Sir F.E. Smith. Carson had said that 'we intend, if the Home Rule Bill is put upon the Statute Book, to take over the government for ourselves,' and he had encouraged his followers 'to break every law that was possible'. Chartres then compared the treatment of Ashe with that of Carson and his associates. 'The reason alleged for not suppressing utterances of this kind was that they had only a contingent application,' Chartres explained; and then continued,

> Mr Ashe was arrested, tried by courtmartial, and sent to jail as a common criminal for making a contingent declaration less emphatic than any one of those we have quoted. The Government that prosecuted him comprised the man who made the declarations we quote, and with him Mr Bonar Law and Sir F.E. Smith, who made similar declarations. Thomas Ashe was done to death, and Sir Edward Carson, Sir F.E. Smith and Mr Bonar Law were rewarded with high office for committing a like offence. This is English government in Ireland in 1917. That has been English government in Ireland for 300 years. If Ireland's heart is aflame with bitter indignation, yet let Ireland's brain be cold and steady. For it is only an Ireland with a brain of ice that can deliver itself from the Power that slew Thomas Ashe.

Extraordinary words from a man who was still working in the Intelligence Section of the Ministry of Munitions; but words that accurately convey the mood in Ireland after Ashe's death.

Following the executions after the Easter Rising of 1916, the nationalist movement was re-organised in 1917. The first bye-election for the ideals of the 1916 Rising had been won by Count Plunkett in Roscommon in February 1917. Several other elections were won for the same ideals during the year, and the Irish Party was losing support and credibility faced by the more radical demand of the Irish people. The British government, particularly after its pro-Unionist stand at the Irish Convention, was perceived as an enemy of the new Irish aspirations. Following the death of Ashe, the nationalist movement was revived in October 1917 under a new republican Sinn Féin organisation and a reformed Irish Volunteers. De Valera was President of both organisations. Home Rule was no longer seen as a satisfactory solution for Irish problems; the policy to be followed was that of republican Sinn Féin. Chartres had shown that he was in sympathy with these new Irish ideals and aspirations.

Sean T. O'Kelly, who had been an associate of Pearse and who had been an influential figure in both the Gaelic League and the Irish Republican Brotherhood in the years leading up to 1916, came to know Chartres well.

He has given further background on his entry into the Irish national movement. Chartres told O'Kelly that the 1916 Rising had had a dramatic effect on him. 'It gave me a great fright,' he said,

> it shook me from the ground up, when I met my colleagues at supper that night and heard such harsh abuse of Ireland and the treachery of the Irish something woke inside me which had been dormant for a long time. That night I realised that I was not an Englishman but an Irishman. All my sympathy was with Ireland and I decided that I would have to fight for her.[3]

On face value we have a genuine conversion experience. It was this experience that led Chartres to seek an interview with Griffith when he visited Ireland in 1917. O'Kelly noted that, after reading Griffith's essays in *Nationality*, Chartres imitated his style so successfully that quite often Griffith published the essays of Chartres as his own when he was busy electioneering.

O'Kelly first met Chartres through Griffith towards the end of 1917. He found him a complete Englishman in appearance: about five foot nine in height, walking with a little lame step because of a knee injury; wearing clothes of the latest London fashion; and speaking with a professorial Oxford accent. Others have testified to the connection between Griffith and Chartres. Robert Brennan, who was at the centre of Sinn Féin activities after 1916 and who played a major part in the successful 1918 election victory, recalls meeting 'Chartres several times in Griffith's office in Dublin' about this time.[4]

One is faced, therefore, by the strange connection between Chartres, a very English gentleman, and Griffith at a time when Sinn Féin was emerging from the shadows of 1916. Clearly, if the conversion of Chartres was not genuine, his appearance at the centre of Irish nationalist affairs would be potentially damaging. And yet there was another connection which placed Chartres even closer to the very centre of the Irish war effort. That connection was with Michael Collins.

Dr Nancy Power, who worked with Chartres abroad in 1921 and 1922 and who knew him extremely well, stated frankly that Chartres had 'got himself transferred from Dublin to London in the interests of Sinn Féin and trafficked in arms back and forward for Collins. This was while he was still in the British service.' She added that 'both Collins and Griffith knew him quite well.'[5] Here we have the answer to our question concerning the acceptability of Chartres.

An amazing answer! He was accepted by the Irish leaders because he was assisting them with gun-running. Nancy Power related that Michael Collins first met Chartres while visiting London at the end of 1918.[6] This meeting between Collins and Chartres is said to have taken place at the home of Crompton Llewelyn-Davies, Solicitor General to the British Post Office. Collins was in London with Sean T. O'Kelly, Robert Barton, and George Gavan Duffy in order to make representations to President Wilson concerning the Paris Peace Conference. Nothing came of this mission, but Collins is said to have met Chartres at the Llewelyn-Davies house.[7] Others at the house have been identified as Sir James Barrie and Auberon Herbert, both of whom were in British Intelligence, and Moya, the wife of Crompton Llewelyn-Davies, who was in close contact—some have hinted at intimate contact—with Collins in 1921 and 1922. Chartres was known, according to Power, by military men close to Collins, but the nature of his work required absolute secrecy. Such is the picture painted by Nancy Power.

Sean T. O'Kelly corroborates her story. He also stated that Chartres first met Collins in 1918, possibly at the meeting referred to by Power, and that he was taken onto the 'information team' that Collins directed. While not mentioning any involvement with arms, O'Kelly records that Chartres visited hotels and posh clubs in Dublin in order to acquire news about military matters. According to O'Kelly, Chartres performed his task satisfactorily and helpfully, and was 'very friendly' with Michael Collins. Nancy Power also related that in February 1919 a group of Irish Labour leaders visited Chartres in London on their way to an International Conference in Geneva. They had a letter of introduction from Michael Collins which, Nancy Power surmises, might have been a request for Chartres to assist the Labour leaders through his wife in Geneva.

Further evidence of a connection between Collins and Chartres is provided by Robert Brennan. He recalled that soon after the attempt on Lord French's life on 19 December 1919, he was sent on a mission to London by Griffith. There he met an IRA man on a separate mission and with him he visited Chartres. In the cloakroom of a club near the Houses of Parliament Chartres showed them a machine gun. It was for inspection purposes only, he said, and was to go to Ireland 'by the ordinary channels'.[8] Possibly Brennan has embellished the story, but his dramatic account of the activities of Chartres has received some credence from the measured testimony of Piaras Béalsaí.

Béalsaí was close to the centre of military affairs during the War of Independence and as biographer of Collins had access to many secret documents. He had spoken to Chartres before the publication of his book on Collins in 1926 and had respected his request that no mention be made of his gunrunning activities. After the death of Chartres, Béalsaí felt free to speak about the relationship between Chartres and Collins during the years 1919–21. 'Collins,' he said,

was in constant touch with him. He visited Collins in Dublin on a
number of occasions. His name was mentioned at meetings of G.H.Q.
and once, if my memory serves me right, in connection with work
the nature of which it is not advisable to make public even at the
present time.[9]

One is intrigued by Béalsaí's statement, but no further information is offered. Béalsaí continued:

it is a remarkable fact that, though Collins had a very capable Assistant Director of Intelligence and several other members of his staff
who were entrusted with the most highly confidential work, he always seems to have dealt with Chartres direct and never through his
staff.

Chartres, in reply to Béalsaí's questions, 'admitted that he had been in the
closest touch' with Collins; and added that 'he had conveyed quantities of
arms and ammunition to Collins on a number of occasions. He had sometimes personally brought over the arms.'[10] A British source noted that
Chartres was not in his early days a Home Ruler, let alone a Sinn Féiner; but
reported that 'it was a notable fact that, at the time when he was at the head
of the Intelligence Section of the Labour Department of the Ministry of
Munitions, his letters were often opened by the censors, and he himself,
whenever he visited Ireland, was shadowed by the police.'[11] Chartres was,
therefore, engaged in a very dangerous enterprise.

Béalsaí drew his own conclusions. He felt that Chartres was loyal to
Collins and that he was sincere. However, he admitted that he was a 'mys-
tery man'. As personal testimony and early career records of this 'mystery
man' give way to documentary evidence, the first faint documentary link of
Chartres with Sinn Féin is to be found in the Foreign Affairs department of
Dáil Éireann and the person of Sean T. O'Kelly.

Paris and Foreign Affairs

Sean T. O'Kelly, who was not only a deputy of the Dáil but also its elected Chairman, was selected to act as republican envoy in Paris by Dáil Éireann early in January 1919. He had been present at the meeting with Chartres in late 1918, but the character of the relationship between Great Britain and Ireland had been dramatically altered in a few short months. Following the December 1918 election victory, the Sinn Féin members elected to the British Parliament had sat in Dublin on 21 January 1919 as Dáil Éireann and constituted a Government of the Republic of Ireland—on the same day the first shots had been fired in the War of Independence. Count Plunkett was Minister for Foreign Affairs. In co-operation with the department of Publicity he attempted to secure recognition for the new Republic of Ireland abroad.

As republican envoy O'Kelly's main task was to present, in as compelling a fashion as possible, Ireland's case to the Versailles Peace Conference. The matter was viewed as one of the most important foreign policy objectives of Dáil Éireann. It was also seen as extremely important by Irish-Americans. Dáil Éireann drew up a comprehensive statement of Ireland's claim, and three American delegates appeared in Paris to support the Irish cause. It was the responsibility of Sean T. O'Kelly to secure maximum publicity for these Irish and American initiatives. He arrived in Paris on 7 February 1919, and was soon assisted by George Gavan Duffy, also an elected member of Dáil Éireann, who, for a short time, was accompanied by his wife, Margaret.[1] Cáit, Sean T. O'Kelly's wife, also joined her husband.

Gavan Duffy, although brought up in France and educated in England, had long been associated with Irish Ireland ideals, but especially so after he had acted as solicitor for Sir Roger Casement in 1916. He was of particular value to Sean T. O'Kelly as he spoke French fluently. Among O'Kelly's other assistants were Victor Collins and M. Caulfield, but these men were soon found to be unreliable. Michael MacWhite, who had served in the French Foreign Legion, was a helpful contact for O'Kelly from the first, and Erskine Childers gave his assistance during the month of August 1919.[2] By the end of his term in Paris he was assisted by Leopold Kerney, Joseph Walshe and Sean Murphy, all of whom were to play a significant role in the department of Foreign Affairs after the Treaty.[3]

One of O'Kelly's first assistants was Madame Anna Vivanti, the wife of John Chartres. Plunkett told the Dáil on 18 June 1919 that she was 'an Italian lady well known as a leading novelist in Italy. She was notified by an Italian lawyer to leave Italy for the good of her health, and we availed of her services.'[4] Michael Collins described her at the time as a 'brilliant writer' who 'has been a great accession to our cause in France as well as her native Italy'.[5] On 15 June Sean T. O'Kelly commented in a long letter to de Valera that 'Madame A. Vivanti will I expect be returning to Italy in about a week, and I have asked her to go via Switzerland.'[6] Having a British visa she was able to travel easily, and she was asked to present copies of *Ireland's Case to the Peace Conference* to the German, Austrian and Hungarian ministries in Switzerland. O'Kelly thanked Vivanti on 30 June 1919 for her 'tremendous work' in Paris; but added that this mission 'ends your official connection with this delegation'.[7] He concluded with the wish and with the confidence that she would keep Ireland's cause in her heart.

On 7 July O'Kelly informed Foreign Affairs that Madame Vivanti had left Paris on Monday last; he praised her 'splendid services'; and gave her about £100 'for the good work she did while here'. In the same letter O'Kelly noted enigmatically that 'yours dated 25th June arrived last night per Mr C'.[8] He added that Mr C had showed him a note from Arthur Griffith asking that his expenses be paid while in Paris and that he be considered for a position on the Irish mission. O'Kelly commented that 'I do not yet know if Mr C can be of much service to us here. I am inclined to think not, but we will try to make all the use we can of him.'

O'Kelly concluded by requesting that he be consulted before any trial appointments were made. Could Mr C be Chartres? One cannot be sure, but it is significant that his wife was deeply involved in the Irish work of propaganda both in Paris and in other European countries. By this time the Treaty of Versailles had been signed, 28 June 1919, without the Irish having had an opportunity to present their case to the Conference, and on the following day the American delegation representing the Irish cause sailed to the States. Doubts were expressed about the value of an Irish office in Paris in this changed situation and the departure of Vivanti may well have resulted from this new scenario.

The difficulties of the task certainly weighed down heavily on Sean T. O'Kelly. On 9 July he informed Foreign Affairs that 'I would like to get home as soon as possible. I am sick and weary of this place.' He was prepared to carry out Cabinet instructions but he wished it to be known that 'I want to get out and get home as soon as ever they feel that they can permit me to do so.'[9]

Gavan Duffy was also affected by the same feelings of disillusionment. He suggested to O'Kelly that 'our work here just now is not serious,' and that they were simply marking time and wasting money. O'Kelly replied on 3 September calling for a combined effort to present Ireland's case in Paris, but both men were clearly under strain.[10] In December 1919 O'Kelly wrote to Griffith offering his resignation, but de Valera, who was in regular contact with O'Kelly from America, informed him on 29 January 1920 that both he and Gavan Duffy should stay in Paris.[11] This news led Gavan Duffy to ask for a move and led him to state that he and Sean T. O'Kelly had not got on well together. He did not apportion any blame but asked not to continue in office as 'I am certain that any attempt to renew a very unfortunate experience will have anything but good results, for there will be no loyal co-operation between the two Envoys and endless friction.'[12] Clearly all was not well in Paris.

The department of Foreign Affairs was also in some disarray. Count Plunkett had endeavoured to formulate a policy with the help of a committee. Among the committee were A. McCabe, Liam de Róiste, J. McBride, J.A. Burke, Terence MacSwiney and Desmond FitzGerald.[13] All of these men had been elected to the Dáil, but the Dáil had been declared illegal by the British in September 1919, making it difficult to move around freely. By the end of 1919, after two meetings with few members attending, Plunkett was left to his own devices. While de Valera from America, and Griffith and Collins in Ireland, also played a part in shaping foreign policy direction, Plunkett made his own specific contribution to formulating a policy in 1920.

In January of that year, for reasons of health, O'Kelly, accompanied by his wife Cáit, went to Rome. Before his departure O'Kelly offered a more measured assessment of Madame Vivanti's potential help to Ireland. She had written on 13 September 1919 offering to work anywhere in the Irish cause. Forwarding her letter to Dublin, O'Kelly made the observation that Madame Vivanti 'in my opinion ought not to be put in any place where she would have responsible work to do'.[14] He still praised her as a good worker but insisted that she needed a well informed person with her. This letter did not terminate O'Kelly's connection with Vivanti. Soon after his arrival in Rome on 6 February 1920 he was to renew contact with her and, through her, with Mussolini.

While the main purpose of O'Kelly's visit to Rome was for health reasons, he also made contact with two former friends, Mgr John Hagan, Rector of the Irish College, and Fr Curran, another member of the College, who were both involved in defending Dáil Éireann's policy at the Vatican in opposition to British influences. O'Kelly, however, was so ill with rheu-

matic fever that Mgr Hagan insisted that he retire to bed immediately, and
during his time in Italy he spent some thirteen to fourteen weeks confined
to bed.[15]. Mgr Hagan and Father Curran were supporting the Irish claim to
independence on two fronts: not only were they justifying Ireland's claim at
the Vatican, but also they were actively seeking military support from Italian sources for the republican war effort. Sean T. O'Kelly played his part in
making the diplomatic approach to the Vatican successful. On 12 April 1920,
advised by Hagan and Curran, he presented a memorandum on Ireland's
case to Pope Benedict XV during a private audience; and from 23 to 27 May
he helped to promote nationalist feeling among the Irish bishops during the
beatification of Oliver Plunkett. Following these developments, O'Kelly
informed de Valera that 'there is no danger now of unsympathetic interference by the Holy See in our affairs'.[16]

Progress on the military side was less satisfactory, but some initiatives
were taken. Count Plunkett had attended the beatification of his namesake
and presumably would have had an opportunity to discuss matters with
O'Kelly. Contacts had been established for military purposes between Donal
Hales, the Irish consul at Genoa, and Michael Collins; and Annie Vivanti
became involved in this search for armed assistance.

She was a friend of D'Annunzio, the Italian revolutionary, and contact
was established between him and Sean T. O'Kelly.[17] O'Kelly asked Vivanti
to sound out D'Annunzio at his headquarters in Fiume to see if arms could
be purchased for Ireland. D'Annunzio agreed to help, if Mussolini gave his
permission. O'Kelly and Vivanti travelled to Mussolini's headquarters in
Milan, where they were welcomed, and Mussolini promised to provide arms
free for Ireland, if a boat and crew could be found to transport them. Plans
were made to buy a boat in Genoa and to find an Irish crew. Having received a letter from D'Annunzio, O'Kelly reported back to Arthur Griffith
on 18 June that as to D'Annunzio's 'offer of "materials"—which I take it
means "munitions" I am enquiring further. I don't know if it can be taken
seriously.'[18]

Despite his doubts O'Kelly enclosed the letter from D'Annunzio to
Michael Collins, and promised to look into the possibility of acquiring cheap
munitions through the port of Fiume. 'Our friends the Egyptians,' O'Kelly
observed, 'are using the port of Fiume for the exportation of arms per Tripoli
to Egypt.' The arrival of a British warship at Fiume, combined with a certain vacillation on the part of D'Annunzio, eventually brought the plans of
O'Kelly and Vivanti to naught. O'Kelly did, however, praise Mussolini for
providing regular space in his paper, *Il Popolo d'Italia,* for the Irish cause.

While these negotiations were taking place, Gavan Duffy wrote to Michael
Collins on 8 March 1920 asking, 'Have you ever thought of using abroad
Annie's husband with whom we spent Christmas 1918? He has great gifts.'[19]

As well as confirming the meeting of Chartres with Collins in 1918, the letter provides the first documented indication that Chartres was considered to be on the Irish side—this, be it noted, while he was still in the British Civil Service. The recommendation of Gavan Duffy may also indicate that some contact had been made with Chartres, either personally or through Annie Vivanti, in order to justify such a proposal. Personal contact was certainly established at this time, for on 5 August 1920 O'Kelly wrote to Gavan Duffy from Pisa, where he was taking the spa waters of nearby Formia for rheumatic fever. He said that he had heard from John Chartres, and that 'Cáit and I are going off to meet himself and madame in Milan' in a day or two.[20] That Chartres should have been at such a location when the prospect of gun-running was in the air, and while he was still in the British service, is to say the least intriguing. O'Kelly concluded his letter to Gavan Duffy by saying that his health had improved and that he hoped to return to Paris some time in September. This time scale was rudely interrupted by the sudden dismissal of Gavan Duffy from Paris.

Gavan Duffy was seen by a messenger from Premier Millerand at 8.30 p.m. on 31 August 1920 and told to leave Paris the next day or to face expulsion.[21] The news amazed O'Kelly and he hurried back to France in order to reverse the expulsion order. Duffy gave his view of the incident. He declared that on 25 August he had sent a letter to Millerand calling on him to intervene in Terence MacSwiney's hunger strike, and that, when he received no reply, he had sent the letter to the press. The British Embassy objected to this action, which had created wide spread publicity, and called for Gavan Duffy's expulsion.[22] All protest on behalf of the Irish proved futile and Gavan Duffy arrived in Belgium on 2 September. Soon afterwards he and his wife went to Rome, where he took up residence at the Hotel Flora and acted as republican envoy.

Thanks to the help of Sean T. O'Kelly, he was quickly in touch with Hagan and Curran at the Irish College. For a short time Michael MacWhite assumed responsibility for the Paris office, but O'Kelly soon returned to his former position and was assisted by the voluntary help of Osmond Grattan Esmonde. Count Plunkett informed the Dáil on 17 September that 'the Irish Republic had rather gained than lost from a propaganda point of view over this matter'.[23]

Chartres appeared on the Paris scene early in 1921. Writing on 18 March, O'Kelly informed Collins that our 'Egyptian friends' are 'keenly anxious' for organisers and instructors in military matters, and recommended that they should be helped. This report may take on added significance since John Chartres was in Egypt in early 1921 and O'Kelly concluded his letter with the words, 'our friend JC will I expect arrive here on 6th April and will stay a day or two here. What would you think of him for Berlin? He is I believe anxious to do work of that kind.'[24] On 18 April O'Kelly reported that Chartres had, indeed, arrived in Paris, but that he was ill in bed with a cold. His wife, Annie Vivanti, had arrived to nurse him.[25] The Paris records, therefore, reveal not only that Chartres was closely involved in the Irish cause, but also that he merited recommendation for a position of responsibility abroad by both Sean T. O'Kelly and Gavan Duffy. It may be also of significance that the recommendations were directed to Michael Collins rather than to Count Plunkett, head of Foreign Affairs. Collins knew the value of Chartres in the sphere of gun-running, and the faint glimpses one has of him from the Paris office still associate him with that area of activity. In the strange world of spies and arms dealers it is difficult to detect a clear pattern of events.

However, in O'Kelly's letter of 18 April a clue is offered to the future placing of Chartres in the Irish service. Having noted that Chartres was ill, O'Kelly added a postscript asking Gavan Duffy for 'Bisonkind's address'. 'Bisonkind' was one of the many code names of John T. Ryan, a leading American arms agent, who was working with Joe McGarrity for the Irish republican cause. He had recently arrived in Germany. It can hardly be a coincidence that it was also in Germany that Chartres was asked to make his first official contribution in the service of the Republic of Ireland. Some consideration, therefore, of the situation in Germany is merited.

Berlin and Foreign Affairs

The placing of a representative in Germany had been an objective of Dáil Éireann for some time. On 16 June 1919 Sean T. O'Kelly had written to de Valera saying that he had been in communication for months with St John Gaffney, the former United States consul at Dresden and Munich. Gaffney was of Irish origins and had been to school at Clongowes College in county Kildare. He had been forced to leave the American consular service after he had supported Roger Casement in 1916, and had been sympathetic to the Irish cause after the Rising. Indeed, he had been nominated by Roger Casement to look after the interests of the Irish Brigade. Under the code name of Thomas Fleming, he resided in Switzerland. While his record was promising, someone appointed by O'Kelly to make a report on him stated that his manner was such that 'he did not think he would make a good impression if appointed as our representative'.[1] O'Kelly felt that 'serious consideration' should be made before he was appointed to any of the larger cities of Germany or Austria.

Another name mentioned by O'Kelly was that of George Chatterton Hill, a former professor at Geneva University. Both Gaffney and Chatterton Hill had played important parts in setting up a branch of the Friends of Irish Freedom in Berlin which was closely linked with the original association set up in America in March 1916. This pro-Irish organisation in Germany had been further strengthened by the formation of the German-Irish Society on 19 February 1917 at the Hotel Kaiserhof in Berlin.[2] Cables were received from General Ludendorff and the Secretary of State, Zimmermann, wishing the society success. St John Gaffney and Chatterton-Hill had contributed to the founding of the society and many distinguished Germans were members; among them were Mathias Erzberger, leader of the Centre Party, Baron von Richtofen, member of Parliament, and Count von Westarp, leader of the Conservatives. The headquarters were established in Berlin and a monthly review, *Irische Blatter*, edited by Chatterton Hill, was produced.

The highpoint of the Society's influence occurred on 17 March 1918, St Patrick's Day, when a meeting was hosted by the German government. On that occasion the Society sent a message to the Kaiser and received a reply that the Kaiser was 'following with keen interest and lively sympathy the fight that brave Ireland is making for freedom'.[3] Defeat in the War had inevitably led to a decline in the fortunes of the German-Irish Society, and had made it necessary for the Irish to re-appraise their position in Germany. In July 1919 Chatterton Hill resigned as general secretary and was replaced by Mrs Agatha Bullit Grabisch, an American married to a German.[4]

The death of Kuno Meyer, the President of the German-Irish Society, in October 1919 removed from the scene one of Ireland's staunchest supporters. Not only had he championed Ireland's claims in cultural matters since the turn of the century, but also, on his tour of America during the War, he had established a close relationship with Joe McGarrity and had supported Ireland's political objectives. [5]

A report on the changed circumstances in Berlin, completed on 25 October 1919, was made to Sean T. O'Kelly. This report was drawn up by an agent code named 'The Traveller,' who was probably Gerald Hamilton. Nancy Power, who later made contact with him, certainly referred to him by that name.[6] O'Kelly expressed certain doubts about the man's reliability, as he had been in trouble with Scotland Yard, but, while not willing to give him any official recognition, believed him to be sincere. In November O'Kelly communicated 'The Traveller's' views to the department of Foreign Affairs in Ireland.

It was proposed, in regard to matters of trade, that a company be created which was to be jointly owned by Irish, American and German interests, and it was reported that a ship was available at the cost of £160,000 to sail between Hamburg and Cork. The port of Hamburg was to figure large in Irish activity in Germany. Having met Baron von Horst, Theodor Wolff, Bernstorff, and Dr Brinckmann, 'The Traveller' concluded: 'I do distinctly feel the necessity of some representative of the Irish Republic living in Berlin.'[7] This recommendation received official recognition in 1920. Count Plunkett, after his visit to Rome in May 1920, drew up a report in which he stated that the Dáil Ministry was keen to appoint consuls and diplomatic representatives in other European countries. In regard to Germany he noted that the position 'has hitherto been such that it is very difficult to make much headway'.[8]

Arthur Griffith, as Acting-President, made the same point in the Dáil on 29 June 1920. Germany, he said, was one of many countries named in which it was desirable to have diplomatic representatives, and he added that the President was looking for thirty men to fill the posts that were required.[9]

On 6 August Count Plunkett again stressed the difficulties involved in
dealing with Germany. 'Slow progress,' he said,

> was being made in the organisation of relations between the Republic
> and Austria and Germany. The manufactures which Ireland might be
> able to get from these countries were treated by England as 'key'
> industries and therefore could not be imported into Ireland.[10]

While Count Plunkett was speaking in generalities, voices in America were
being far more specific about German 'manufactures'. On 16 August John
T. Ryan, the 'Bisonkind' whose address Sean T. O'Kelly had sought from
Gavan Duffy, wrote to Joe McGarrity announcing that he was leaving on a
mission to Germany. In a rather cryptic letter he said that he had $10,000 to
spend, that he intended to send 'a good shipment of the right goods' to the
'Old Homestead' and he hoped that this would upset 'Mr King and his wife'.[11]
'Old Homestead' was Ireland; and 'Mr King' was presumably England. Here
we have a very specific purpose of Irish policy in regard to Germany: arms
were sought to wage the War of Independence against England.

Ryan, a lawyer, had been a captain in the United States army during the
Spanish-American war and had seen action in the Philippines. He was, therefore, experienced in military matters. Ryan was also one of the three Clan
na Gael executive in 1916 who had been in touch with Captain Spindler and
the Casement expedition.[12] He was wanted for 'aiding and assisting German
spies' in New York after the outbreak of war. A poster from this time stated
that he was 45 years old; was five feet ten inches tall and weighed 190 pounds;
and was almost bald, as well as having a Van Dyke beard. Two photographs
show that this description was accurate. Some of his aliases were given: 'Phil-
ippine Island Ryan', 'William West', and 'William Roberts or Robertson'.[13]
He was clearly an important, interesting and potentially dangerous man.

Ryan had taken the side of Joe McGarrity, abandoning the policy of
John Devoy and Judge Cohalan, when the Clan na Gael had split in 1920.
He was in touch with McGarrity in June 1920 and informed him that he had
communicated with 'Topman' (de Valera) and Jordan (possibly Dr Patrick
McCartan) about a projected journey. One project that was considered was
a mission to Russia, and Ryan was proposed by McCartan as a possible member of that mission. Germany, however, was to be Ryan's European destina-
tion.

Before Ryan arrived in Germany another emissary of the Irish Republic
had done so. Nancy Power visited Germany for a few months in November
1920. There was no doubting her republican credentials. She had been in
contact with the insurgents in the General Post Office in 1916 and, like her
mother, Jennie Wyse Power, was a dedicated member of Cumann na mBan.[14]

She was a graduate of the School of Irish Learning which, through its founder Kuno Meyer, had strong German connections. Her doctoral studies at Bonn University in Germany had been interrupted by the War and she returned to complete her examinations. Arthur Griffith, however, had asked her to contact Gavan Duffy to see if she might be of any help in Germany. Gavan Duffy read to her a long report on the German situation by a friend of his, Gerald Hamilton, 'The Traveller'. Following her visit to Gavan Duffy, Nancy Power was followed by police and arrested upon her arrival in Cologne by the British occupying forces. She was then released. After Christmas she received a letter from Gavan Duffy requesting her to go to Dortmund to recover a sum of money that Jurgens, a shipping dealer, had been paid for providing arms, but which had not been transmitted. She failed to make contact with Jurgens and the attempts to recover the Irish money from him form part of the story of Chartres in Berlin.

Ryan, meanwhile, had arrived in Germany on 18 December 1920 and, although having difficulty contacting 'Old Homestead' [Ireland], did make contact with some of Joe McGarrity's connections. He also met Gavan Duffy, who had left Rome to undertake a European reconnaissance tour on 18 January 1921.[15] During this tour Duffy visited Basle, Berlin, Copenhagen, Paris, Odense, Madrid, Salamanca, Barcelona and Genoa before returning to Rome on 8 March.[16] Gavan Duffy was again travelling with Gerald Hamilton, and they were under surveillance from detectives who were in contact with Colonel Maude, the head of British intelligence. Ryan, who was deeply suspicious of Hamilton, insisted that he would only meet Gavan Duffy on his own. After some difficulty and some confusion this was arranged, and they concluded their business successfully. Fate was not so kind to Talaat Pasha, a prominent Young Turk leader resident in Berlin. He agreed to meet Gavan Duffy with Hamilton accompanying him. Soon afterwards Pasha was shot dead outside his house. The rumours were that Hamilton had betrayed him and that Hamilton was a secret British agent.[17]

Beneath the official memoranda and formal statements made to Dáil Éireann about foreign policy in regard to Germany, events in Germany itself were evidently far more complex and far more dangerous than revealed on paper. That should be borne in mind when one notes Count Plunkett's report of January 1921 in which he stated that

> our relation with [the] central powers necessarily is restricted to trade and even trade is seriously impeded by the bad condition of the exchange and the impediments imposed by England ... The press of Germany shows the state of terrorism imposed by the allies on the defeated nations and it is nearly impossible to get a clear statement of events in Ireland into the papers.[18]

Beneath the rather opaque language of this report, other realities were shaping Irish considerations. Two events on 10 February 1921 conspired to make the implementation of this hidden agenda more likely: firstly, Robert Brennan was appointed Under Secretary for Foreign Affairs with a special office and staff, thereby creating a more efficient service; and, secondly, a report making specific recommendations for Germany was drawn up by Gavan Duffy.[19] While in Berlin, as well as meeting John T. Ryan, whose arrival must have stimulated a response from Ireland, Duffy met various helpers of the Irish cause. Among those he mentioned were Mrs Archibald, Aubrey Stanhope, Miss Smedley from America, Gerald Gifford who was 'hard up', Michael O'Brien, a student who was proving 'most useful to Professor Jetter', and Professor Julius Pokorny 'one of the best and keenest friends' of Ireland. Gavan Duffy also collected various memoranda from those working in the Irish interest.

Written reports were submitted by Jurgens, despite the issue over his misuse of Irish money, Chatterton Hill and Gifford. Jurgens claimed that 'we intend to prevent any English intervention in trade with Ireland'; and, on a practical level, he proposed that Ireland should be electrified with high voltage electricity—an interesting proposal in the light of the future hydro-electric scheme at Shannon. Duffy summarised the reports and concluded that 'I am convinced it is most necessary to have a political and a commercial representative as soon as possible in Berlin; and a press bureau is badly needed, for hardly any Irish news gets through.'[20]

In regard to the press bureau Chatterton Hill had submitted a request that such a bureau should be set up, and he made a desperate plea that he should get the job: 'my present position,' he wrote, 'is a fearful one.'[21] Gavan Duffy, however, observed that Chatterton Hill was 'addicted to drink', unscrupulous, and 'at daggers drawn' with St John Gaffney. This view of Hill's unreliability had been expressed earlier, in August 1920, when Michael Collins had withdrawn his name from the Irish pay roll, and had advised that 'he should not expect any further payment from us'.[22]

Despite these clear warnings Chatterton Hill's petition was successful and he was appointed to editorial work in the German Propaganda Bureau by a decision of the Dáil Ministry of 8 March 1921.[23] The Ministry decision also granted £1,000 per annum for propaganda work and nominated Colonel Emerson as financial director. Having regard to the strictures of Gavan Duffy and Collins, the appointment of Chatterton Hill appears inexplicable. Ironically the decision to select him provoked immediate action in order to offset the dangers presented by his appointment! Gavan Duffy, possibly as yet unaware of Hill's appointment, again urged the appointment of a strong man in Berlin on 11 March.[24]

De Valera, who certainly knew of the appointment, was quite clear that Chatterton Hill was 'so bad' that action was needed immediately to limit any damage that he might do. He informed Michael Collins of this on 2 April 1921.[25] Robert Brennan confirmed this view to Collins on 6 April, informing him that Dr Nancy Power was proceeding to Berlin to take control of the situation for the present.[26] Realisation of the need for an Irish presence in Germany was matched by a realisation of the difficulty of establishing a base in Weimar Germany, which, to a high degree, was under Allied and especially English control. This control was tightened in the early months of 1921 when the Weimar government fell behind in the payment of reparations imposed at the Versailles Treaty. Three ports on the Ruhr were occupied in March and on 5 May the London Ultimatum was presented to Germany by which they were to make repayments at the rate of £100 million per annum.

The government of Josef Wirth that came to power at this time was committed to a policy of fulfilment of the Versailles terms, and was also inclined to secure Britain's good will to balance the demands of the French. It was also faced with internal divisions on two levels: on the one hand, there were bitter conflicts between the forces of the left and the right; and on the other hand, the power of the central government was strongly challenged by the separatist ambitions of provincial assemblies.[27] It was against this background that John Chartres became republican envoy to Berlin.

John Chartres and Nancy Power in Berlin

Dr Nancy Power took the first steps that shaped the beginning of the Irish republican office in Berlin and which culminated in the appointment of Chartres. She left Dublin on 11 April 1921 and arrived in Berlin on the 16th.[1] Power related that she was told by Brennan

> to go first to Paris and there I would meet Mr Chartres who, it was desired, should act as envoy in Berlin. Mr Chartres was at the time on his way back from Egypt where he had been for reasons of health. If he was agreeable to go direct to Berlin I could turn back to Dublin but if he decided otherwise I was to go to Berlin and start the Bulletin. I went to Paris and saw Mr Chartres. I had never met him before ... He said first of all he would have to get more definite instructions and secondly he would have to resign from the British Civil Service. He wished so to arrange matters that he would be actually in Berlin when his resignation was received. I quite understood that he could not take up the appointment in mid-Channel so I went on to Berlin and he came to Dublin.[2]

De Valera was concerned that she had departed with 'very inadequate instructions', and to redress that failing Robert Brennan wrote to Nancy Power on 29 April conferring on her 'full discretionary powers'. Arrangements were also made that she should receive £250 for immediate expenses.[3]

Brennan's letter also showed that the appointment of Chartres had not been absolutely finalised. While noting that 'J. C. is here at present; he may join you later,' Brennan also stated that it was likely that St John Gaffney would go to Berlin 'in our interest'.[4] Gaffney had left Germany in September 1920 and returned to America. While there he had offered his 'services to the Irish Diplomatic Mission' which had recently been set up in Washington.[5]

It would appear that he was offered an appointment because on 28 April he wrote to de Valera under the code name of Spillane stating that he was sailing on the *Kronland* on 14 May, and would go to Paris to receive his instructions. He added that he 'would prefer to be commissioned as Envoy in G[ermany]' as he knew the Foreign Office officials there. He concluded by casting doubts upon the reliability of Chatterton Hill and Colonel Emerson, and requested that in future he be referred to as 'Fleming Clune' and not as Spillane.[6]

Upon his arrival in Europe he spent a week with Sean T. O'Kelly in Paris before making the journey to Basle, Switzerland, arriving there on 30 May. While he was at sea, the decision was taken to appoint Chartres to Berlin. On the very same day, 29 April, that Brennan had written to Nancy Power raising doubts about the appointment of Chartres, Michael Collins wrote an enigmatic note to de Valera stating that he was seeing that night the only person that he knew who was capable of carrying out the Berlin appointment: he was 'a South of Ireland Unionist and a Protestant'.[7]

Chartres might well be described in such terms; and it will be recalled that Collins would have had on his desk the letter from Sean T. O'Kelly of 18 March recommending Chartres as the man for Berlin. The decision to appoint Chartres was finally made in May. On 16 May de Valera wrote to Michael Collins, stating that

> I saw Mr C[hartres] last evening. He is of opinion that he could do best work for us in B[erlin], and that his opportunities for helping in your special department would now be slight. The impression made upon me was that we should send him to B[erlin] at once.[8]

In making his decision de Valera may well have been influenced by his own personal knowledge of John T. Ryan and of his mission to Germany. Moreover, de Valera's reference to the contribution of Chartres towards the 'special department' of Collins confers an official type of seal on the earlier evidence that Chartres was involved in gun-running. De Valera continued, in words that were applicable to Gaffney, 'if the man comes from America we can send him to the Southern part of the country. He wouldn't be by any means as discreet or as able, I think, as Mr C[hartres].'[9] Collins was called upon to consult with de Valera to confirm the appointment of Chartres as soon as possible.

While matters were being resolved in Dublin, Nancy Power was busily engaged in the initial work of setting up the Irish office in Berlin. She was eminently qualified to carry out the task assigned to her. She spoke German fluently; she had many contacts in the German academic world on account of her studies; and her mission at the end of 1920 had given her an insight into the political realities that governed Irish-German relations. It was with this experience behind her that Nancy Power opened the Berlin office of the Irish Republic on 16 April 1921. Her first objective, having regard to the priorities identified by Gavan Duffy, was to produce a journal of Irish news.

Despite rumours of peace initiatives, the War of Independence was still being bitterly contested, and it was important that the Irish side of the story should be heard in Germany and in other parts of Europe. It was hoped that she would be assisted by Dr Chatterton Hill. However, he took umbrage when it was made clear that he was to be an assistant and he left Nancy Power to cope on her own. Colonel Emerson, an American who had thrown in his lot with Germany at the outbreak of war and had founded a League of Oppressed Peoples, was also expected to help. Differences had arisen, however, between him and Chatterton Hill, and he was not in Germany when Power arrived.[10]

The political situation in Germany in early May was also unstable, Power noted, but the uncertainty was resolved, she said, 'when it became clear that the strife with the Entente was to be of a diplomatic character'.[11] Despite these difficulties Nancy Power quickly set up a bi-weekly Bulletin with the help of Professor Pokorny, a leading figure in German Irish studies. This Bulletin was circulated both to the Berlin newspapers and to the provincial press and they incorporated this Irish news into their columns. The provincial newspapers were particularly responsive to the Bulletin material. With the help of Gifford, she also published, at the request of J.J. O'Kelly, acting Chairman of the Dáil, the Address to the Nations made in the first Dáil of January 1919. This was sent to members of the Reichstag, the Prussian and Bavarian Landtags, the Bishops, the members of the German-Irish Society and also to influential people in Austria and Switzerland. 'It created great interest,' Nancy Power recorded, 'and several papers published resumes, or long extracts.' Her work was evidently carried out efficiently and successfully.

Apart from this type of work, Nancy Power also made several very interesting contacts. 'I interviewed,' she declared, 'Admiral von Tirpitz, who discussed with me a form of propaganda which would be excellent if it could be carried out.'[12] She could not reveal more in writing, but wished to discuss the matter further. In her memoir she relates that Tirpitz wanted someone who had known Terence MacSwiney to visit Germany and talk to the many underground groups that existed. He felt that such talks would generate great sympathy for Ireland. Nancy Power also reported that Captain Spindler would welcome some sign of recognition for the services he had undertaken as captain of the *Aud* in the Casement expedition of 1916.[13]

As well as these valuable comments on the German scene, Nancy Power also made several interesting remarks on those acting in Ireland's interests.

She mentioned 'Professor Getter', John T. Ryan, whose work she remarked was 'not, strictly speaking, within my province', and she came into close contact with him. She recalled that he 'believed that the entire German police and the entire allied organisations were doing nothing but searching for him all over Europe. He saw me and strangely enough he did not resent me. He resented most people.'[14]

She was, in fact, grateful to Ryan for his advice, based on his influential contacts, and recognised that he 'had the interests of Ireland sincerely at heart'. Ryan was acutely aware of the power of the allies in Germany in the aftermath of the Treaty of Versailles, and, after one particular police inquiry that led Nancy Power to spend a few days in Paris, he exclaimed, 'You have got to remember that the Allies have their feet on the German's necks.'[15] Ryan was not the only contact Power made who had an air of mystery surrounding him.

She also met Gerald Hamilton. She recommended that his advice be followed as he knew everyone in Berlin. Referring to him, as Gavan Duffy did, as 'The Traveller', she acknowledged that she had received 'a very large amount of assistance' from him. She felt that he could be trusted—Ryan and Chartres were soon to give another view; and she added that 'Sean T. [O'Kelly] agrees with me that his sincerity is beyond question.'[16]

By chance Nancy Power also met St John Gaffney. She left Berlin on 27 May to return to Ireland via Paris, and there encountered Gaffney who was on his way to Switzerland. He did not make a good impression upon her. She related that 'all I had heard of his vanity and bumptiousness confirmed itself when I saw him'.[17] Power was afraid that he might go to Germany before Chartres and thus make trouble. These fears proved groundless, but may have stimulated Power to consult with Chartres with some urgency.

Nancy Power met Chartres in the house of Con Curran immediately upon her return to Dublin on 30 May 1921, and fully briefed him on the current German situation. No doubt she also mentioned her fears about Gaffney.[18] She also gave him a statement of accounts. Armed with all this information Chartres left for Berlin. According to Nancy Power he received his credentials on 1 June, and a letter from Collins to de Valera on 4 June mentioned that Chartres had left Dublin.[19] On 7 June Sean T. O'Kelly, from his headquarters in Paris, informed Collins that he was 'expecting the arrival of J.C. to-night', and presumed that he would resume his journey within a day or two.[20]

The transition from British civil servant to Irish republican envoy was not announced publicly. Apart from any reluctance on the part of Chartres to publicise his change of allegiance, the envoy's position in Germany was of an unofficial character and it was advisable to keep a low profile. The position, however, was important, and for Chartres it marked a new and challenging departure in the life of a man who was in his late fifties. Despite the rumours and doubts associated with his name, the remarkable feature of his formal entrance into the Irish ranks is the acceptance accorded to him by so many influential Irish leaders—could Griffith, Collins and de Valera all be wrong about him? could leading men on the ground, like Sean T. O'Kelly and Gavan Duffy, be deceived? The recognition that Chartres had won from Griffith, Collins and de Valera meant that he could rely on support in the highest quarters as he entered upon his appointment in Berlin; and the contacts that he had established with Sean T. O'Kelly and Gavan Duffy meant that he was able to operate at ease and with confidence in the area of foreign affairs.

Chartres was clearly at home in the European scene. The odd glimpses that we have of him and his wife in Paris and Italy, still living out their amicable but unusual relationship, show him to be familiar with Europe and involved in sensitive matters touching upon Irish policy. These sensitive matters had touched upon armaments, and, with John T. Ryan in Berlin, it must have been a positive recommendation that Chartres had run guns into Ireland for Collins. Moreover, he had some knowledge of German, having spent some time studying there. If his qualifications for the job were of the highest order, less is known of his personal feelings.

An insight into those feelings, however, is provided by a remarkable book that was presented to Collins and de Valera in draft form in the early days of June 1921. It was written by Chartres and was entitled *The Bloody English*. Collins had not seen the book, but he had talked to Chartres about the title, commenting that 'It's the best I have ever heard.'[21] This acknowledgement by Collins that he had met Chartres, made on 4 June, is the first documentary evidence on his part indicating that personal contact had been established between them. De Valera had read the book, or parts of it, and remarked that 'As regards the title, I didn't express any opinion on it. There is a good deal pro and con. I daresay inasmuch as the feeling against the English is rising, the title will rather attract than repel.'[22]

Although it did not appear in published form until 1922, and then under a pen name, the book shows that Chartres had a violent aversion to things English.[23] In the preface he justified the title 'bloody English' on account of the bloody deeds carried out by Englishmen in the pursuit of Empire. Critical objection to English imperial policy was complemented by a vicious attack on English morals. Sexual immorality in schools and the activities of soldiers in brothels were narrated with a disturbing intensity. Rational criticism of colonial policy was matched by a hatred of the English race that was almost neurotic. Granted that Chartres was a genuine convert to the Irish cause and was not trying to deceive anyone, then it has to be said that, as he

entered upon his Berlin appointment, his opposition to things English was
not only implacable but also verging on the paranoid.

While en route to Berlin, Chartres wrote to Robert Brennan on 11 June
1921, acknowledging an advisory note concerning J.T. Ryan, alias Professor
Jetter, and signing himself 'E.S.', the code name that he used for all his correspondence, and which matched the pen name of the author of his book,
'Edward Seaton.'[24] Contact was clearly going to be made with Ryan. Brennan
advised Chartres to contact Sean T. O'Kelly for more information about
Ryan, and he clarified the status of Chartres in relation to St John Gaffney,
who had already settled at Basle in Switzerland: Gaffney was instructed not
to interfere with Chartres in any way.[25]

This message appears to have been accepted by Gaffney because at the
end of June he informed de Valera that he would 'call on Mr C[hartres] and
offer him any aid or advice I can in his Mission'.[26] Michael Collins, in his
capacity as Minister of Finance, was also in touch with Chartres. On 21 June
he sent him a draft cheque for £41 13s. 4d., his monthly salary, and instructed
him that it would always be sent separately from the ordinary expenses.[27]

Other letters on financial matters followed and it was evident that, in the
midst of his other activities, Collins was endeavouring to have all accounts
accurately presented. It was also clear that he had a close relationship with
Chartres that was not simply based on financial matters. Despite the difficulties Nancy Power and Chartres had made a good start. This was reflected
in a report of the Foreign Affairs department for June 1921 which was prepared by Robert Brennan and presented to the Dáil on 17 August. It recorded that 'a Press Bureau has lately been established in Berlin where the
initial work regarding the issuing of a "Bulletin" having been caried out by a
talented young Dublin lady is being continued by the newly appointed envoy.'[28] Towards the end of the month Chartres requested an intelligent and
hard working assistant, and suggested Máire Comerford, with whom he had
been in contact earlier in the year. Although Chartres was happy to recommend Comerford, she was extremely suspicious of him, regarding him as 'a
plant' by British Intelligence. Several communications on the appointment
were received from Brennan. Eventually it was agreed that Nancy Power
was more qualified than Máire Comerford and that she should return to
Berlin, leaving early in September.[29]

In the meantime Chartres was busy. In a letter of 4 July he reported on
his progress. He gave a detailed account of his propaganda work. He was
amazed to find that there was still an 'outwardly friendly attitude towards
the English'.[30] In seeking to explain this anomaly, he suggested that

> the Germans have always had that form of snobbery which admires
> foreign ways, and this sentiment has not been extinguished by the

war so far as England is concerned. There is a sort of feeling that what is English is best, and English character is taken at the English valuation.

France, Italy and Egypt had seen the light, Chartres said, but 'in Germany the lesson remains to be learned'. This benign attitude of many Germans towards England made it harder to promote support for things Irish in opposition to England. Moreover, Chartres reported 'the Irish cause has suffered here from the character ... of some of those who have championed it.'

From these general observations, Chartres drew very definitive conclusions. 'The objectives of our propaganda must be three,' he declared, firstly 'to make known the facts of the Irish situation'; secondly, 'to make clear the qualities and ideals of the Irish nation', and, thirdly, 'to illumine the real character of the English'.[31] He was happy enough with the Bulletin, but suggested a less direct way of advocating Ireland's case.

Instead of focusing on Ireland it would be more effective to introduce the Irish question by highlighting English injustices towards Germany. This he had attempted to do by several articles to the papers. Chartres also had clear views concerning his diplomatic role: 'a main objective of our diplomacy,' he wrote, 'is to secure recognition.' He maintained that it would be extremely difficult for any country to act individually against England, and proposed that a group of powers should be contacted. They should then, in co-operation with the United States, be encouraged to grant recognition to the Republic of Ireland.

Chartres identified America as playing a vital role in this policy. He believed that recognition of Ireland 'would be in fundamental harmony with American political doctrine', and 'would be enormously popular in America'. Moreover, he felt that such a policy would have an advantage for America 'because it would take the Irish question out of American party politics.' Hope in the effectiveness of this policy was engendered by the belief of Chartres that as 'America is profoundly suspicious of English dealings with Japan, it would be all to the interest of America to have an independent, neutral country interposed between American and British shores.'[32]

Chartres reported that he had discussed this approach with Sean T. O'Kelly in Paris, with 'A' in London, possibly Art O'Brien, the Dáil representative, and with Ryan in Berlin. They were all favourably inclined to such a policy. Writing, as he was on 4 July, there was a certain realism behind this proposal when there were grave suspicions between America and England over naval strength and control of the seas. However, Charles Hughes, the American Secretary of State, had seen the British Ambassador on 23 June and made determined efforts to resolve Anglo-American differences. Interestingly enough, these efforts were linked with the Irish situation: basically the English were informed that unless they modified their naval alliance with Japan, America might recognise the Irish Republic. Francis M. Carroll has noted that 'it is significant that the Secretary of State took pains to link the two issues in his talk with the British Ambassador and that the arrangements both for the truce between the British and the Dáil and for the Washington Conference on naval disarmament and Asian affairs co-incided on 11 July 1921.'[33] These developments, while confirming the valid-ity of Chartres' analysis, necessarily modified his initiatives on the diplomatic front. The need for propaganda in Ireland's interest remained, however, as did other aspects of his mission. One of these aspects concerned John T. Ryan.

The relationship between Chartres and Ryan is, in some ways, the most fascinating feature of his time in Berlin: it is also the most difficult to deci-pher. Parts of Chartres' letter of 4 July, and a great deal of the correspond-ence between Berlin and Dublin, were written in numbered code and are quite literally indecipherable. However, contact was certainly made with Ryan, alias 'Professor J', alias 'Jetter'. At the end of June Chartres saw Ryan and they discussed the agent called 'Traveller, no. 70'—presumably this was Gerald Hamilton. Chartres recounted their impressions. 'After observing this gentleman closely,' Chartres declared,

> I was driven to very unfavourable conclusions. So fully was I per-suaded that on June 26th I telegraphed to Paris 'Convinced traveller dishonest.' A day or two later I had an opportunity of discussing him with Professor J. [Ryan], whose impressions confirmed my own. Ryan said, 'Anyone dealing with that man does so, in my opinion, at his peril.'

That was the message that Chartres sent to Dublin. An agent, number 32, had told him of 'immorality, police inquiries and blackmail', concerning 'The Traveller', and Chartres earnestly recommended that 'he should be given no commissions or information of any kind'.[34]

Further evidence of contact between Chartres and Ryan is provided by Patrick McCartan. Passing through Germany in July, while returning from his abortive mission to Russia, McCartan made the interesting observation that Chartres had only got 'his passport extended' because of Ryan's influ-ence with the German authorities. He then added the surprising observa-tion that neither he nor Ryan were aware that Chartres was acting as representative for Dáil Éireann. McCartan also gave Ryan $7,500, presum-ably for the purpose of securing arms.[35]

Another small sign of a contact between Chartres and Ryan is afforded by the fact that Chartres suggested to Brennan that important letters be sent to the address of Michael O'Brien, who was living in Berlin. O'Brien was also in touch with Ryan, and had already acted as a liaison between him and Nancy Power.[36] Although no tangible evidence is revealed in these letters to connect Chartres directly with gun-running, the connection with Ryan indicates that he must have been aware of such activities. A last laconic note may indicate something more. It read: 'Waterford Resolution. This has been received and is being transmitted.'[37] In the light of Waterford being the port to which armaments were soon to be shipped from Germany, it may conceal very relevant information.

The record of Chartres in Berlin after his letter of 4 July is scanty. Some brief letters were despatched by Chartres in which he reported that de Valera was held in the 'greatest respect' in Germany, and in which he advised that a representative be sent to India for a meeting of Gandhi's Congress Party.[38] Brennan's letters were equally brief but kept Chartres aware of developments in Ireland. On 27 July he informed Chartres that the delegates had crossed over to England to meet Lloyd George, and reported that 'the quietness here is absolute'.[39] During this period it is known that the wife of Chartres was with him. She was a great help at a social and personal level until she left for Italy on the last day of July.[40]

Chartres was also kept informed of developments in Ireland by direct personal contact with Michael Collins. On 6 August Collins informed Chartres that 'the Truce is worse than the War;' and he concluded that 'the next moves will probably be more exciting still. I think the victory will be with us.'[41] To this Chartres replied on 20 August that recent events had generated much respect for Ireland, and added that 'one is proud and thankful to belong to such a country.'[42] His embrace of the Irish cause appears to have been complete, and, as if to illustrate his commitment, Chartres ended his letter with the Irish words 'Mise le Meas mór'—I with great respect—a practice that he was to continue.

J.T. Ryan still featured prominently in the correspondence between Berlin and Dublin. On 8 August 1921 Chartres received a coded message with a reminder of the 'absolute necessity for secrecy'. He was told 'to make the Professor Jetter acquainted with the contents'.[43] Chartres replied on 24 August stating that he was receiving great assistance from Jetter.[44] By this time Chartres, following the first meeting of the Second Dáil on 17 August, was listed formally as the representative for Germany. There were eight other representatives: apart from Chartres, they were Sean T. O'Kelly in Paris, Gavan Duffy in Rome, Harry Boland in the United States, Art O'Brien in London, Dr Patrick McCartan for Russia, Eamon Bulfin in the Argentine and Frank W. Egan in Chile. There were also official Press bureaux together with other propaganda agencies, and efforts were made to co-ordinate these activities with the departments of Trade and Publicity. All in all the Foreign

Affairs department had come a long way from the early days of January 1919, and, on hearing the report in the Dáil, Sean Milroy declared that all 'must be impressed profoundly by the enormous work accomplished by this Department. They have, I think, deserved well of Ireland.'[45]

Despite the progress in the Foreign Affairs department, Arthur Griffith replaced Count Plunkett as Minister for Foreign Affairs on 26 August 1921.[46] The change was part of the overall policy to have a smaller and more efficient cabinet. The leading figures in the republican movement retained their posts, while the lesser figures assumed offices without cabinet status. Although the change did not affect Chartres—indeed his position may well have been enhance by his personal acquaintance with Griffith—it did have major implications for the cabinet.

One indirect, but critical, effect of this policy was to remove the more advanced republicans from the cabinet— men like Plunkett, who was moved to Fine Arts, J.J. O'Kelly, Countess Markievicz, Art O'Connor and Sean Etchingham. Their voices were not to be heard at cabinet level during the Treaty debate, whereas they had been in attendance to voice their objections to Lloyd George's terms in August. Robert Brennan, however, remained in his post as Under-Secretary. In that capacity he advised Chartres on 25 August to see Sean T. O'Kelly, when he returned to Paris, in order to obtain a fuller picture of diplomatic developments in Ireland.[47] O'Kelly had spent some time in Dublin and as a Dáil deputy had attended the meetings of the Dáil. The negotiations between de Valera and Lloyd George had finished, and, as Brennan informed Chartres, the situation was very precarious: peace might be achieved or war might be resumed. If war was to be the option, then arms would be needed.

On 5 September Chartres began a detailed report to Brennan, which was only completed on the eighteenth of the month. His base was the Eden Hotel, Berlin. He reported that the Bulletin was now in printed form and was being used by certain papers, such as the *Deutsches Tageblatt*, the *Deutsches Abendblatt* and the *Westen*. He wrote,

> For the moment, newspaper publicity has received a check through the suppression for fourteen days of a number of papers—among them some of those most sympathetic towards ourselves—following the shooting of Erzberger.[48]

Erzberger was assassinated on 26 August. Chartres provided no further details, but the murder of Erzberger, the former friend of the German Irish Society, indicated the extremely fragile and volatile condition of the Weimar Republic. Many political groups of both left and right were extremely opposed to the Weimar regime, which they believed was too sympathetic to

the allies diktat at Versailles. Erzberger, as a signatory of the Versailles settlement, became a symbol of German humiliation and this led to his assassination by right-wing military forces.

It was in this delicate situation that Chartres attempted to promote Irish
interests, even writing articles for the papers himself; and it may be significant that his views were most welcome in the paper, *Deutsches Abenblatt*,
which belonged, in Chartres' view, to 'the extreme right'. Chartres made
four specific suggestions to advance Ireland's standing in German eyes: firstly,
he requested exclusive interviews by the President and others to be used for
propaganda purposes; secondly, he wanted articles of general human interest, for example on Irish games or music, and illustrated with photographs;
thirdly, he proposed lecture tours with lantern slides on Irish history; and,
fourthly, he announced that his book *The Bloody English* was being translated into German and that Tirpitz was willing to write a preface for it.
Chartres suggested that the book be first published in America in English,
signed in his own name, and then placed on the German market in translation. He concluded by noting that much interest had been generated in Germany by the Anglo-Irish negotiations, and observed that 'the undeviating
adherence to principle in the President's communications seem wonderful
to the Germans'.[49]

The remark, 'Germany has much to learn from Ireland,' was to be heard
frequently on German lips, and on a personal level, Chartres reported that
there was much sympathy for Ireland. However, on the official diplomatic
level the Weimar Government could not afford to show sympathy to Ireland. Chartres, in outlining the diplomatic realities that dictated this policy,
made clear the political realities that governed the functioning of the Weimar
regime. 'The subservience of German Ministers and officials to the English
is extreme,' he wrote, 'is, in fact, almost incomprehensible.' It was only
understandable, he wrote, in the light of the terms of the Versailles Treaty.
Chartres reported that the German aim

> partly through policy as a measure against the French and partly
> through sheer fear of the consequences of a more independent atti-
> tude, is to stand as well with the English as possible ... the *mot d'ordre*
> seems clearly to be to play the English game to the limit.

This attitude made it impossible for Chartres to announce his position publicly. He explained that

> l have been assured in different quarters that to announce oneself
> openly as the envoy of the Irish Government would lead to private

protests from the English and would probably result in my having to leave the country.

In the course of elucidating the political climate in the country, Chartres also revealed the precariousness of his own position. He stated that

> I have had only a temporary permission to stay here and until a permanent authorisation was obtained I could have been obliged to leave not by an act of revocation or expulsion but by the simple device of not renewing the passport for a further short period.

He hoped to receive permission to extend his residence permit in a few days, but he was in no doubt that, if the British made any protest against his conduct, 'the present German Government would give way at once and do whatever was required of it.' Chartres, therefore, was forced to act cautiously and circumspectly. Ryan agreed with this approach; he 'was anxious that no disturbing steps should be taken for a time'.[50] Concluding his letter on 18 September, Chartres noted that Nancy Power had not yet arrived. She was soon to do so, however.

In early September Robert Brennan gave Nancy Power various instructions concerning codes for Chartres, to whom she was to report.[51] When she returned to Berlin at the end of September she found that considerable developments had taken place on the arms front. She recalled that

> Mr Briscoe was in Berlin but I thought it better not to make any contact with him. He was there for the purpose of purchasing arms; and it appeared to me better that the open and underground movements should not come together.[52]

The Irish 'underground movement', as Power puts it, was very strong in Berlin at that time. Robert Briscoe, Sean MacBride and Charles McGuinness, a qualified sea captain, operating under the name of 'Captain Thompson', were all in Berlin for the purchase and shipment of arms. They were in touch with J.T. Ryan, although the level of their connection is uncertain.[53]

Briscoe, a Dublin-born Jew of Lithuanian origin, had worked in Germany before the War and spoke the language fluently. Furthermore he knew his way around Berlin and had many useful contacts. Through an association with Liam Mellows, Director of Purchases of the IRA, he was approached by Michael Collins and agreed to smuggle guns into Ireland from Europe. This was in early 1920. A company named 'Kenny, Murray Ltd' was set up in Ballinasloe as a front for this operation.[54] Once in Germany Briscoe established contact with Major Hassenhauer of the Orgesh, one of the many secret organisations of disaffected German military personnel who resented the Allied intervention in their country.[55] The Major was willing and able to provided guns and ammunition in return for money. Through this source Briscoe had directed many small supplies of arms into Ireland in the past.

When he returned to Germany in September 1921, it was with the intention of supplying arms on a much larger scale. McGuinness had a vital part to play in this new type of operation. He had been seen by Mellows and Collins soon after the Truce and had arrived in Germany in September. The plan was that he would buy a ship for the delivery of arms. He was given £30,000 for this purpose.[56] It would appear almost certain that Chartres, granted his connection with Ryan, must have been aware of these developments. However, events in Ireland were dramatically to change the circumstances of Chartres.

The Truce of 11 July had been followed by the abortive talks between de Valera and Lloyd George. However, after much background activity and following a meeting of Irish delegates with Lloyd George at Gairloch in Scotland on 12 September, it was decided to make a further attempt to hold a conference between Britsh and Irish representatives. Collins wrote to Chartres the next day commiserating with him at 'not being in at the final'; and, having noted some problems with codes, explained that 'I meant you to use that cipher for me only. Kindly note this particularly and oblige.'[57]

Whatever formal links Chartres had with Foreign Affairs, it is evident that he also had a direct line to Collins. He made use of this line on 18 September to give his view to Collins that 'clearly a conference without conditions was the only possibility. I believe England can be pushed further ... the diplomacy for Ireland has been magnificent.' He concluded by wishing Collins good luck 'in his wonderful fight for Ireland', and asked him to deduct £100 from his salary towards the new Dáil loan.[58] The conference was called for early October and events conspired to bring Chartres back to London for the final act. At a ministry meeting of Dáil Éireann on 30 September 1921 it was decided that Chartres should be recalled from Berlin 'in connection with the Peace Delegation;' and he was summoned to Dublin on 3 October.'[59]

He was to be second secretary to the conference. Originally the names of Harry Boland and Kevin O'Higgins had appeared as possible candidates, but the final selection was for Erskine Childers, Fionan Lynch and Chartres, who arrived back in Dublin on Thursday 6 October.[60] As a qualified common lawyer, it was intended that Chartres would give legal advice. According to Nancy Power, Chartres had told Griffith that he was not a constitutional lawyer, but was prepared to do his best on constitutional matters.[61]

This appointment of Chartres gave even more prominence to his change of allegiance. As Jennie Wyse Power confided to her daughter, Nancy, 'to my amazement your boss is included in the secretariat—so he is in the open at last.'[62] Robert Brennan wrote to Nancy Power on 7 October regretting that Chartres had been called away, and asked her 'to carry on alone.'[63] While Nancy Power, John T. Ryan and Robert Briscoe were acting in their diverse ways for Irish interests in Berlin, John Chartres was required to direct his energies towards the London treaty negotiations.

The Plenary Conference Meetings

The Quest for External Recognition
11–24 October 1921

John Chartres attended a meeting with de Valera at about 11 p.m. on 7 October in the company of Childers and Gavan Duffy. They discussed the draft of a Treaty which would serve as the basis for the negotiations that were to be conducted by the plenipotentiaries. Gavan Duffy had also been recalled from his assignment in Foreign Affairs to act as one of the plenipotentiaries. As a solicitor, who had later trained as a barrister, his legal qualifications equipped him well to contribute to the negotiations. The document that resulted from the meeting was described as the 'Combined alternative drafts for work on by Delegation.'[1]

The plenipotentiaries—Arthur Griffith, the Chairman, Michael Collins, Robert Barton, Eamon Duggan and Gavan Duffy—had received their credentials and instructions earlier in the day of 7 October.[2] Griffith, as Minister of Foreign Affairs, Collins, as Minister of Finance, and Barton, as Minister of Economic Affairs, were members of the Dáil Cabinet. The entire entourage, Collins excepted, sailed for England together on the following day. As well as the delegates a large gathering of junior secretaries, domestic helpers and bodyguards made the journey.

Chartres and most of the delegates were housed in 22 Hans Place, while Michael Collins and his aides were based in 15 Cadogan Gardens. One of these aides, the teen-aged Sean MacBride, had like Chartres been recalled from his mission to Germany.[3] The houses were located in the residential area of Kensington and were some ten minutes walking distance apart. It was noted that on Sunday, 9 October, Chartres along with Erskine Childers and Robert Barton attended Matins at St Luke's Chelsea, while the Catholics in the group went to Mass at Brompton Oratory.

Childers recorded that all the party, except Chartres and himself, went for a car drive in the afternoon in the countryside. He and Chartres arranged the office, classified the books, and typed out the President's draft Treaty. They worked late, retiring to bed at 2 a.m. On 10 October they went to Downing Street and discussed procedures for recording the confer-

ence meetings with Tom Jones and Sir Maurice Hankey. Ironically Hankey
had last seen Childers while fighting on the same side with him on the beaches
of Gallipoli. Jones felt that Childers and Chartres 'were very stiff and most
cautious in all their utterances'.[4]

They had good reason to be reserved. Apart from a fear that they might
concede something of material advantage to the Republican position, they
must have realised the incongruity of two men born in England, and associated with England in the last War, presenting to men of similar upbringing
the Irish claim for independence. After a second visit to Jones, agreement
was reached on procedures, and the British announced that Sir Edward Grigg
would replace Hankey as one of the English secretaries. He soon gave way
to Lionel Curtis. Arthur Griffith informed de Valera that Childers and Chartres had seen their opposite numbers on the British side, and that they had
'made arrangements re. the meeting tomorrow.'[5]

For Chartres the transition from position of responsibility in the British
intelligence service to envoy for the Republic of Ireland in Berlin, and from
there to secretary on Ireland's behalf in the peace treaty with England was
sudden and remarkable. Although the *Irish Independent* did focus at this time
on the background of Chartres, it does not seem to have caused any wide-
spread comment. The position of secretary may not have seemed sufficiently
important to merit investigation and possible controversy. However, Chartres was to act not only as secretary, but also in his capacity as a lawyer; and
in that capacity he had a special responsibility for drafting the constitutional
terms for Ireland's relationship with the British Crown. It is this role of
Chartres that makes his change of loyalty so remarkable and so worthy of
inquiry: one year he was acting in British interests to uphold the Crown
against the Irish rebels; the next year he was acting in Ireland's interests to
weaken the claims of the British Crown in Ireland. The first plenary conference of the negotiations took place at 10 Downing Street on 11 October
1921 at 11 a.m. Chartres was there.

The plan of the seating arrangement shows that Chartres sat between
Arthur Griffith and Michael Collins, although some distance behind them.
Lloyd George was facing him. Other members of the English delegation
were Sir Austen Chamberlain, who did not attend the first meeting, Lord
Birkenhead (F.E. Smith), Winston Churchill, Sir Hamar Greenwood and
Sir Gordon Hewart. The secretaries to the English delegation, Tom Jones
and Lionel Curtis, sat, like their Irish opposite numbers, some distance from
the table.[6] Chartres attended all but one the seven plenary conferences that
took place between 11 and 24 October.[7] He was also present at the only
meeting of the committee on Financial Relations on 19 October, and attended one of the five committee meetings on the observance of the Truce
which took place between 12 October and 10 November. Robert Barton

recorded that both Chartres and Childers took long-hand notes of the plenary conference meetings, which were later written up and transmitted to de Valera in Dublin. Chartres was, therefore, at the heart of things.[8]

The first meeting of the plenary conference was designed to promote a working atmosphere, rather than to provoke controversy. As Griffith reported to de Valera after the first meeting, 'The meeting has left on my mind the impression that the English Government is anxious for peace'; and added, 'The question of the Crown and Ulster did not arise. When they do, the sailing will be rough.'[9] Griffith was very soon to be proved correct. That very afternoon, at the second sitting of the conference at 4 p.m., Lloyd George threw into a discussion on defence the observation that 'Royalty is very useful. They are getting to recognise that in the Dominions.'[10] He then proposed that Lionel Curtis draft 'an agreed statement about Dominion status'. Such a statement was bound to raise the issue of the Crown.

De Valera wrote to Arthur Griffith on 14 October suggesting a plan of procedure for the Irish side. He made particular comments about Ulster and the Truce, but also proposed a plan of campaign over the Crown. He urged that it should be treated as part of 'the broad question of "Association"'.[11] De Valera maintained that both Childers and Duffy agreed with him in this approach, and he expressed the view that the drafts which he gave to them and Chartres on the eve of their departure should form the basis of negotiation. The planned procedure was extremely complex, but it merits consideration for two reasons: firstly, to elucidate the context in which Chartres acted; and, secondly, to show that, from the very first great thought had gone into the idea of Association. De Valera maintained that he had briefed Childers, Chartres and Duffy to view the drafts in the following light: the A draft contained 'the preliminary counter proposals'; the B draft was 'the breaking proposals'; and the S draft indicated 'a contemplated signed Treaty'.

While the drafts contained no direct recommendations regarding the Crown, Ireland's position in regard to England was, however, stated very precisely. On the one hand, Great Britain 'recognises Ireland as a sovereign and independent state'; on the other hand, 'Ireland agrees to become ... an external associate of the British Commonwealth.'[12] The focus of attention was to be on loyalty to the Association rather than to the Crown itself. This line of approach had been adopted by de Valera since 27 July , when, in the course of his earlier discussions with Lloyd George, it had suddenly dawned on him that the concept of Association might resolve all difficulties. His biographers have given a vivid description of the origin of de Valera's concept:

he was tying his bootlaces, sitting on the side of his bed at Glenvar, when the word 'external' flashed into his mind. It would clarify all that he had been trying to say ... The whole idea was that Ireland would be *associated with* the Commonwealth but not a *member* of the Commonwealth. [13]

In pursuance of this policy he had, therefore, laid down very clear guidelines, and expected to be consulted on all issues of importance; but he ended the letter of 14 October with the observation that 'we must depend on your side for the initiative after this.'

John Chartres had already shown initiative. On 14 October, the same day as de Valera's letter, Chartres had submitted a memorandum on the Crown to Arthur Griffith. [14] The dilemma as he saw it was that, 'We desire technically as well as substantially, to preserve the Republic and the President. The English desire technically not to sacrifice the King.' The problem was to reconcile these conflicting aspirations. Chartres proposed a compromise based on two assumptions: 'assume that Ireland is acknowledged to be a sovereign, independent state ... and assume that this sovereign and independent Ireland is prepared to associate herself for certain purposes with the British Commonwealth of Nations.' [15] Based on these two assumptions Chartres suggested a solution:

> It is clear that Ireland cannot associate herself with the British Commonwealth without associating herself with the monarch who stands at the head of the Commonwealth. To the extent, therefore, to which this association extends, the King could be recognised as the official head of the whole combination.

Such a recognition, Chartres contended, would not take away from the independence of the Irish Republic or of its President. 'Our national independence would have been secured and our honour saved.' [16]

He also expressed the hope that Ulster might be induced to come into this arrangement. The memorandum was clearly in accord with the thinking of de Valera: the problem of the Crown was to be resolved in the context of Association, as de Valera wished; and in that context it was eminently sound. Barton acknowledged that Chartres 'was mainly responisble for the formula by which Ireland as an external associate was to give recognition to the King as head of the Association'. [17] From the Irish point of view, indeed, it may be said to have offered a possible way forward.

It contained one fatal weakness: it underestimated the strength of England's commitment to the Crown. Chartres assumed that 'the English would probably be content with a very partial and shadowy recognition of the

Crown'.[18] This was not the case; and, as the negotiations proceeded, it was to prove impossible to reconcile Irish aspirations for independence with English loyalty to the Crown.

Ulster, rather than the Crown, however, dominated discussion at the plenary conference of 14 October, and Griffith reported back to de Valera on the days happenings. De Valera replied immediately again making mention of the Crown. He reinforced his earlier instruction: it should be treated in the context of external association; and the draft treaty A offered the best line of procedure. He concluded by saying that 'I expect the battle-royal on the main treaty will take place during the coming week.'[19] He was to be proved right.

The fifth plenary conference meeting assembled at 10 Downing Street at 3.30 p.m. on Monday 17 October. The main topic of discussion was Ulster. The next plenary meeting was not held until Friday, 21 October. In part the slight break was caused by the other committee meetings that occurred at this time. On 17 and 18 October meetings concerning the Truce and Defence were held; and on 19 October a meeting of the Finance committee took place. Chartres attended this as secretary.

Henry Mangan, who also attended the meeting as a financial adviser on the Irish side, recalled that Michael Collins put in a large claim from the British for the over taxation of Ireland. Sir L. Worthington-Evans responded to this by remarking 'Oh! Mr Collins, you want to bring the claim back to Brian Boru.'[20] Laughter from the English side, and even smiles on the Irish side, followed this remark. As the meeting ended Mangan was alone at the conference table with Collins, when Chartres suddenly 'came up, looking very annoyed, and in a low but intensely angry tones said to Collins: "Did you see how they laughed at us? It was infamous."' That was how Mangan saw the scene, and he concluded that the emotions of Chartres 'were out of tune with those of the other Irish representatives.' Mangan, it should be noted, was highly suspicious of Chartres; nevertheless it would appear correct to say that Chartres, at this time, was extremely sensitive to, and critical of, all British representatives.

While this difference among the Irish officials was purely personal, more serious grounds for acrimony arose over the Defence meetings, and these differences had serious implications for the conference as a whole.[21] The Irish representatives were Emmet Dalton, J.J. O'Connell and Eoin O'Duffy. They were selected by Collins and not by the Minister of Defence, Cathal Brugha. They were also loyal to Collins. Diarmuid O'Hegarty, who was secretary to that committee, was a member of the IRB and, therefore, in the Collins camp as well. Brugha had good grounds to be unhappy and uneasy with this development.

After the Easter Rising Brugha and de Valera had attempted to organise the new Irish nationalist movement free from the influence of the secret body of the IRB, and their attitude on this matter was one of the main issues dividing them from Michael Collins, who was President of the IRB. In April 1919 Brugha had taken the initiative in requiring all members of the Irish Volunteers to take the oath of loyalty to Dáil Éireann. This action, although resisted by Collins, made the Volunteers responsible to the republican Dáil and effectively created the Irish Republican Army.

Following the truce of 11 July Brugha had attempted to enforce his control over the Army in opposition to that of Richard Mulcahy, the Chief of Staff, who was loyal to Collins, threatening to dismiss him twice.[22] Collins, by persevering with the IRB organisation, was sanctioning a divided loyalty among the fighting men, and his efforts to influence the Defence committee at the Treaty negotiations indicated that beneath the surface a struggle for control of the military was taking place. Possibly one can detect in this dispute over the Defence committee the first sign of a serious division in the Irish ranks, and the realisation by those involved that at the end of the day it would be those who controlled the Army who would be able to implement their policy. At the end of November, at the climax of the Treaty negotiations, the issue over control of the army was to surface again in a far more dramatic form.

Chartres, in the midst of these other activities, still firmly set his sights on the problem of the Crown. On 20 October he submitted a further and more detailed memorandum.[23] The preface might indicate that he had gone over to the English side completely for he wrote that 'the following observations are based on the assumption that it has been decided to recognise the British King.' However, in the four points that he made, it was evident that he placed this recognition of the King inside the framework of external association. In short he developed the idea expressed in his memorandum of 14 October and he expanded it cleverly.

Chartres seized on a statement that Lloyd George had made in his correspondence with de Valera on 26 August 1921, and tried to turn it against Lloyd George and in favour of the Irish position. 'Ireland would control every nerve and fibre of her National existence', Lloyd George had written, '... She would', in fact, he continued, 'within the shores of Ireland, be free in every aspect of national activity, national expression, and national development.'[24] Chartres then posed the question, 'In an Ireland as free as this from external control what room would there be for the King?' He maintained, moreover, that Ireland should not be treated as a Dominion, and concluded that Ireland's 'freedom must be technical as well as substantial. There will be no Veto, no Viceroy, no Union flag. The King will have no concern, however technical, in Irish legislation, nor be the head, however shadowy, of the Irish army ... Only so can our independence be secured, our people satisfied and our honour saved.'[25]

If the internal independence of Ireland was to be argued for in this absolutist manner, Chartres did concede that there was an external sphere in which some connection with England could be acknowledged. Again he turned to a letter of Lloyd George to develop his proposal. Lloyd George had written to de Valera that 'Our proposals go even further, for they invite Ireland to take her place as a partner in the great commonwealth of free nations united by allegiance to the King.' Chartres suggested that it was 'in this further sphere and only here that contact could be established between Ireland and the British Crown.' In this very precisely defined relationship Ireland was to 'associate herself with a group of free nations united together by the British Crown ... [and] we should acknowledge the head of the Partnership, that is, the King'.

Chartres developed this proposal in practical terms. He proposed that

> as an external act of recognition Ireland should vote a modest annual amount to the Civil list. It would not be a tax levied by England in Ireland. It would be a sum voted annually by the Irish Government to the King, not as King of Ireland, or as any factor in the Government of Ireland, but by way of contribution in respect of those "affairs of agreed common concern" outside Ireland in which Ireland would be associated with the partnership of States over which the King reigns.

An air of optimism coloured Chartres conclusions: he felt confident that Ireland's case was a good one—a fair one; and he also felt that Lloyd George would be happy to see his proposal as a way out of a difficult problem. 'If we provided him with a case of this kind,' Chartres argued, 'and let him know that the alternative was failure, he would probably strain every nerve to see it through.'[26] The same weakness that Chartres had shown in his first memorandum of 14 October was again manifested: he underestimated the resolve of Lloyd George and his team to uphold the prerogatives of the British Crown. Even if Lloyd George might have been happy to look for a way out, and there is no proof that he was, he had no room for manoeuvre in a Cabinet that was a coalition of Liberals and Conservatives. Ireland's case on the Crown, nevertheless, was to be fought on the grounds and the assumptions that were defined by Chartres in accordance with the guide lines of de Valera.

It might have been expected that the Crown would be discussed at length at the sixth plenary conference on Friday 21 October which began at 12 noon. It was not to be, however. The conference was disrupted by the star-

tling revelation of Lloyd George that the there had been a major infringe-
ment of the Truce by the Irish. 'Our first proof comes from Germany,' he
said angrily; 'the German police have seized a ship with arms on board for
your people; it contains field guns, rifles, pistols and large quantitities of
ammunition.'[27] Chartres was not at Downing Street to hear this complaint.

It is hard to believe that his absence from the meeting was not connected
with the gun-running allegation by Lloyd George. The incident was occasioned by the arrest at Hamburg of Charlie McGuinness in possession of a
large supply of arms on board a ship. Having made contact with Robert
Briscoe in September, he had bought a ship, the *Anita*, and loaded it with
arms. It was to the seizure of this ship and the subsequent trial of McGuinness
that Lloyd George referred on 21 October. Collins instructed Sean MacBride
to travel to Hamburg immediately to assess the situation.[28] In these circumstances it was not surprising that Chartres also made plans to leave London.

He could not leave immediately, however. The conference of 21 October ended with Lloyd George at last raising questions about allegiance to
the Crown, and demanding answers. Chartres had to make his contribution
to this debate before he could depart. Lloyd George asked the Irish delegates to present a memorandum before the next meeting that would deal,
firstly, with 'the question of allegiance to the King'; and, secondly, the issue
as to 'whether Ireland is prepared to come freely and of her own accord
within the fraternity of nations known as the British Empire'.[29] There was
also a recognition by Lloyd George that Michael Collins had presented 'a
formidable document' on defence which challenged English assumptions,
and which needed clarification.[30]

Faced by questions concerning not only the Crown and Defence, but
also the matter of gun-running, the Irish delegates met at 3 p.m. in the rooms
of John Chartres. Requests for instructions from de Valera were drafted and
Michael Collins set off for Dublin with them.[31] Over the weekend of 22 and
23 October Chartres and Childers were extremely busy. As well as focusing
on a memorandum on the Crown and Dominions status, they were also
occupied in drafting memoranda on Finance and Defence.

On both days Tim Healy, who was in touch with Lloyd George, visited
them. Attempts by Healy, who regarded the outlook as black, to act as an
official intermediary were prevented by the opposition of Childers and
Chartres. They objected to him presenting their memorandum to Lloyd
George. Healy departed to present his scheme of a Channel Island-type solution to Lloyd George on the next day.[32]

Meanwhile Childers and Chartres renewed their efforts to complete their
memorandum. They worked until 2 a.m. assisted by Gavan Duffy. The next
morning Childers was up at 7 a.m. typing up the draft proposals. At 9.30
a.m. Griffith brought his introduction to be typed, and at 10.30 a.m. there

was a meeting of the delegates. Many changes were needed in the Defence memorandum which effectively meant, according to Childers, that 'neutrality [was] scrapped'.[33] He and Chartres revised the new draft and had it ready by 3.15 p.m. The Irish memorandum was then rapidly transmitted to Lloyd George and presented to him at 3.20 p.m., too late in the day to receive sufficient consideration before the meeting began at 5 p.m.

In many ways the Irish memorandum of 24 October was simply a statement of the question: it recalled the origins of the Conference—to ascertain 'how the association of Ireland with the community of nations known as the British Empire may best be reconciled with Irish National Aspirations'; and noted that they were now no nearer a solution. It was claimed that Ireland was 'an ancient and spirited nation'; that, despite explicit promises, England was not conferring full Dominion status; that partition was unacceptable; but it accepted that 'Ireland will consent to adhere for all purposes of agreed concern, to the League of Sovereign States associated and known as the British Commonwealth of Nations.' In return for this association, it was proposed that 'Ireland be recognised as a free State'.[34] There was no explicit mention of the Crown. It was to the Crown, however, that Lloyd George immediately directed his questions. The following discussion took place:

> *Lloyd George*: Take the word 'adhere'. Does that mean that if all other conditions are satisfied you are prepared to come inside the Empire, as New Zealand, and Canada?
> *Griffith*: That is not quite our idea of association.
> *Lloyd George*: Association is not the position of Canada and Australia. What is the distinction between association and coming inside the Empire?
> *Griffith*: We should be associated with you—outside that a free people. They are bound by the link of the Crown.
> *Lloyd George*: By 'adhere' you don't accept the link of the Crown?
> *Griffith*: We would accept the Crown as head of the association.[35]

The cross examination of Griffith by Lloyd George continued. Throughout the interrogation Griffith attempted to maintain the formula of 'the Crown as head of the association'—an external association. In preserving this stand he was acting in accordance with the instructions of de Valera and the memoranda of Chartres.

At this vital stage in the negotiations, when the nettle of the Crown was finally being grasped, there was a sudden change in the procedure of the Conference. Lloyd George and his colleagues withdrew and an arrangement was made for him and Chamberlain to see Arthur Griffith and Michael

Collins from 6 p.m. until 7.15 p.m. While these talks were taking place Childers and Chartres wrote up the minutes of the earlier meeting.[36]

A significant stage in the negotiations had been reached: the plenary conference meetings had ended. The Crown and other central issues of the negotiations were to be resolved by meetings between the British representatives and, apart from a few broader based meetings, Griffith and Collins alone.

The Sub-conference Meetings

The Republic at Risk
25 October – 24 November 1921

Alfred, 'Andy', Cope, Assistant Under-Secretary at Dublin Castle, played a leading part in the setting up of the sub-conference meetings. At the request of Griffith and Collins, made through Duggan, Cope made the arrangements for this first private meeting with Lloyd George. The British Prime Minister, for his part, was convinced that more could be done with Griffith and Collins alone, and he was particularly anxious to exclude Childers from the conferences because he was too extreme in his demands.[1] Cope's vital part in this stage of the negotiations was to presage a future role in the conference that was to prove equally important.

He had been a detective with a long and successful career in the Customs service before he was appointed to the new Dublin Castle administration of May 1920. In this capacity he had made many secret contacts with the Sinn Féin leaders in order to bring about the Truce. After the imprisonment of Griffith and Duggan in December 1920, Cope had established contact with them, and, through them, opened lines of communication with Michael Collins. Most significantly, in the critical days before the Truce was secured on 11 July 1921, Cope on his own initiative ordered the release from prison of Griffith and Duggan. He did this so that they might bring pressure upon de Valera to accept a cease fire. At that time Duggan remarked to Cope that 'our labours were nearly over'.[2]

Following the signing of the Truce Cope intervened decisively on several occasions, notably at the Gairloch meeting in September, to keep the peace talks going. He was also in personal contact with Michael Collins, meeting him with Duggan soon after the Truce was declared on 11 July.[3] While it is also true that both de Valera and Childers were arrested for short periods before the Truce, and also released at the request of Cope, there is no evidence of any enduring relationship between them and him. The relationship of Cope, however, with Collins, Griffith and Duggan was a significant factor in the coming negotiations.

For the present Griffith informed de Valera of the outcome of the first sub-conference meeting with Lloyd George and Chamberlain on 24 October. 'The burden of their story,' Griffith wrote, 'was that on the Crown they must fight.' 'I told them,' he added, 'that the only possibility of Ireland considering Association of any kind with the Crown was in exchange for essential unity.'[4]

De Valera gave his response on 25 October. His secretary noted that an 'important dispatch [was] sent to Plenipotentiaries by special courier. President very much disturbed over communications received from delegation.' Griffith was informed by de Valera that

> we are all here at one that there can be no question of our asking the Irish people to enter an arrangement which would make them subject to the Crown, or demand from them allegiance to the British King. If war is the alternative, we can only face it, and I think that the sooner the other side is made to realise that the better.[5]

This letter provoked a storm among the delegates. Some of them felt that their powers as plenipotentiaries were being restricted; and Griffith, Collins and Duggan, according to Barton, were very angry. In reply it was made clear that the delegates viewed de Valera's observations on the Crown as 'inconsistent with the powers given them on their appointment'.[6] They stated that 'obviously any form of association necessitates discussion of recognition in some form or other of the head of the association'; but they maintained that their instructions conferred upon them 'this power of discussion'. The letter concluded, 'we strongly resent, in the position in which we are placed, the interference with our powers'.[7]

While all the delegates signed the letter, there was a marked difference of approach amongst them, indicating lines of division that were to endure to the end of the negotiations. Barton and Duffy felt that de Valera's letter did not call for such a firm reaction—feeling, indeed, that Griffith had exaggerated the threat of war; but Griffith, Duggan and Collins were bitterly opposed to it. Collins, indeed, claimed that those in Dublin were trying to 'get me to do the dirty work for them', and threatened to return to Dublin.[8] De Valera endeavoured to placate the delegates in a letter to Griffith on 27 October. 'There is obviously a misunderstanding,' he wrote. 'There can be no question of tying the hands of the plenipotentiaries.' His memoranda, de Valera stated, 'are nothing more than an attempt to keep you in touch with the views of the members of the Cabinet here', so that they might act in a manner to secure a unified Cabinet decision at the end of the day. It was also agreed that de Valera should not go to London.[9]

It was in these critical circumstances—the delegates divided amongst themselves and dealing with Lloyd George as a divided group—that Chartres prepared a further note on the Crown. In some ways it was a response to a British memorandum which, according to Childers ,was 'very stiff', and which had been received on 27 October.[10] Moves were made by the English Government to have further dialogue and Andy Cope of the Irish Office attempted to contact Barton or Duggan. Eventually Childers saw Cope and was persuaded to see Lloyd George on the following day. They talked for one hour and Childers reported back to two meetings of the delegates which took place in the morning and afternoon of 28 October. In the evening Childers and Chartres worked from 8 p.m. until 1 a.m. drafting a memorandum in reply to that of the English. The other delegates, according to Childers, went to the theatre.[11]

This 'Further Memorandum' was completed the next day and transmitted to the English. It was a one-page document which clarified the Irish position in response to the British memorandum of the 27 October, and it contained some of the observations made privately by Chartres in his note of 28 October. The English memorandum had declared that 'the first question of Imperial importance is allegiance to the Crown. The Crown is the symbol of all that keeps the nations of the Empire together.'[12] Chartres had proposed, in reply, on 28 October that a free Ireland,

> in complete control of her own destiny and in unfettered and absolute possession within her own shores of all legislative and executive authority, should for the purposes of the treaty of association voluntary recognise the Crown as the symbol and titular head of the combination of signatory states.

It was this formula, with very slight emendations, that formed the basis of the 'Further Memorandum' drawn up by Chartres and Childers on 29 October, and which has been called by Pakenham the 'Chartres Crown'.[13] This memorandum, which Chartres and Childers had worked so hard upon, denied from the outset that the English memorandum constituted an adequate reply to their earlier proposals of 24 October.

Concessions were then made, on the Irish side, in regard to Defence: it was, for example, agreed 'that the British Government should have, under license from the Irish Government, such coastal facilities as may be agreed to be necessary'; and flexibility was shown in regard to finance and trade. However, it was firmly stated that 'the unimpaired unity of Ireland is a condition precedent to the conclusion of a Treaty of Association'; and it was then proposed that:

> the Irish Delegates are prepared to recommend that the Elected Gov-
> ernment of a free and undivided legislative and executive authority,
> should, for the purposes of the association, recognise the Crown as
> symbol and accepted head of the combined signatory States.[14]

While the British Government was preparing to make a response to this
'Further Memorandum', De Valera communicated his own view of it to
Griffith. He was not entirely satisfied. 'We are not quite certain,' he wrote,
'what exactly the last three lines may involve, and accordingly refrain from
making any comment.' [15] The last lines focused on the recognition of 'the
Crown as a symbol and acepted head of the combination of signatory States'.
While de Valera made no comment, he referred Griffith to his letter of 25
October, which had provoked so much controversy, and in which he had
asserted that there could be no subjection to the Crown or allegiance to the
King. He was, therefore, not entirely happy.

During the next five days—30 October to 3 November—there were five
meetings of the sub-conferences. Griffith and Collins met their British coun-
terparts alone and without the presence of secretaries. It was in this context
that vital decisions were made concerning the approach to the Crown and
Ulster. The move towards sub-conferences was accompanied by several secret meetings of other individuals in which Andy Cope figured prominently.
Immediately after the 'Further Memorandum' was presented, Cope urgently
requested that Duggan should meet Tom Jones. This was done, and it was
made clear to Duggan that the Memorandum was 'most unsatisfactory'.[16]

On the next day, Sunday 30 October, Cope called upon Griffith and
Collins to meet Lloyd George and Birkenhead at Churchill's house. They
met at 10 p.m. and a private conversation took place between Lloyd George
and Griffith. Childers called it a 'very critical day, perhaps the most critical
for Ireland of all days in centuries'.[17] He complained that he and Chartres
were at work until 2 a.m. summarising the content of the meeting. Lloyd
George had called for a response to the issues of the Crown, the Empire and
the Navy. In his draft reply Griffith, while firm on the unity of Ireland, had
offered to recommend 'recognition of the Crown', and 'free partnership
with the British Commonwealth', if satisfactory formulae could be devised.[18]

The next day at a meeting of the Irish delegates Griffith proposed that he
should write a private letter to Lloyd George on the subject of loyalty to
the Crown which would reflect his exchange of views with Lloyd George.
Jones and Lloyd George had talked about such a letter as the best way forward on 29 October.[19] Gavan Duffy made a protest about such a procedure
and, according to Childers, he, together with Gavan Duffy and Chartres, sat
up until 1 a.m. 'discussing opposition' to the proposal.[20]

The issue became more acute on the morning of 2 November. Over breakfast Griffith informed Childers that he saw no reason for another delegates meeting. However, he adjourned to Childers' room and they were joined by Gavan Duffy and Barton and later by Collins and Duggan. Gavan Duffy renewed his criticism of Griffith's private letter because 'it went back on our own Memos'.[21] He maintained that in the joint memorandum of 29 October they had 'very carefully limited the recognition of the British crown'; and he argued that the vagueness of Griffith's proposal served 'to undermine the stand we have taken'.[22] He also asserted that Association had not been discussed at the Conference proper, and that the British had presented no answer to the Irish memoranda. Faced by this protest by Duffy, which was also supported by Barton and Childers, Griffith used very abusive language, but agreed to modify his personal letter. However, despite these issues, the letter was redrafted and presented to Lord Birkenhead by Griffith and Collins at 11.20 a.m. that morning.

That evening Griffith and Collins met Lloyd George, Birkenhead and Chamberlain at 10 Downing Street. Griffith's private letter was again redrafted, a third and final draft, in accord with British recommendations. Childers sat outside the meeting with Jones and Grigg. He was very depressed feeling that the Irish position had 'weakened badly', and that no one had supported him.[23] Following the meeting Griffith returned to the Irish headquarters and Chartres typed up the agreed private letter on Irish official paper. It was finished at 11 p.m. and sent immediately to Birkenhead's house where Lloyd George was dining. Childers stayed up late, discussing developments with Gavan Duffy and Chartres, and sadly recorded that the 'position is bad'.[24]

Griffith's letter, in regard to the Crown, stated that he was prepared 'to recommend that Ireland should consent to a recognition of the Crown as head of the proposed association of free States'; and that he would also recommend 'a free partnership of Ireland with the other States associated within the British Commonwealth'.[25] He also agreed to help the British with naval facilities. These proposals were 'conditional on the recognition of the essential unity of Ireland'. On the face of it this appears a reasonably strong commitment to the unity of Ireland, but, in fact, it was a watering down of his first draft formula, which had read that he could not accept association with the Crown or the Commonwealth, 'if the unity of Ireland were denied in form or in fact'.[26] In the later letter at 11 p.m. the appeal for unity was made before Ulster was mentioned, and subsequently a form of political recognition was, in fact, accorded to the North East of Ireland. Griffith conceded that he would acknowledge 'existing parliamentary powers', 'while reserving for further discussion the question of area'.[27]

The implications of this change in formula, which was made after Collins and Griffith had met Birkenhead on the morning of 2 November, were all too clear to Collins. He was obviously aware that something had been lost and was very disappointed. Commenting on the feelings of Collins and Griffith, Lloyd George said that 'they must be satisfied at present with the nominal unity of the whole of Ireland and that it would take time to make it real'.

Collins, for his part, maintained that neither he nor Griffith was being supported from Dublin. He noted on 4 November, 'not much achieved. Principally because P.M. [Lloyd George] recognises our over-riding difficulty—Dublin ... From Dublin I don't know whether we're being instructed or confused. The latter I would say.'[28] While at first glance, the grounds for criticising Griffith appear slight, the move from the agreed memoranda of the delegates was significant. De Valera, however, was not unduly critical of Griffith's new approach when, on 9 November, he commented on all that had passed since 27 October. Indeed he praised the way that the Ulster question had been handled. The Delegation had managed the matter 'admirably', he wrote; but he did express some anxiety about the Crown.

He concluded 'as far as the "Crown and Empire" connection is concerned, we should not budge a single inch from the point to where the negotiations have now led us.'[29] In this opinion he was reflecting the fears of Barton, Gavan Duffy and Childers. They were acutely aware that the carefully phrased Irish memoranda, based on the Treaty drafts drawn up on 7 October, had taken second place to a formula devised by Griffith—a formula which had been influenced by the British, and which was far more flexible in regard to Ireland's demands. That the delegates had managed to restore something of the original aspirations was reassuring; but that confidence was tempered by the fact that Griffith and Collins were shaping the final document in private consultation with the British negotiators. It was the acceptance of the sub-conferences in place of the plenary conferences that potentially threatened the Irish Republic, and Griffith's private letter to Lloyd George may well be described as critical stage in the Treaty talks.

There was good reason to be worried. Barton was convinced that the meetings of Collins and Griffith with the British between 30 October and 2 November 'sealed the doom of the Republic'.[30] He might have felt even more anxious for the Republic, if he had been aware of the connection of Griffith, Collins and Duggan with 'Andy' Cope of the Irish Office. The sending of Griffith's letter was followed by an increased level of personal contact with Dublin. On 4 November Collins and Gavan Duffy, who was still talking of 'the difficulty of the situation', departed for Dublin. On the same day Chartres left for Berlin, arriving there on 5 November. He was expected to be away for about ten days.[31] Childers, while informing his wife of these developments, noted that 'there appears to be a likelihood of a detente for some days now,' and that observation was to prove correct.[32] Chartres, however, was to be extremely busy.

Soon after Chartres arrived in Berlin de Valera received a message emanating from there that the Republic was at risk in the Treaty negotiations. A telegram was sent on 8 November 1921 from 'Jetter', John T. Ryan, to Joe McGarrity in Philadelphia. It read:

> Only great pressure on trustees in L[ondon] by directors at home will save surrender of free title to old homestead. All trustees weakening including M.C. Topman stands firm and strong. Correct official information from inside.

The trustees were the delegates in London; 'old homestead' was Ireland; MC was Michael Collins; and 'Topman' was de Valera. McGarrity telephoned Harry Boland in Washington and he cabled the news to de Valera.[33]

Although Ryan was later to tell Robert Brennan that he had received the information from the German Foreign Office, it may, granted its claim to be official and from the inside, with some degree of certainty be ascribed to John Chartres. Credibility is given to this assumption by the fact that Nancy Power passed on at this time virtually the same message to her mother—and the source was Chartres. Her mother could 'scarcely credit' the account of Chartres, and was unwilling to believe that Collins could 'give the great article away'.[34] Chartres was certainly in a position to deliver the news.

On 5 November Nancy Power reported to Dublin from Paris that 'owing to enemy pressure, it was necessary for me to leave B[erlin] for a day or so.' She also added that she had important despatches from 'Professor Jetter' to deliver in Paris, and while on this mission had met 'Magner', who was on his way to Berlin. 'Magner' was her code name for Chartres. She stressed the value of 'Mr Magner's presence at Berlin', and was concerned to learn that 'his return is regarded as temporary'.[35] His presence was badly needed in Berlin because the gun-running affair had taken a new turn. Power conveyed to de Valera a supplement from J.T. Ryan about these new events. De Valera was anxious over these new developments, but could only urge Nancy Power 'to see that the disturbances such as the recent one do not occur'.[36]

While the reasons for Power's sudden movements and the meaning of de Valera's enigmatic message are not entirely clear, it is known that Robert Briscoe and Charlie McGuinness had another ship, laden with arms, sailing for Ireland at this very moment. The ship, the *Frieda*, sailed from Hamburg on 28 October. After an extremely hazardous ten-day journey, McGuinness berthed the ship near Cheekpoint, in Waterford Harbour on 11 November, and contact was made with Liam Mellows.

McGuinness made extravagant claims as to the size of its cargo, but, at a conservative estimate, it was carrying 200 rifles and 10,000 rounds of ammunition. One of those involved stated that the arms were distributed throughout the South and the West. He also remarked that an express messenger was sent to the delegates in London, informing them of the successful mission and encouraging them to hold out. Official figures for the importation of munitions, published in December, showed that in the five months of the Truce more munitions were brought into Ireland than in the previous eleven months. The figures also show that this landing by McGuinness was extremely significant: his contribution of 200 rifles made up the major part of the total number of 313.[37] McGuinness sold the *Frieda* immediately after his arrival in Waterford, and bought a tramp steamer, the *City of Dortmund*. It was planned to use this for normal trade and also for the transport of chemicals for military purposes.

By the end of the month McGuinness had returned to Germany and was in touch with Briscoe again in order to continue their gun-running operations. While no signs of contact have been established between Chartres and the Briscoe operation—neither Briscoe nor McGuinnes mention Chartres in their books—he must have been aware of their activities. Nancy Power acknowledged this to be the case when she wrote that the presence of John Chartres 'was necessary in view of a storm which had arisen following the discovery of an attempt to run guns from Germany to Ireland'.[38]

Despite his preoccupation with the armaments issue, Chartres also carried out duties of a more routine character. On 10 November he sent to Dublin a statement of accounts for the months of September and October. However, there was an attempt to recall him on 15 November to which he replied that departure was impossible. He was, nevertheless, summoned back to London on 18 November by a telegram from Arthur Griffith.[39] Chartres was reluctant to return. He had informed Griffith that, 'it seems to me that I ought to deal with the situation that has arisen here unless there is a definitely greater need for my services elsewhere.'[40] He felt that he had no more to add either to the two memoranda that he had composed or to his contributions to the official Irish memoranda. 'On the subject of the Crown,' Chartres concluded,

> I have put forward ideas which, I think, would deprive the English of any sufficient ground for the renewal of hostilities, and at the same time would keep the monarchy out of Ireland and so preserve intact our republic and its freedom.[41]

Despite his protest, Chartres returned. Following his departure from London on 4 November there had been, as Childers had sensed, a lull in the conference meetings, but a marked increase in visits to Dublin. Collins had departed on 11 November in the company of Duggan, and was followed on the next day by Barton and Childers, Barton having seen Cope before his departure.[42]

During this visit Collins met Mark Sturgis, Assistant Under-Secretary at Dublin Castle and a close colleague of Cope, in the Gresham Hotel. Sturgis remarked that Collins 'is just like the big young pleasant prosperous self-satisfied cattle dealer in a big way of business with which Ireland is full'. He struck Sturgis as 'strong, brave and quite ruthless'.[43] Also staying in the hotel and also in contact with Collins was Moya Llelwynn Davies in whose London house in December 1918 Chartres had made contact with Collins.[44]

On his return to London Collins and Griffith saw Lloyd George on 15 November, and on the following day, as a result of these private meetings, the British Government submitted Draft Treaty proposals. Divisions still existed in the Irish ranks. Barton, Gavan Duffy and Childers still maintained that they did not 'know enough of what is going on'. Collins, for his part, made a similar complaint, but his was directed once again against de Valera. 'Dublin,' he declared, 'is the real problem. They know what we are doing, but I don't know exactly the state of their activities'—a strange statement granted that he had just returned from Dublin.[45] The group associated with Childers wished for a return to the full conference framework and they accused Griffith of delaying the return of Chartres. Barton complained explicitly to Griffith that 'you won't agree to any appeals to J.C. [John Chartres]'. It was against this background that Chartres had been recalled on 18 November.[46] On the same day Collins again left for Dublin.

At the time Barton, Duffy and Childers perceived that Chartres was on their side, but Griffith too had need of him. Not only did the British draft treaty of 16 November call for consideration, but also Griffith had entered upon certain commitments concerning Ulster in private conversations with Lloyd George.

The force of the previous memoranda of Chartres had been weakened by Arthur Griffith's involvement in the exchange of views between Lloyd George and James Craig. The Irish side had hoped that, by accepting some form of allegiance to the King and some form of partnership inside the British Empire, Ulster might accept an all-Ireland Parliament, thus securing a form of Irish unity. A settlement on these lines, to which Griffith had given his measured approbation, had been proposed by Lloyd George to Craig on 10 November.[47] It was linked with a promise of a Boundary Commission to re-assess the six county area. Lloyd George's letter read:

Ireland would give her allegiance to the Throne and would take her place in the partnership of Free States comprised in the British Empire ...

The unity of Ireland would be recognised by the establishment of an all-Ireland Parliament, upon which would devolve the further powers necesary to form the self-governing Irish State.[48]

The reply of the Ulster Cabinet was brief and to the point. It stated that 'so long as the suggestion of the Government contains a reference to the establishment of an all-Ireland Parliament they feel it would be impossible for them to meet in conference on the subject.'[49]

This reply was delivered on 11 November. On the same day Craig wrote a three-page letter spelling out his objections. Unionists were more than ever, he said, opposed to an all-Ireland Parliament, and he maintained that the way forward lay through the Government of Ireland Act of 1920. 'The possible unity of Ireland,' he wrote, 'is provided for by the establishement of the Council of Ireland under the Act of 1920 together with the machinery for creating a Parliament for all Ireland should Northern and Southern Ireland mutually agree to do so.'[50]

In such a proposal the future destiny of Northern Ireland lay in the hands of the Unionists. They had understood this when they had accepted the 1920 Act, and they were not going to abandon the initiative that they had secured. Rather than accept an all-Ireland Parliament, Craig said that Ulster would prefer, as a lesser evil, to leave reluctantly the Imperial Parliament and set up its own Parliament with Dominion status.

Griffith discussed the Ulster reply with Lloyd George privately on Monday 12 November.[51] Although Griffith's expectations should have been reduced to more realistic proportions, he was still content to comply with the agenda proposed by Lloyd George. The British Prime Minister had to contend with a meeting of Unionist diehards on Thursday 17 November in Liverpool, and he had requested that Griffith should not present obstacles before this encounter. Griffith promised that he 'would guarantee that while he [Lloyd George] was fighting the "Ulster" crowd we would not help them by repudiating him.' This information was passed on to de Valera on 12 November, and Griffith added that 'before I left I told him [Lloyd George] that as I was helping him over the "Ulster" difficulty, he should help us over the "Crown and Empire".'[52] Griffith, in fact, did more. He gave an assurance stating that he would not allow any difficulty over Ulster and the Boundary Commission from preventing a settlement of the other issues.[53]

The next day, 13 November, Griffith approved a short memorandum drawn up by Jones which formalised his assurance on Ulster. This concession was to prove of great consequence in the final days of negotiation. A further exchange of letters between Lloyd George and Craig failed to alter his stance. Lloyd George informed Craig on 14 November that:

> we have received with great regret your refusal to enter into conference with us unconditionally. To demand as between two sets of Ministers of the Crown a preliminary limitation on freedom of discussion is contrary to the spirit of mutual loyalty and co-operation which animates His Majesty's Government in all parts of the Empire.[54]

In reply to Craig's suggestion that two separate Dominions be created in Ireland, Lloyd George replied that:

> your proposal would stereotype a frontier based neither upon natural features nor broad geographical considerations by giving it the character of an international boundary. Partition on these lines the majority of the Irish people will never accept, nor could we conscientiously attempt to enforce it.[55]

Craig based his defence of Northern Ireland on the rock of the Government of Ireland Act of 1920, and the suggested line of procedure produced by the British on 16 November reflected this reality. It was in this context that Chartres was called upon to make his contribution.

The twelve proposals of the British Government of 16 November—variously called 'tentative suggestions' by Griffith and 'draft of the proposed Treaty' by de Valera—made no explicit mention of the Crown.[56] Ireland was to have 'the status of a self-governing Dominion', like Canada, but the Crown was clearly designed to retain its traditional place within the Dominion structure. Provision was also made for Northern Ireland to opt out of the Southern Ireland state. De Valera gave his reaction to Griffith on 17 November. He felt that it was time to draft 'our final word': the British attempt to proceed by the Dominion Act should be resisted; and the best way of doing that would be by modifying 'the draft Treaty "A" which we had prepared before you left'.[57]

The Irish delegates gathered again on 21 November to make a response to the British proposals. Collins had returned from Dublin with a rough draft of a treaty from de Valera. The atmosphere was extremely tense. Griffith, highly emotional, attacked Childers viciously, accusing him of causing the European War through his book, *The Riddle of the Sands*, and claimed that he was now trying to provoke another war. At one stage in the argument Childers threatened resignation.

After a break they resumed discussions at 5 p.m. and Chartres joined them in the middle of their debate. At 11 p.m. he began typing up a formula from a mass of tangled papers and did not retire to bed until 3 a.m. after a long chat with Childers.[58] His return to London was made known to those working in Foreign Affairs. On 22 November Brennan informed Sean T. O'Kelly in Paris that 'John C. has returned safely'; and he commented that Chartres 'was rather surprised at our message bringing him back'.[59]

On the same day, 22 November, the formula that Chartres had typed out, which reflected the aspirations of Childers, Duffy and Barton, was submitted to a meeting of the delegates. It was entitled 'Heads of Agreement'.[60] After much discussion and emendation the title was changed to a 'Memorandum by the Irish Representatives', resulting in some diminution in the Irish claims. Nevertheless, the memorandum not only signified an attempted return to the principles contained in draft Treaty 'A', but also it marked a reversal of the negotiating trend promoted by Griffith. The 'essential unity of Ireland' was asserted; it was claimed that authority in Ireland derived from the Irish people; and only qualified recognition was given to the Crown as 'the symbol and accepted head of the Association' to which Ireland belonged as an 'associated' state.[61]

The Irish ten-point memorandum was handed in to 10 Downing Street at 12.30 on Tuesday 22 November. Lloyd George was extremely angry and Tom Jones was instructed to inform the Irish that 'the document filled him with despair'. This news was conveyed by Griffith to de Valera: Lloyd George, he said, 'was in despair about the document' because 'it did not accept the Crown or the Empire. It brought them back to where they were six weeks ago.'[62] Birkenhead and Chamberlain also found it 'impossible'.

Jones had a private discussion with Griffith and Collins in an attempt to resolve the problem. The editor of his diary observed that in many ways it was 'the most exacting moment of the whole negotiation'.[63] At the meeting Griffith defended the approach on the Crown and Empire as 'honourable to both sides', but there were signs that Griffith was defending a concept to which he was not fully committed. He was also under considerable pressure from Lloyd George. The indications were that he missed the freedom of manoeuvre which he had previously enjoyed. He wrote to de Valera that 'owing to the Crux over the Crown and Empire, they [the British] feel their position weakened if not gone. In view of your letter of October 25th I cannot discuss the alternative with them.'[64]

The question of de Valera coming to London to resolve the issue was raised but was not acted upon. De Valera later justified his absence from London on the grounds that Griffith had been instructed not to sign a document that contained allegiance to the English Crown, and that his own presence in Ireland would be needed to persuade hard-line republicans to accept any form of allegiance, even that based on External Association. In other words, Irish unity would be best preserved by his presence in Dublin, whether the negotiations were concluded successfully or not.[65]

On 22 November Griffith felt that there was a high probability that the negotiations might be terminated unsuccessfully. He added that he, Collins and Barton were formally to meet Lloyd George and his colleagues on the next day, 23 November, and concluded that 'we shall argue the acceptability of the arrangement re Association we have proposed, but I have little hope of any good result'.[66] Griffith did not inform de Valera of all that had transpired. According to Jones, whose intervention was critical, Griffith 'insisted that he was not going back on the private "letter of assurance" that he had given the P. M' on 2 November.' Nor did he mention that he and Michael Collins were to see Lloyd George and his colleagues privately that night. 'Andy' Cope, incidentally, spent the evening trying to get Duggan to see the merits of the British position.[67] Tension and division, therefore, were apparent in the Irish ranks. Although the Irish Memorandum of 22 November reiterated the original Irish demand to some degree, the secret meeting of Griffith and Collins perpetuated the more flexible line of policy that was associated with the sub-conferences.

Childers made an attempt to block this renewal of negotiations via the sub-conferences by an initiative on the morning on 23 November. He presented to a meeting of the Irish delegates a document entitled 'Concessions contained in our proposals of 22 November'.[68] The tone of the document was set by the opening paragraph which proclaimed that 'Ireland's full claim is for a Republic, unfettered by any obligations or restrictions whatsoever.' This was followed by a detailed analysis of the way in which the Memorandum had abandoned this original aim in regard to the Crown, Ulster, Defence and other matters. Griffith so 'strongly disagreed with it' that, losing his temper completely, he heaped abuse upon Childers. Apologies were offered and Griffith, Collins and Barton left for a meeting at Downing Street. Childers asked Chartres to go with them. He did and discussed legal matters with Jones. Lloyd George 'informed them of the grave view he and his colleagues took of the reply', but the meeting was positive and arrangements were made for a further meeting with legal representatives present.[69] Collins, according, to Barton 'suggested having a constitutional lawyer meaning Chartres', whereas Barton, himself, stressed that Gavan Duffy should attend as he was not only a lawyer but also one of the delegates.[70] Collins finally agreed and both Chartres and Duffy were members of the delegation that met the British team on Thursday 24 November at the House of Lords.

The meeting on 24 November was attended by Griffith, Collins, Gavan Duffy and John Chartres on the Irish side, and by Lord Birkenhead and Sir Gordon Hewart on the British side. It was the first sub-conference meeting that either Chartres or Duffy had attended. Before the Irish left their head-quarters there was a blazing row between Griffith and Gavan Duffy over the composition of the delegation—Gavan Duffy maintaining that a meeting of all the delegates should decide the matter; and it was evident that suspicions ran high in the Irish ranks.[71]

Before the meeting Griffith advised Chartres to see Cope. Chartres did so and gave Cope an outline of his approach to the question of the Crown. Cope responded by saying that 'Lloyd George would tumble over himself to get such a settlement.'[72] At the meeting Chartres tried to defend the view of the Crown that he had expressed in his various memoranda. He gave no sign that he had been diverted from this line of approach by the changes in direction that had taken place since he had left for Berlin.

He repeated his original distinction: namely, that in 'purely Irish affairs' Ireland 'must be absolutely independent'; but that 'Ireland would be prepared to recognise the British Crown as the head of the aggregate of States to which she would adhere.'[73] Even the word 'adhere' that had provoked Lloyd George's critical questioning earlier was used once again. In reply to questioning Chartres defended Irish independence strongly: 'the Crown should have no existence whatever' within Ireland, he said. Again he used the words of Lloyd George, that Irishmen 'were to control every nerve and fibre of their national life', to prove his point.[74]

Birkenhead then turned to the role of the Crown as a symbol. 'The British people,' he said, 'attached the greatest importance to the symbol of the Crown.' When Chartres replied that recognition of the King 'as head of the aggregate of States' could be accompanied by some outward act of loyalty, such as a financial grant, Birkenhead bluntly said that 'it would not meet the great difficulty'.[75] Both Collins and Griffith defended the view put forward by Chartres: Collins said that Ireland was making 'a great concession'; and Griffith appealed for 'a big gesture by England'. Griffith specifically identified his appeal with the principles expressed by Chartres, stating that

> for external affairs, such as peace and war and defence, Ireland would recognise the British Crown as proposed, while for internal retaining the Republic. They might prefer to translate 'Saorstát na hÉireann' by 'Free State',

Immediately Birkenhead agreed that 'the title "Free State" could go into the Treaty'.[76] Griffith's use of the word 'Republic' was used subsequently by Barton to show that Griffith realised that, while the isolated republic was not attainable, a Republic based on external association might be, and that this was attained in de Valera's later Document number 2. The contention of Barton was that Griffith and Collins did not fight hard enough to obtain this type of Republic.[77]

The word 'Republic', however, was to give way in both form and reality to that of 'Free State', as it became impossible to make any progress on the central issue of the Crown. It was evident that a critical stage in the negotiations had been reached. This was recognised by the British as well as the Irish. Tom Jones frankly acknowledged the gravity of the situation when he wrote that

> the outcome of the discussion was a promise by Sinn Féin to provide a formula embodying their conception of the Crown and allegiance. For the first time this issue was made absolutely clear to both sides and it was hard to see how any formula can reconcile our position and theirs.[78]

Chartres and Gavan Duffy wrote up the minutes of the meeting, and the same evening Griffith, Collins and Barton departed for Dublin.

The Final Round of Meetings

Recognition of the English Crown
25 November – 6 December 1921

The next day, 25 November, a dispute arose over the record of the previous day's meeting which had significant implications. Chartres maintained that he had met Birkenhead and Sir Gordon Hewart in the morning, Tom Jones being present, and exchanged notes. He claimed that his account was accepted by Birkenhead as recording the meeting 'with remarkable fidelity', but that the British record was not accepted.[1] Jones saw Chartres privately at 11.45 and made the following record:

> I had half an hour with him, for the first time with any real intimacy. I pleaded with him on the subject of allegiance but found him utterly irreconcilable on allegiance to the King in Ireland. He had seen such things done in the King's name by the King's servants in the last two years that he would rather, as he put it, go underground tomorrow than consent to any intervention ever again by this country in the domestic affairs of Ireland. He spoke with great earnestness and there was no misunderstanding the depth of his conviction.[2]

Later in the day Tom Jones questioned the accuracy of Chartres' account of the previous day's meeting. The specific example of inaccuracy that he cited concerned the words of Sir Gordon Hewart.

It was stated that Hewart had 'assured the Irish delegates that they must not suppose that the British Government was contemplating the alternative of war'. Jones stressed that what he had said was 'that the Irish delegates must not suppose that the British Government was contemplating with equanimity the alternative which was war'.[3] Jones claimed that the threat of war was more real than the record of Chartres indicated, and he wished this reality to be presented to the Irish delegates who had returned to Dublin for a Cabinet meeting.

A sharp exchange of letters took place between Jones and Chartres, with Chartres maintaining that Jones 'has persisted in his misrepresentation of a conversation to which he was not a party'. Extremely angry that his report had been labelled 'incomplete and inaccurate', Chartres concluded that 'in these circumstances Mr Chartres cannot continue the correspondence with Mr Thomas Jones.'[4] That evening Childers, Gavan Duffy, Chartres and J. O. Byrne had a long discussion about the formula that would be sent to Downing Street in reply to the meeting of 24 November.[5]

While these developments were taking place inside the diplomatic forum, Michael Collins made an overture to the British which was 'personal and unofficial'. An undated memorandum containing his views on association with England was transmitted to Birkenhead by Austen Chamberlain on 25 November.[6] Chamberlain commented that 'this is extraordinarily interesting though sometimes perverse and sometimes Utopian. Who (outside our six) would guess the name of the writer?' Barton and several of the Irish delegates did not, indeed, believe that Collins was the real author.[7]

The memorandum began with an historical introduction and maintained that 'the history of Ireland as an independent nation which is now at last receiving recognition, is utterly different from that of the Colonies.' Collins continued

> the only association which it will be satisfactory to Ireland to enter will be based, not on the present technical legal status of the Dominions, but on the real position they claim, and have in fact secured ... It is essential that the present *de facto* position should be recognised de jure, and that all its implications as regards sovereignty, allegiance, constitutional independence of the governments should be acknowledged.

Such an association, Collins maintained, would be a novelty, but it would provide a new pattern for national co-operation. It might, he said, 'form the nucleus of a real League of Nations of the world ... into such a league might not America be willing to enter?', he asked in conclusion.[8] Although doubts must surround the authorship of the memorandum, the most interesting fact is that any initiative that was purely 'personal and unofficial' was made by Collins at all.

On the same day, 25 November, as the private memorandum of Collins was sent to Lord Birkenhead, the Irish Cabinet met in Dublin. The Treaty negotiations were discussed; but there was another item on the agenda: it concerned the Army. De Valera and Cathal Brugha, the Minister of Defence, had summoned Griffith and his Cabinet colleagues to Dublin on 22 November to consider the question of a New Army. The letter to Griffith made it clear that it was to be no ordinary Cabinet meeting: the entire General Headquarters Staff of the Army was to attend.[9]

While tensions and differences were appearing among the delegates in London, it was evident that in Dublin some Cabinet members were concerned about the loyalty of the Army, if a critical division occurred in the Irish ranks. The draft formula for the new commissions made Brugha's aims perfectly clear. 'In view of the possibility of further fighting,' he stated, 'and in order to put the army of the Saorstat in an unequivocal position as the legal defence force of the nation under the control of the civil Government, the Cabinet has decided to issue fresh commissions and to offer re-enlistment to all ranks.'[10] These commissions were to date from 25 November, the eighth anniversary of the founding of the Irish Volunteers.

This action of de Valera and Brugha marked a continuation of their struggle with Collins and the IRB for control of the Army. The minutes of the Cabinet for 25 November 1921 record that action was taken on two fronts—the Army and the Treaty negotiations. A compromise was made concerning changes in the Army. Richard Mulcahy, the Chief of Staff, and his fellow officers at Headquarters, mostly members of the IRB, were vigorously opposed to any change and strongly resisted the new policy. Brugha, while acceding to these wishes and confirming the officers in their positions, did secure a resolution which stated that 'the supreme body directing the Army is the Cabinet', and declared that 'the Army of the Republic has but one allegiance, namely, to the elected Government of the Republic'.[11] In this manner Brugha did manage to impose some civilian control in the person of the Minister of Defence over the Army which was to be known as the 'Re-Commissioned Army'.

There was rather less compromise over the issues raised by the Treaty negotiations. Concerning the British Crown, the Cabinet resolved 'that Ireland shall recognise the British Crown for the purposes of the Association as symbol and accepted head of the combination of Associated States'.[12] This proposal was in accord with the principles expounded by Chartres at the House of Lords meeting on the previous day, and which Lloyd George had described as unacceptable. Faced by such a resolution, war, if Hewart's observation meant anything at all, remained a possible alternative for the British. It was in these circumstances that the delegates returned to London.

Childers and Chartres had not been idle in their absence. When Griffith returned on 26 November, however, he showed little interest in the draft formula drawn up by Childers, Duffy and Chartres. 'He told us nothing,' Childers recorded, and he said that 'he would draft one of his own'. That night Childers went to bed early, while the rest of the delegates played roulette. The next day, Sunday 27 November, Childers allowed himself a game of whist in the evening with Barton, Duffy and Chartres.[13]

On Monday 28 November the Irish delegates gathered at 1 p.m. to finalise their response to the British proposals. Childers felt that Griffith was giving away too much of Ireland's case, and he complained that he received 'little help from any one else'.[14] After some debate a Memorandum by the 'Irish Delegates on their proposal for the Association of Ireland with the British Commonwealth' was despatched to Jones at 5 p.m. It reflected the recent Cabinet decision and reiterated the Irish standpoint of 24 November.

Three points were made. One of which declared that 'Ireland will agree to be associated with the British Commonwealth for all purposes of common concern, including defence, peace and war, and political treaties, and to recognise the British Crown as Head of the Association'.[15] A note was added claiming that Ireland was not in a comparable position to the other Dominions, and expressed the hope that Ireland's concession in regard to naval bases might be met by some gesture of conciliation from Britain in regard to the Crown. It was not to be. On seeing the memorandum in the early evening of 28 November Lloyd George exclaimed 'This means war.'[16]

Steps were taken by the British team to produce a better Irish response. Later that evening, largely owing to the overtures of Jones and Cope, Griffith and Duggan visited Lloyd George at Chequers. Childers had told Jones that Griffith and Collins were not prepared to attend such a meeting—Collins was actually away—but the matter did not end there. According to Childers, 'it is pretty clear that AG [Griffith] and ED [Duggan] took steps, possibly through Cope (or Cope may have taken the initiative) to re-open the matter.'[17] The suspicions of Childers were well founded: Jones acknowledged that he and Cope had made further contact with Duggan, who was with Griffith and Tim Healy at 15 Cadogan Gardens. Much to the chagrin of Childers, Griffith declared that a meeting was to take place and that it was to be noted as 'official'.[18]

Before their departure there was a meeting of delegates at 6 p.m. The seriousness of the situation was made clear by Griffith, who declared that at the moment things were 'impossible'. He felt that they were caught in a dilemma: either they made some surrender on the Crown, or Lloyd George would offer a plebiscite on Dominion status with war as the alternative. Griffith felt that they would lose a vote on such terms of reference. Duggan concurred with this analysis. Some mild remonstrances were made by Barton, Duffy, Childers and Chartres, but they were reassured by Griffith's promise that he was going to insist that the Crown was to have no place in Ireland. He and Duggan then departed to see Lloyd George and Birkenhead. They were at Chequers for about two hours, leaving at 11.45 p.m. The British team stressed that the Crown in Ireland was to be no more influential than in any other Dominion, and this assurance appeared to mollify Griffith and Duggan. Lloyd George went to bed feeling better: a negotiating position had been retrieved.[19]

The next day, Tuesday 29 November, the British went to work to produce a final draft of Articles of Settlement on the assumption that the King
was 'to have the same rights and powers in Ireland as in Canada and Australia'.[20] They had gathered from their conversations with Griffith and
Duggan that the formal Irish Memorandum of 28 November did not express Ireland's final position. While the British representative were working
on their plans, Griffith reported to the Irish delegates at 11 a.m. on his previous night's meeting with Lloyd George. Collins had returned to London
and was present. Griffith reported that Lloyd George had not found the
Irish Memorandum to be acceptable. He had said that it 'brought them further apart'; and that 'we must be either in or out of the Empire'.[21]

According to Griffith the British 'declared the document we had sent in
earlier was impossible for them. No British Government could attempt to
propose to the British people the abrogation of the Crown. It would be
smashed to atoms.'[22] The British also said that the Oath of Allegiance was
'an immense difficulty for them.' On the one hand Griffith stood firm, telling the British that 'we had no authority to deal with them on any other
basis than the exclusion of the Crown from purely Irish affairs'; but on the
other hand he entertained the idea of change by not rejecting their offer that
'the Crown in Ireland should be no more in practice than it is in Canada or
any Dominion'.[23]

The British proposal was that Ireland should enjoy responsible government inside some form of Dominion structure, and that there should be an
oath to that constitution and indirectly to the King. Some caveats were made
against conceding too much to British demands. Gavan Duffy warned against
concession on Defence; Childers produced a paper on 'Law and Fact in
Canada,' which examined the independence of the Canadian government;
and Chartres submitted the draft of a scheme 'for stripping [the] King of all
power'.[24] The twelve-point note of Chartres showed 'how the exclusion of
the crown and of Imperial supremacy might be effected by means of positive enactments in harmony on practically all points with Dominion
constitutional usage'.[25] These twelve points were obviously made in an attempt to uphold Irish aspirations against the British request that the Irish
should accept Dominion status.

Chartres made no concessions to the British demands. Rather he tried
to turn the British proposals against themselves by citing Dominion precedent in favour of the Irish position. For example, he stated that 'in Ireland
no royal veto shall be exercised on Irish legislation (Dominion precedent)';
and proposed that 'the Irish Government shall have the unrestricted right
to make commercial treaties (Canadian precedent).' The first point that he
made was that 'Ireland shall recognise the Crown as the Symbol and ac-

cepted Head of the Community of Nations (including the Irish Nation) constituting the British Commonwealth.'[26]

Faced by the changing circumstances that occurred during the negotiations, faced too by the vacillation of Griffith, there are no signs that Chartres moved away from the pristine position advocated by de Valera—namely that Ireland's internal independence would be upheld, but that external acceptance of the Crown would be tolerated. Griffith, however, departed for the sub-conference that afternoon with Collins and Duggan influenced more by his evening meeting with Lloyd George than by the critical qualifications of Chartres and Childers. At the Downing Street meeting Lloyd George re-affirmed his previous views of the situation. He, Birkenhead and Chamberlain, according to Griffith,

> specifically offered to put a phrase in the Treaty ensuring that the Crown should have no more authority in Ireland than in Canada. They offered us a form of Oath of Allegiance different from their one, which we stated would not do.[27]

There was a degree of urgency about the meeting as it was planned that the British proposals should be formulated as quickly as possible and then brought back to Dublin for Cabinet consideration. While the British draftsmen finalised their proposals, Griffith reported back to a meeting of the Irish delegates at 6.30 p.m. He asked Childers, Gavan Duffy and Chartres to draft 'an alternative form of oath'. Childers noted that it was the first time that Griffith had asked him for advice of any kind. After the meeting Griffith urgently requested de Valera to call a Dáil Cabinet meeting for Saturday, 3 December.[28]

The next day, Wednesday, 30 November, the Irish delegates played roulette after dinner as they awaited copies of the British proposals. Jones delivered them personally at 10 p.m. and talked with Griffith, Collins and Duggan. He did not communicate with Childers. One hour later Griffith presented an envelope of documents, unsigned, undated and without address, to Childers, Barton, Duffy and Chartres. They discussed the contents until 1.15 a.m. Childers found them unsatisfactory. Apart from some concessions over a boundary commission and safeguards regarding Ulster, he felt that the Oath was not acceptable and that the arrangements for Defence were hopeless. They were, Childers felt, the same terms that Lloyd George had tried to impose on 20 July in the course of his discussions with de Valera.[29]

The rigidity of Childers' response was too much for Collins. He had been feeling the strain in recent days, observing that 'more and more the responsibility rests with me', and he privately protested that 'the advice and inspiration of C [Childers] is like farmland under water—dead. With a purpose I think—with a definite purpose. Soon he will howl in triumph—for what it is worth.'[30]

On the morning of Thursday 1 December there was a meeting of the Irish delegates in Childers' room. Discussion of the proposals took place and Childers voiced his anxieties, but his role as secretary was criticised by Griffith and Collins. Childers was effectively marginalised by Griffith at a private meeting with Lloyd George in the early evening, at which he asked J.O. Byrne, rather than Childers, to draft objections. When Griffith returned to 22 Hans Place, further discussion took place among the delegates. Childers argued that their position was becoming impossible, and Chartres, in the words of Childers, 'threw in a few words about vital matters which they do not understand'.[31]

This was to be the last recorded intervention by Chartres in the conference negotiations. Childers obviously felt that Chartres was still trying to uphold fundamental principles which Griffith and Collins did not fully understand, but the momentum in favour of accepting the British proposals could not be overturned. That night, at 9.30 p.m., Griffith and Collins returned for another meeting with Lloyd George. Childers sat outside the negotiating room, effectively symbolising his lack of influence, and, as if to highlight his ineffectiveness, Cope sat down with him urging him 'to support peace'. Childers was acutely depressed. 'I thought of the fate of Ireland,' he wrote, 'being settled hugger-mugger by ignorant Irish negotiators and AG [Arthur Griffith] in genuine sympathy with many of the English claims.'[32] Such was the personal and somewhat jaundiced view of Childers as he departed for bed at 2.30 a.m. with the final amendments to the British proposals to hand.

The next day, after further contacts with their British opposite numbers, the Irish delegates departed for Dublin. They left in different groups: Griffith and Duggan with the final proposals; Collins, Duffy and Childers later in the day. On the same day Chartres left London. He informed the Foreign Affairs department that he was leaving 22 Hans Place on Friday 2 December and returning to Berlin.[33]

Although Chartres was not involved in the final drafting of the Treaty, it is instructive to examine the last stages of the negotiations in order to assess the ultimate outcome in relation to his own proposals on the Crown. When the Irish Cabinet met on Saturday 3 December, they tackled the challenge presented by the British Articles of Agreement. Over the issues of the Crown and allegiance the British had defended their stand along the lines indicated to Griffith on 29 November. The first article stated that 'Ireland shall have the same national status in the Community of Nations known as the British Empire as the Dominion of Canada.' The proposed oath denied the validity of the distinction between internal and external allegiance that the Irish had attempted to make throughout the negotiations. It read 'I ... solemnly swear to bear true faith and allegiance to the Constitution of the Irish Free State; to the Community of Nations known as the British Empire; and to the King as Head of the State and of the Empire.'[34]

The meeting opened by the delegates and Childers giving their views on the draft Treaty. They did, incidentally, refer to the 'Treaty' rather than to the 'Articles of Agreement' in their discussions. Griffith, Duggan and Collins were fundamentally in favour, although Collins was not entirely happy. He was noted as saying that he 'would recommend that Dáil go to country on Treaty, but would recommend non-acceptance of Oath'.[35] Gavan Duffy, Barton and Childers were opposed to acceptance of the Treaty.

After lunch the advisability of the acceptance of the Treaty was discussed. The Cabinet alone attended this session, although Kevin O'Higgins, as assistant in Local Government, was also present. De Valera maintained that the Treaty 'could not be accepted in its then form'. He added that he personally 'could not subscribe to the Oath of Allegiance'; nor could he accept the permission granted to North East Ulster 'to vote itself out of the Irish State'. He 'took his stand upon last Irish proposals which meant external connection with the Crown'.[36] In that context he proposed an amended oath to read: 'I ... do solemnly swear true faith and allegiance to the constitution of the Irish Free State, to the Treaty of Association and to recognise the King of Great Britain as Head of the Associated States.'[37] De Valera congratulated the delegates but advised that they should proceed as they had done when rejecting Lloyd George's first proposals on 20 July 1921. They should put up counter proposals and be 'prepared to face the consequences—war or no war'.

The approach of Griffith was markedly different. He did not find the British document 'dishonourable', and he 'would not take the responsibility of breaking on the Crown'. He proposed that 'the Plenipotentiaries should sign and leave it to the Pres.[ident] and Dáil to reject'.[38] Cathal Brugha was critical of this procedure as being potentially divisive—in the Cabinet, in the Dáil and in the country at large. When the Cabinet conclusions were formulated, it was evident that the policy of Griffith had been rejected. It was 'decided unanimously that [the] present Oath of Allegiance could not be subscribed to', and it was also agreed that Griffith was 'to inform Mr. Lloyd George that the document could not be signed'.

Collins did not accept the clarity of these decisions. On leaving the Cabinet meeting he was reported as saying, 'I've been there all day and I can't get them to say Yes or No, whether we should sign or not.'[39] Griffith was of the same mind. Together, in the days following the Cabinet meeting, they combined to formulate a plan of procedure. They agreed, firstly, that their own solution on the lines of Dominion status should be pursued; that the views of those in Dublin were not to be taken as sacrosanct; and they calculated that a majority of the Irish people would support them. Collins was particularly scathing about the direction given from Dublin. 'The Treaty,' he said, 'will not be accepted in Dublin—not by those who have in mind personal ambitions under pretence of patriotism'; and, he added, 'still less do I agree to being dictated to by those not embroiled in these negotiations'. He concluded by asserting that 'the advantages of Dominion Status to us, as a stepping stone to complete independence are immeasurable'.[40] This approach was inevitably to lead to conflict with the other delegates.

When the delegates arrived back in London on the morning of 4 December it was Gavan Duffy, Barton and Childers who drew up a draft reply to the British Articles. It was titled, 'Amendments by the Irish Representatives to the Proposed Articles of Agreement', and it embodied the decisions made at the Irish Cabinet meeting.[41] Griffith, Collins and Duggan were not happy with the proposals and made some amendments. However, the finished document, which was called 'the Irish counter proposals', contained an amended oath which was almost identical to that formulated by de Valera and was made in accordance with the principles of Chartres. The recognition paid to the King was limited: he was recognised as 'Head of the Associated States'. Indeed Collins later referred to this formula as 'de Valera's oath of allegiance'.[42] It was very similar to the various formulae that had been presented by Chartres. Griffith, Collins and Duggan refused to present this memorandum to Lloyd George, and Griffith only joined Barton and Gavan Duffy when it was clear that they were prepared to see Lloyd George alone.

On hearing the Irish proposals at 5 p.m. on 4 December, Lloyd George retired with his colleagues, Chamberlain, Birkenhead and Sir Robert Horne, and returned to pass judgement on the Irish amendment. The Irish form of the oath, Lloyd George said, was 'a refusal of the fundamental conditions' presented by the British over the period of the negotiations. The amendments, as a whole, he declared bitterly 'constituted a refusal to enter the Empire and accept the common bond of the Crown. They were but the same proposals which had already been discussed and rejected.'[43] The talks were effectively at an end. Griffith concluded by informing de Valera that

> the conversation came to a close, we undertaking to send them copies of our proposals to-morrow and they undertaking to send in a formal rejection tomorrow. They would, they said, inform Craig tomorrow that the negotiations were broken down.[44]

According to Barton, the absence of Collins and Duggan, especially of Collins, made the British aware that the split in the Irish ranks could still be exploited. In short they realised that the Irish stand on the oath and on other matters might not be their last word. The private meetings of the British with Griffith and Collins, combined with the personal assurances of Griffith and the private memorandum of Collins, would have encouraged them to make progress by exploiting the divisions on the Irish side. This they did. At midnight on the evening of 4 December a private meeting took place between Griffith and Jones. Griffith frankly made clear to Jones that the Irish delegation were deeply divided: 'he and Collins had been completely won over to belief' in Lloyd George's promises; and required help to overcome 'Barton and the doctrinaires', and to win over others in Dublin.[45]

It was against this background that Collins met Lloyd George alone on the morning of 5 December. The minutes of their conversation reveal that Collins spoke strongly about Ulster and the essential unity of Ireland without receiving any precise concession from Lloyd George, although the renewed offer of the Boundary Commission—raised earlier on 12 November—appears to have mollified the anxieties of Collins. In regard to the oath, little is recorded apart from Lloyd George's insistence, and Collins's apparent acceptance, that it should be seen within a Dominion framework.[46] Pakenham relates, however, that Collins 'handed Lloyd George a new form of oath which a legal friend had suggested to him.' It has been suggested that Crompton Llewelynn Davies, the husband of Moya, may well have been this legal friend, and that he may also have been responsible for some of the other submissions of Collins at this time.[47] Other sources record that Collins had kept the IRB regularly informed about the negotiations and that the new oath had been drawn up in accordance with their wishes. These had been conveyed to Collins after the Cabinet meeting of 3 December by Sean Ó Murthuile, the secretary of the IRB.[48]

This new formula of Collins was more acceptable to Lloyd George. While he had been prepared to end the negotiations after the conference which Barton and Gavan Duffy had attended with Griffith, he was now, just twenty-four hours later, prepared to consult with his cabinet and meet the Irish delegates in further conference. The role of Michael Collins was clearly decisive. His failure to attend the morning meeting weakened the Irish case; his private meeting with Lloyd George indicated that any final settlement was likely to accord with his own proposals.

The Articles of Agreement that faced the Irish delegates on the afternoon of 5 December placed Ireland inside a Dominion structure. The oath read

> I ... solemnly swear to bear true faith and allegiance to the Constitution of the Irish Free State; to the Community of Nations known as the British Empire; and to the King as Head of the State and of the Empire.[49]

In the course of the final two sub-conferences of 5 and 6 December, at which Griffith, Collins and Barton were the Irish representatives, the oath was modified slightly but significantly in Ireland's favour to read:

> I ... do solemnly swear true faith and allegiance to the Constitution of the Irish Free State as by law established, and that I will be faithful to H.M. King George V, his heirs and successors by law, in virtue of the common citizenship of Ireland with Great Britain and her adherence to and membership of the group of nations forming the British Commonwealth of Nations.[50]

This formula reflected the thinking of Collins. The minutes of the meeting by Barton record that, when Griffith raised the question of the oath,

> Birkenhead said that Mr. Collins had handed in to him that morning a form of oath on which he [Mr Collins] had been working and then produced it with his (Birkenhead's) alterations. We objected to the final words being 'British Empire' and suggested 'British Commonwealth of Nations'.[51]

This formula was clearly an attempt to be all things to all men, and did, indeed, modify the rigidity of the British demand for recognition. By blurring the distinction between internal and external recognition of the King, it was hoped to induce as many Irishmen and Englishmen as possible to see that their principles had not been compromised.

Not all the delegates were happy with the formula, but they did sign it. Griffith, Collins and Duggan with varied degrees of willingness—Griffith after he was asked to stand over his written undertaking on Ulster; Barton and Duffy signed reluctantly, and after Lloyd George had threatened the renewal of war if the terms were not accepted. Childers was resolutely and bitterly opposed to the agreement. It ran counter to the main thrust of the policy with which he had been associated since the conference began. Mystery surrounds the final involvement of de Valera. Often it is asked why no phone call was made from the delegates to de Valera before they signed.

He was staying in Limerick on the night of 5/6 December at Strand House, the residence of Stephen O'Mara, senior, and was accompanied by Cathal Brugha and Richard Mulcahy. In fact de Valera, himself, informed Joe McGarrity that he had received a telephone call announcing that an agreement had been made, and the O'Mara family record that a call did come from London during the night and was answered by de Valera. An indication that such a contact took place is to be found in a cable received at 411 Fifth Avenue, New York, by Stephen O'Mara, junior, on 6 December. It was from his father and read: 'Full agreement reached by Irish and British delegates at early hour this morning.'[52] Whatever the level of knowledge that de Valera had on the morning of 6 December, the final terms were those with which Griffith and Collins had become identified.

While both Griffith and Collins had been prepared officially to argue the case for External Association until late in November, their private initiatives had alerted the British to the possibility of an alternative policy. The beginning of the sub-conferences on 24 October marked the beginning of a new departure. This was confirmed by the individual actions of both Griffith and Collins: Griffith, most notably by his private letter of 2 November and his assurance on Ulster of 12 November; Collins, most particularly by his memoir to Birkenhead of 25 November and by his private discussions with both Birkenhad and Lloyd George on 4 and 5 December. It was their policy, facilitated by Jones and sustained to a high and intriguing degree by Cope, that carried the day.

Despite the explicit injunction of the Irish Cabinet meeting of 3 December, Griffith and Collins were prepared to put their names to the Agreement with the British. They believed that their compromise was the best for Ireland and they were prepared to let the people decide the outcome. Collins, for his part, had also endeavoured to ensure that the Army remained under his and IRB control. Confusion and division ensued in the ranks of the politicians, the Army and the people. Irishmen could, and did, claim that by pledging their allegiance to the 'Free State' and their faithfulness to the King they were not abandoning the Republic. Other Irishmen claimed that allegiance to a 'Free State', which accepted the role of the English King, and faithfulness to that King, which was based on a 'common citizenship', was a betrayal of the Republic.

Individual reactions varied enormously. Those who had sworn loyalty to Dáil Éireann, the Government of the Republic, and meant it in both substance and form found compromise the most difficult. Those who had declared for the Republic but equated that profession of faith with some form of Irish independence found it easier to come to terms with something less than the Republic. The misgivings of the former were accentuated by the fact that the 'essential unity' of Ireland had not been secured; the doubts of the latter were assuaged by the promise contained in the Boundary Commission. Division was inevitable.

The Cabinet accepted the Treaty terms by four votes to three on 8 December 1921: Griffith and Collins were supported by Barton and Cosgrave, with de Valera, Brugha and Stack against acceptance. Members of the Dáil were soon to gather and make their own decisions. Chartres in Berlin had to determine his own position on this most delicate of issues.

Berlin: Charles Bewley and the Irish Race Congress

Chartres was not called upon to make a decision on the Treaty immediately. His first concern, after his return to Germany in the early days of December 1921, was to restore the efficient functioning of the Berlin office. He found that the Irish representation in Berlin had changed significantly. He, as republican envoy, and Nancy Power, as secretary, were still running their department, but Charles Bewley had been appointed as Irish consul with special concern for trade.

Bewley was a member of the well known Dublin Quaker family but, while a student at Oxford University, had become a Catholic. He qualified as a barrister and had actively supported the republican courts which had been created by Dáil Éireann after 1919. He had been notified of his appointment on 17 October 1921 at a salary of £750 per annum, far higher than the envoy or of a Dáil deputy.[1] In early November he was advised to travel to London and to contact J.L. Fawsitt, the former trade consul to the United States.[2] He was to meet him at 22 Hans Place, where Fawsitt was engaged in the fiscal terms of the Treaty, and to get a briefing from him concerning the role of a trade representative.

Despite the presence of Chartres in Hans Place, it would appear that he was not consulted about the appointment, nor was he asked to tender advice on the scope of Bewley's work. Explanation for the appointment of Bewley may originate in a visit that he paid to Germany in the summer of 1920 in which he had met Chatterton Hill. No mention is made of this visit in Bewley's own account of his time in Germany, nor does he mention that Chatterton Hill had subsequently approached him in October 1921 asking for financial assistance. Some sign of a connection between them is indicated by a request from Chatterton Hill to de Valera on 23 November 1921 that he might assist Bewley in his work as consul.[3] At that time Chatterton Hill had just arrived in Dublin and was evidently in some distress. He pleaded with de Valera 'not to let me starve', and, after listing his career record in the service of Ireland, claimed that he only sought justice. Whatever the reason for Bewley's appointment it was clear that it emanated from the department of Trade rather than from the department of Foreign Affairs. The difficulty of defining spheres of operation between the two departments, combined with personal differences, led to strained relations between Chartres and Bewley.

Bewley, while giving a highly personal impression of their first meeting, accurately conveyed the antipathy that came to exist between them:

> I walked into the lounge of the Eden [Hotel], to keep our appointment. In an armchair, reading *The Times*, sat a middle-aged man with a monocle attached to a black ribbon, whom I would have taken for an English tourist if I had not known him to be the Irish Republican 'envoy'. I introduced myself.
>
> 'Trade representative?' said Chartres. 'Yes, yes! My friend Gavan Duffy wrote me that you would arrive here.'
>
> He spoke with the throaty voice and Oxford accent of the English upper-middle class, while he surveyed me graciously through the monocle.
>
> 'I should like to make it plain,' he went on, 'that our duties lie entirely apart. I have no connection with trade matters, and I hope you understand that you have no concern with political matters, which are my exclusive responsibility.'
>
> I had hoped for much assistance from him, but I found my reception slightly disconcerting. However I said meekly that I quite understood that our activities would henceforth lie in different spheres. [4]

Almost inevitably the demarcation lines between the activities of Chartres and Bewley proved difficult to draw, and failure to resolve them amicably proved a major source of difficulty in the months ahead. The problems were not, however, immediately apparent.

After his return to Berlin in December, Chartres occupied himself diligently with the day-to-day tasks of envoy. On 2 January 1922 he dispatched a seven-page report on the Berlin mission. Almost four pages were devoted to recording the reaction of German newspapers to the Treaty. While praising the ability of Lloyd George, they inclined to the view that Ireland had made gains. Many of the papers praised the courage and patience of the Irish and presented historical sketches of the past relations between England and Ireland. Comparisons were made with Germany. The *Oberbeyrische Gebirgsbots* declared that 'it is a great example for Germany for it proves that a nation cannot be lost if it preserves its national consciousness.' Chartres noted that 'in a great deal of this writing it is easy to discern the part played by the Bulletin in disseminating the Irish national idea'.[5]

Some papers perceptively attributed Irish gains to American influence on England. The *Rostocker Anzeiger* stated that but for America 'the English would not have hesitated to crush the Irish rebellion with all the resources of modern warfare'; and the *Deutsches Velksblatt* of Stuttgart declared that Lloyd George abandoned his policy of force because 'there is another Ireland beyond the reach of England's power; an Ireland in America'. From the German point of view it was hoped that England, having freed herself from the burden of the Irish problem, would be able to intervene more positively in Europe. This opinion was expressed by the *Westfalischer Merkur* which stated that 'Lloyd George is no benefactor or even friend of ours, but he is not the worst of our opponents, and it can be only agreeable to us if he finds time and strength to furnish a heavier counterpoise to the French policy of force.' France, after Versailles, was seen to be Germany's most bitter enemy. The rest of the memorandum was given over to practical suggestions for the future.

Significantly Chartres noted that no reply had been given to his detailed memorandum of 5 September. The primacy of the peace talks had inevitably meant that developments in foreign affairs were placed on hold. Moreover with Griffith, the Foreign Minister, and Chartres, the envoy, involved in the peace negotiations, and with Robert Brennan, the Under Secretary for Foreign Affairs, absent from his post for some time owing to illness, there was little scope for progress. Chartres asked that his suggestions made in September should be acted upon. In that memorandum he now stressed particularly the idea that exclusive interviews should be given to the German press by the President, for example, which would show that Ireland was not anti-German; he proposed articles on general human interest on Ireland such as on music and sport in order to create 'a pro-Irish atmosphere, which of course would help the political work'; and he repeated his call for magic lantern lecture tours. Photographs, Chartres observed, were very valuable for stimulating an interest in Irish affairs, and he also called for prompt information. He cited approvingly the example of Erskine Childers who had sent him signed copies of the Treaty agreement, thus enabling him to place the information with newspaper syndicates.[6]

The Bulletin, Chartres maintained, had continued to make a beneficial impact. 'It has,' he stated, 'been going now for many months twice a week to every German paper of any importance, and the steady, regular supply of facts, statistics and comment has undoubtedly had a marked effect.' He praised particularly the 'great efficiency' of Nancy Power, and added, 'I wish to place on official record my appreciation of her excellent work during that trying and uncertain period.'

Chartres also made a mention of Bewley that was surprisingly positive in the light of Bewley's recorded impressions. Having talked with Bewley it was agreed that an announcement of his arrival would appear in the Bulletin to bring him, in the words of Chartres, 'into contact with interested persons in the various manufacturing and trading centres throughout the country'. This apparently even-handed approach was matched by a similar approach to the Treaty debates. Chartres explained that the Bulletin gave 'extracts from leading speeches in the Dáil for and against the treaty'. Flexibility was still possible in the uncertain political climate of the time. The same consideration applied to the dealings in arms. Chartres reminded Brennan that during his recent visit to Berlin they had agreed 'that certain matters of a special character were to be placed in the responsible charge of Professor J'—John T. Ryan. Chartres continued:

> I suggest that when this plan is carried out a clear line of delimitation should be drawn marking off these functions from my own. My personal relations with J. have been very cordial, and misunderstandings may be avoided in the future if the course I here recommend is followed.

Chartres also submitted a detailed statement of accounts of the Berlin mission up to 1 January 1922, and on 3 January received £80 as part of his salary directly from Michael Collins.[7] The performance of these routine duties and the January report show that the Berlin mission was being conducted on very efficient lines. Chartres appeared happy to accept the new situation created by the Treaty and, indeed, appeared to have made an attempt to perpetuate a policy of continuity with the past. This was expressed not only in his wish for his September memorandum to be acted upon, but also in his willingness to allow J.T. Ryan to function as before.

A letter from Brennan to Chartres on 10 January 1922 encouraged this continuity of policy. Not only did Brennan praise the 'excellent report' of 2 January, but also he noted in regard to Ryan that 'I made the recommendation that he be made responsible for the activities you mention to the proper authorities and received an assurance that the recommendation had been already carried out.'[8] One can discern behind the coded language that gun-running, the specialised business of 'Professor Jetter', was to be confined to his hands, but for Chartres to be associated with gun-running in any form was extremely risky. Indeed, this information was unearthed by the Intelligence Department of the Free State Army during the Civil War. Brennan ended his letter by informing Chartres that Gavan Duffy was the new Minister of Foreign Affairs, and concluded by saying, 'I do not yet know whether there will be any change in the activities of the foreign establishments, but for the present you are to carry on as usual.' This Chartres attempted to do, but the appointment of Gavan Duffy and the divisions in Irish ranks following recognition of the Treaty were to make continuity of policy impossible.

When the Treaty terms were finally accepted by 64 votes to 57 on 7 January 1922 and Arthur Griffith became President of a new administration on 10 January, Chartres was prepared to serve as envoy of this new administration with Gavan Duffy as the new Foreign Minister.[9] Willingness to continue in office, however, did not, in all cases, signify whole-hearted commitment to the Treaty: Sean T. O'Kelly and Harry Boland, for example, who had openly spoken against the Treaty in the Dáil debates, also remained in office. Indeed the policy of the ministry of Foreign Affairs under Gavan Duffy exemplified the divisions caused in Irish ranks by the Treaty.

Gavan Duffy, himself, despite his experience in foreign affairs, was a most unlikely candidate for a post in the pro-Treaty administration. He had been allied with Barton and Childers in opposing the initiatives of Griffith and Collins during the Treaty negotiations; he had been reluctant to sign the Treaty; and during the Treaty debate he had only advocated the Treaty with some reluctance. 'I am going to recommend this Treaty to you very reluctantly but sincerely,' he had declared on 21 December 1921, 'because I see no alternative ... We lost the Republic of Ireland in order to save the people of Ireland.' Moreover, Gavan Duffy hoped that in the framing of the new Constitution for the Irish Free State the King of England would be relegated 'to the exterior darkness'.[10] He had repeated these views on 10 January, when he played a prominent part in the debate over the appointment of Arthur Griffith as President:

> I made my own position pretty clear on the Treaty, I do not like it; I never did like it ... we had to accept it because we saw no real alternative ... Anyhow the Republic goes on, and must go on until it is superseded by the Free State.[11]

This approach was markedly different to that of Griffith. Speaking at the close of the debate on the Treaty on 7 January, when he was still the Foreign Minister, he criticised two foreign representatives, presumably O'Kelly and Boland, who had publicly opposed the Treaty. He quoted with approval a letter from MacWhite, the representative in Geneva, whom he described as 'the man who has done more for us on the Continent than any other man'. Griffith, himself, denied that there ever was a functioning Republican Government, and cited MacWhite to prove that all European countries regarded the Treaty as a triumph for Ireland which should be accepted as the basis for joining the League of Nations.[12]

On the one hand Griffith, the President of Dáil Éireann, was happy to move on from a Republic to a Free State; on the other hand Gavan Duffy, the Foreign Minister of Dáil Éireann, was only prepared to make the move with reluctance and in a manner which removed the English King from influence in Ireland. This ambivalence at the source of power inevitably had an impact upon the Irish representatives abroad.

An incident on the day after Gavan Duffy's appointment illustrated the problem. Duffy had been advised at a Cabinet meeting to interview the foreign representatives concerning their duties and had asked Art O'Brien, the Irish representative in London, whether he would be willing to continue in service under a change of government—the implication being was he prepared to accept the Treaty. O'Brien replied that the question should not have been put by the 'Minister of Foreign Affairs of the Republican Government', and he refused to reply.[13] In many ways Chartres could face the question put to O'Brien with equanimity. He was in good standing with Griffith and Collins and he had expressed satisfaction with the Treaty. However, he also had some anti-Treaty connections that might prove embarrassing or even harmful.

On 7 January 1922, the very day that the Treaty was approved, Chartres's book, *The Bloody English*, appeared in the *Irish Press* of Philadelphia in serial form. The articles were signed Edward Seaton, 'True Born Englishman'.[14] The *Irish Press* was published by Joe McGarrity, friend and colleague of J.T. Ryan, through whom possibly Chartres had made contact with McGarrity. By associating himself with McGarrity, Chartres was identifying himself not only with the most influential Irish American opposed to the Treaty, but also with one of de Valera's closest allies. Moreover, the contents of the articles were, as has been noted, so hostile to England that it was difficult to reconcile them with any acceptance of the British Crown. Indeed, if the articles conveyed the real views of Chartres towards the English, then any doubts as to the conversion of Chartres to the Irish cause are removed.

The connection between Chartres and John T. Ryan was also potentially damaging. Around this time Ryan wrote to McGarrity giving him his views on Ireland after the Treaty and on Chartres in particular. 'The old fellow's heart is all right,' said Ryan, and he praised his role in the Treaty negotiations. He maintained that Chartres 'was for the Republic to the end', but was unaware of the secret contacts between Griffith and Collins with Lloyd George.[15] Ryan then explained that Chartres was prepared to accept the title of 'Irish Envoy' instead of 'Envoy of the Irish Republic' because he considered that de Valera would not win the election on the Treaty.

Of the work of Chartres in Germany Ryan was extremely critical describing it as 'a joke'. He blamed Nancy Power for this state of affairs, claiming that Chartres was 'absolutely dominated' by her. 'I know the weakness which brings this result,' Ryan hinted suggestively, 'but will not put it on paper.' Ryan had no time for Nancy Power, writing that she was 'a vixen and was one of the cabal which has been working against Mr Topman [de Valera] for a year. She has no ability ... is shy and selfish and has a shifty glance.' Bewley was also dismissed as an 'out and out un-Free Stater', while Briscoe was dismissed as 'a cheap Jew'.[16] Much of this outspoken criticism was ill informed and derogatory, and may be put down to Ryan's bitter opposition to any one who supported what he termed the 'un-Free State'. For Chartres to have been involved with someone who was so bitterly opposed to the Free State, and who was so closely linked with McGarrity, was not the ideal pedigree for a pro-Treaty representative abroad. Some might be prepared to call his loyalty into question.

The first major event to test not only the loyalties of Chartres and Power, but also the loyalties of all those embroiled in the division over the Treaty was the Irish Race Congress that met in Paris on 23 January 1922. What had been planned in 1921 as a rally to signify the unity of the Irish throughout the world served only to illustrate the differences that divided them. The pro-Treaty group had consolidated their position by approving of the Treaty in a meeting of the Southern Ireland Parliament, and by setting up a Provisional Government, with Michael Collins as Chairman, on 13 January to implement the terms of the Treaty; the anti-Treaty group also made efforts to create an organised opposition which led eventually to the formation of Cummann na Poblachta with de Valera as President.

For most of the year 1922 there were two governments in southern Ireland: the Provisional Government with Collins as chairman; and the republican Dáil Government with Griffith as President. Gavan Duffy as Minister of Foreign Affairs in the Dáil Government was in a most delicate position. There was no minister of Foreign Affairs in the Provisional Government and, as minister for the Dáil ministry, he had to conduct a policy that was acceptable to all his colleagues—some of whom were in the Provisional Government, or sympathised with it, and were planning to dismantle the Dáil government which he represented. Fear of party differences spreading to the Paris Congress began as soon as the division had taken place over the Treaty and the election of Arthur Griffith as President of Dáil Éireann. On 12 January 1922 a meeting of the Dáil cabinet proposed that Gavan Duffy should contact de Valera and come to some arrangement about sharing out the eight representatives to be sent from Ireland.[17] This was done, and the Irish delegation was divided into two groups of four—later the number was increased to five; the pro-Treaty group was headed by Eoin MacNéill; the anti-Treaty group by de Valera.

More explicit instructions were given to Gavan Duffy on 16 January by a Cabinet directive that 'the Minister for Foreign Affairs is to settle definitely with President de Valera regarding the undertaking that party politics will not be introduced' at the Congress.[18] It proved impossible, however, to keep party politics out of the conference. Even before the first preliminary meeting of the Congress at the Grand Hotel, Paris, on Friday 20 January had taken place, Gavan Duffy had taken steps to see that the new Dáil ministry was adequately represented in the planning of the conference. He had requested that Desmond FitzGerald, Minister of Publicity in the new ministry, replace Robert Brennan as representative of the government and liaison officer with the Congress.

Brennan, who had already declared his support for de Valera, immediately resigned as Under Secretary for Foreign Affairs, and left for Paris to engage in work at the conference.[19] His departure was the first clear sign that foreign policy was to be conducted along different lines after the acceptance of the Treaty. Gavan Duffy had good reason to be anxious about the influence exercised upon the conference by de Valera's supporters. Art O'Brien, who had taken issue with Duffy over the claims of the Republic, enjoyed a presiding role at the first meeting of the delegates, and on the next day, 21 January, presided over a very important meeting on General Procedure and Agenda. As a result of this meeting the anti-Treaty group secured leading positions as chairmen of the discussion groups, which began on 23 January, and of publicity arrangements.[20]

While preparations were being made for the conference, Chartres was preparing to leave Berlin for Paris. Before he departed he wrote to Michael Collins on 21 January. Chartres left no doubt as to where his sympathies lay. He recalled his conversations with Collins in 1920, and he congratulated him on the take over of Dublin Castle from British troops. He continued

> I cannot help sending you a word of warm personal congratulation. The flag will have to be carried, and I am sure will eventually be carried a little further. Meanwhile the victory actually gained and the opportunities it offers for national recovery and consolidation are dazzling. I think I know something of the magnitude of your own contribution to what has been gained and the great inspiration it has been to others. I congratulate you again and wish you all good fortune in your work for Ireland.[21]

With a flourish Chartres signed himself in Irish Eoin macSeartarris.

Chartres is listed as one of the Irish envoys abroad who attended the opening session of the Congress in the Hotel Continental, Paris, on 23 January 1922; so too, incidentally, is Bewley, who is listed as a trade consul.[22] Little is known of Chartres' contribution to the conference, but the proceedings themselves indicate very precisely the clash of principles that divided Irish people at that time. Gavan Duffy had prepared a message for the Congress which conveyed warm greetings to all and called upon all Gaels to 'cement yet more strongly the bonds linking to the Motherland its children'. The minutes record that this message from the 'Minister for Foreign Affairs of the Irish Republic' was read to the conference by Sean T. O'Kelly 'Envoy of the Irish Republic'.[23]

Clearly in the minds of those who drew up the minutes the Republic was not dead despite the Treaty, and that was the attitude of many at the conference. Constitutionally there was some basis for their conviction because the Provisional Government had not yet produced the constitution for the Free State that was to replace the government of Dáil Éireann; and many hoped that the new constitution might preserve the Republic by omitting any reference to the English King. Gavan Duffy shared that hope and his first memorandum on foreign policy bore testimony to these sentiments.

This was drawn up on 25 January 1922. Gavan Duffy declared that:

> while the policy of the new Government of the Republic is friendly to the Provisional Government set up under the Treaty with England, this Government has undertaken the duty of maintaining the existing Republic and the efficiency of its machinery until the Irish People shall have determined whether or not to accept the proposed 'Irish Free State'. Moreover, if in the meantime the British Government should fail to carry out its engagements, Ireland must be in a position to resume the struggle without delay.[24]

However, Gavan Duffy did also call for a more friendly approach in relation to England, and he did show a realistic awareness of the problems caused by divisions over the Treaty declaring that

> as national unity is now broken by the emergence of two political parties in the Republican State, members of the diplomatic service will be under the obligation of reflecting faithfully the policy of the Government, whatever their personal opinions on party politics. It will be their duty to refrain from propaganda either for or against the Treaty.

Despite these qualifications the memorandum stated frankly the republican character of the Dáil Government. This was made clear in Gavan Duffy's injunction that 'the Irish representatives abroad will continue to represent the Government of the Irish Republic and that Government alone.'[25]

Granted that this was the attitude of Gavan Duffy, it was to be expected that the delegates to the Paris Congress should feel that the political debate was far from over. Coincidentally the major debate on political aims and ideals took place on 25 January 1922, the very day that Gavan Duffy had formulated his foreign policy document.

The motion before the Congress on that day was that the first aim of the new organisation should be 'to aid the people of Ireland in the attainment of their full political, cultural, and economic ideals.' The chairman of the session was Eamon de Valera.[26] Debate centred around the word 'full': Eoin MacNéill argued that this might imply that only the 'absolute maximum' Irish aspiration might be supported, and this could lead to clashes with the majority of the Irish people. By implication he was referring to decisions on the Treaty, and others were more explicit in relating 'full' to the extreme republican demand. Party divisions became apparent as those opposed to the Treaty, such as Mary MacSwiney, Countess Markievicz and Art O'Brien, spoke for 'full' ideals; and those in favour of the Treaty, such as MacNéill and Michael Hayes, expressed more caution.

Towards the end of the debate a startling revelation was made. The original proposer of the motion, P.S. Cleary from Australia, stated that he had not included the word 'full' in his draft. This elicited from de Valera the response that

> I am the real culprit in this matter, because I put the word 'full' in last night, and I know exactly why I put it in. The reason I put it in was that there are in Ireland more than 75% of all those at present in Dáil Éireann who do not think that we have yet realised our ideal to the full, and the only people who would have any reason to object to that word 'full' would be those who say 'We have got our ideal and we have finished with it.' I do not believe that any nation will ever achieve their political ideal. The point was to get something to enable the two parties to work together, and it was with that object that I put that word in.[27]

After some further criticism of the word 'full', de Valera asserted that 'I assure you I don't preach this formula now from a party spirit. I have not been accustomed to a party spirit, and I will never be a party leader.' Despite these disclaimers of de Valera, which make interesting reading in the light of his later career, it was evident that he had acted surreptitiously in order to make the new organisation more acceptable to him and to his supporters. A more explicit attempt was made to fashion the organisation to de Valera's likeness by Art O'Brien when he proposed that

> the delegates from the existing political organisations of the world regret that the delegates from the Irish Government who recently went to England found it impossible to obtain a settlement based on Ireland's full claim.[28]

This effort, again focusing on the word 'full', proved abortive; but a compromise formula was eventually agreed on for the aims of the new organisation. It stated that the first objective was 'to assist the people of Ireland to attain to the full their national ideals, political, cultural and economical.'

The Congress closed on 28 January with unanimous agreement that the organisation be called 'Fine Ghaedheal' [Family of the Gael] with the motto: 'Beyond all telling is the destiny God has in mind for Ireland the peerless.'[29] The fine words, however, could not conceal the deep divisions dividing the participants. Fine Ghaedheal was effectively still-born. Instead of providing a platform for Irish unity, the Paris Congress served only to draw more finely the demarcation lines that divided the Irish parties over the Treaty. However, by defining more precisely the demarcation lines, the Congress, taken together with Duffy's memorandum, did illustrate the confusion that lay at the heart of Irish politics in January 1922. The Republic was not yet dead: it had still to be acted for, and could still be argued about.

Those involved in the Dáil government, especially those engaged in foreign affairs, experienced this dilemma most acutely. Chartres had pledged his allegiance to Collins and, as a result, the dilemma did not touch upon him too immediately. For other representatives abroad it was far different. Art O'Brien and Sean T. O'Kelly were reported by MacNéill to have acted at the Paris Congress against the interests of the Government. He wrote a letter of protest on 2 February and raised the matter at a Ministry meeting on the following day. MacNéill suggested that they should be dismissed from their posts in London and Paris respectively.[30]

MacNéill did not, however, have it all his own way. On the same day, 2 February, as he drew up his report, Sean T. O'Kelly sent a long letter to Gavan Duffy. In it he complained that it was reported that an Irish delegation, made up of MacNéill, Michael Hayes, and Michael MacWhite, had visited M. Poincaré, President du Conseil, and M. Millerand, president of the French Republic, on 31 January. O'Kelly stated that

> if Messrs MacNéill and Hayes called on M. Poincaré or M. Millerand as representatives of the Provisional Government of the Irish Free State, of course I have nothing to say to the matter, except this, that I

think their visit might have been deferred till the Irish Free State had been established. I am sure at any rate you will at once recognise the anomalous position in which such a visit places you, as Minister of Foreign Affairs of the Irish Republic, as also myself, the representative of that Republic in Paris.[31]

O'Kelly maintained that the official Government delegation had shown him scant courtesy and added that 'not one of the members of the official Delegation announced their coming on their arrival here.' He concluded by asking Gavan Duffy 'whether it was with your knowledge and consent that these gentlemen called upon either the President of the Republic or its Prime Minister, and if so in what capacity they called'.

This issue between O'Kelly and Duffy touched upon the heart of the matter: were they ministers and envoys of the Republic or of the transitional Provisional Government? The incident resurfaced again in March. For the present as Chartres left Paris after the Congres, he must have been aware of the tortuous path that he had to tread. On the one hand he could return to his task with some confidence and a clear conscience as he was fully supportive of Collins and Griffith; but, on the other hand, his stridently anti-British articles in the *Irish Press* of Philadelphia were in direct variance with Duffy's instruction about anti-English propaganda. Fortunately for Chartres the articles were not signed.

Once in Berlin Chartres had to deal with an incident concerning Charles Bewley. Trivial as the affair might appear on the surface, it served to demonstrate not only the difficulties of moving from the government of the Republic to that of the Free State, but also the tensions between the Irish government departments of Foreign Affairs and Trade and Commerce. It also raised the matter of Irish attitudes to anti-Semitism. The issue centred around differences between Bewley and Robert Briscoe, who was still in Germany and who was still involved in the arms business. As Chartres was leaving the Grand Hotel in Paris on 28 January, Bewley handed him a memorandum giving his version of the incident.[32] Chartres had earlier received Briscoe's version of events. Having heard both sides of the story, Chartres sent a report to Gavan Duffy. He related that

> shortly after his arrival here Mr Bewley became acquainted with Mr Briscoe, who for a considerable time past has been engaged upon special work for the Irish government. Subsequently Mr Bewley visited a music-hall in Berlin [the Tauenzien Palast] and in the bar where both he and Mr Briscoe are known, expressed his antipathy to Mr Briscoe—who is a Jew—so violently that he was obliged to leave the premises. Later, he apologised to Mr. Briscoe and also returned to the

music-hall where he apologised to the proprietor for the scene he had caused and the offence he had given to customers present.[33]

Bewley, in his submission to Chartres, frankly acknowledged the charge that Briscoe had made against him. He stated that he made it in the context of rebutting the claim that Briscoe was the Irish consul in Germany, and had added that 'it was not likely that a Jew of his type would be appointed'. Chartres concluded that

> such behaviour in a public place by a gentleman known to represent officially a department of the Irish government reflects injuriously upon our country's reputation here. Moreover, an anti-Semitic outburst by an Irish official in a country where Jews are very numerous and very influential was an extraordinary indiscretion from the point of view of Irish material interests. I should be sorry to press the matter so as to cause Mr Bewley permanent injury but on Public Grounds I must express the opinion that if it were possible to transfer him to some other sphere of activity such a step would correct the mischeif[sic] that has been done, and would be in the interests of decorum, national dignity and commercial prudence. At present all of these interests have suffered at Mr Bewley's hands.[34]

The advice of Chartres was not acted upon because the incident had taken on a broader dimension.

Briscoe had reported that on 20 January, while attempting to resolve his personal differences with Bewley, he had visited his office and there encountered Jurgens, the Hamburg merchant who had tried to double-cross the Irish over the provision of guns. Charlie McGuinness, his associate in gunrunning, had accompanied him to Bewley's office. Briscoe maintained that he had warned Bewley that Jurgens was not to be trusted and that he was still dealing with the affair.[35] On the face of it, even stronger grounds might appear to exist to censure the conduct of Bewley, but he had acted cleverly to safeguard his own position. His actions were to produce an effect later in the month of February. In the meantime Chartres made his formal report for the month of January.

Chartres acknowledged Gavan Duffy's memorandum of 25 January and inquired whether the paragraph about anti-English propaganda applied 'to the publication of authentic recent news.'[36] He then asked if news without any comment 'in the normal propaganda way' was still acceptable. Progress was being maintained, Chartres said, in securing publicity through the Bulletin and syndicated articles, but he again made a plea for the information he had requested in September and January. Evidently nothing had been done to supply him with special articles and photographs. Chartres made his point well and developed a new line of direction for the department of Foreign Affairs. He stated that

> in former reports I have dwelt upon the importance of creating, apart from politics, a general atmosphere of sympathy with Ireland, and I beg to emphasise this point once more. We do not know when we may need the support of national opinion in foreign lands, and I should like to do everything practicable to make Ireland known, apart altogether from political issues.

As well as these remarks on the conduct of Irish policy, Chartres made his usual comments on German politics, focusing on the appointment of Rathenau as Foreign Minister. He reported perceptively that this appointment 'is the most important recent event in German politics for it has split the Coalition'.[37] He related how the reconstituted Wirth administration of November 1921 was only made possible by the accession of the Deutsche Volkspartei party under Stresemann to the coalition of the Centre and Democratic parties. This alliance no longer existed because Stresemann felt that the appointment of Rathenau had been made without the promised consultation with his party. Chartres predicted the fall of the Wirth administration, if it could not carry out its new taxation programme, and he emphasised the important role of Stresemann's party in shaping political developments. He also made clear that the situation in Germany was extremely difficult with strikes affecting the railways, water supplies, the electricity and the telephones.

Chartres also transmitted his regular survey of the German press. He continued to be remarkably objective, possibly even dangerously so. If Foreign Affairs wanted only to hear of acceptance of the Treaty, Chartres was not going to oblige them. He did recount, giving many examples, that the general view of the press as regards the Treaty 'continues to be that it is a great victory for Ireland within the sphere of practical politics'; but he also cited many instances of the press praising de Valera—this 'romantic figure' of 'classic greatness'. An article by Senatsprasident Flugge in *Der Tag* on trade was also reported:

> Hitherto Ireland's foreign trade has all passed through England. Ireland will now turn to other lands. We hope Germany will be among them. Ireland has immense stores of undeveloped mineral wealth. It is probably not out of the question that German experts may be required for their utilisation.

Chartres concluded his report by asking, if in the altered circumstances following the Treaty, he might end his personal position of living in 'a sort of semi-transparent incognito'.[38] All in all his report, like his previous ones, was comprehensive and thought-provoking. The quality of the memorandum was recognised by Gavan Duffy who thanked him for his 'valuable analysis', and advised him that he need no longer remain incognito and that he might continue to publish news items, while keeping an eye on their tone.[39] Privately Gavan Duffy was even more fulsome in his praise of Chartres. On 22 February he asked Desmond FitzGerald, as Minister of Publicity, to respond to the 'excellent proposals' of Chartres whom he described as 'the best man we have on the continent'.[40]

The good standing of Chartres had also been enhanced by a report from Michael MacWhite, the Irish envoy to Switzerland. He wrote to Gavan Duffy on 3 February 1922: 'It is no easy matter,' he informed him, 'to make practical suggestions with reference to the rearrangement of the work of your Ministry abroad. To obtain suitable and experienced men to carry on this work in the different European capitals is easier said than done.

> To begin with a permanent Under Secretaryship will most probably have to be established in Dublin. By the nature of things, the man for this position should enjoy the confidence and respect, not only of yourself, but also of the foreign representatives, and be of undoubted reliability more especially because of the critical period ahead of us. He should likewise have some technical and organising experience. The only man I can think of whose qualifications are equal to the occasion is Mr Chartres—but I do not know his opinions on the present political situation, nor do I know him sufficiently well to recommend him. [41]

Political attitudes were all-important. The following day MacWhite submitted another proposal to Gavan Duffy. He informed him that he had met Sir Eric Drummond, General Secretary of the League of Nations, and he made the recommendation that Ireland apply for membership of the League.[42]

Gavan Duffy was encouraged to act on the advice to join the League of Nations, and he had already taken steps to appoint an Under Secretary to replace Robert Brennan. Although Gavan Duffy turned to Joseph Walshe, one of Sean T. O'Kelly's assistants in Paris, rather than to Chartres, to fill the post of Under Secretary the recommendation of MacWhite could only have been beneficial to Chartres.[43] Chartres needed all the assistance that was going as the lines of division over the Treaty hardened in the month of February. The treatment of Harry Boland and Sean T. O'Kelly was to serve as a warning to all foreign representatives.

A visit by Joe McGarrity to Ireland which began on 12 February 1922, when he met and attempted to reconcile not only Collins and de Valera on a national level, but also Collins and Boland on an IRB level, was not successful.[44] As McGarrity was engaged in these meetings, his paper, the *Irish Press*, continued its extracts from Chartres' *The Bloody English* with an article which attacked the morals of the English soldiers and gave details of their use of brothels in Egypt. These were not sound political opinions for the climate of the time; nor was it desirable to be too closely identified with McGarrity's views, although his attitude was not yet totally incompatible with the pro-Treaty position. Boland, who was solidly aligned with de Valera in opposition to the Treaty, urged McGarrity to bring the re-organised Clan around to the anti-Treaty position.

On 16 February, while McGarrity was still in Ireland, Boland was dismissed as envoy to America. He was replaced on 7 March by Professor Timothy Smiddy, although his appointment was made directly, and possibly significantly, by a decision of the Cabinet rather than by Gavan Duffy.[45] One says 'significantly' because earlier in the year, on 27 January, Gavan Duffy had sounded out Stephen O'Mara, junior, for the post in America stating that

> the Cabinet feels that at the present time there should be someone responsible representing the Republic in the United States: there is no question of any representative of the Free State being sent out so far as my Government is concerned, and I have not heard of any such intention on the part of the Provisional Government.[46]

Times had changed rapidly: it was evident that Smiddy would not represent the republican position in America.

The balance of power was moving in an anti-Republican direction, and this affected the fortunes of Harry Boland and Sean T. O'Kelly. Both men were not only diplomatic representatives but also members of Dáil Éireann. Their positions became almost untenable with the development of party politics. In O'Kelly's case the position may have been accentuated by the fact that Gavan Duffy had been his assistant in Paris in 1919 and 1920, and personal difficulties between them had developed at that time. These differences had been accentuated by the problems that had arisen at the Irish Race Congress in Paris.

Apart from the major issue of Gavan Duffy's attitude to the ministerial visit to the French President, there had been other incidents. O'Kelly had objected to the appointment of Walshe as Under Secretary for Foreign Affairs on the grounds of principle: namely, that 'the staffs of the separate delegations abroad were appointed and controlled by the heads of each delegation'. To 'second' Joseph Walshe to Dublin was 'an interference with the previous practice', and should not have been undertaken without consultation, so argued O'Kelly.[47]

Gavan Duffy replied that there was no place for such a practice at the present time; but, as if to make his point, O'Kelly announced on his own initiative that Osmonde Grattan Esmonde would replace Walshe as first secretary, and that Sean Murphy, on the staff of the secretariat of the Irish Race Congress, would take over as second secretary on 1 February.[48]

At about the same time the issue arose which led directly to the dismissal of both O'Kelly and Boland. Gavan Duffy questioned O'Kelly on 26 January about a joint letter signed by himself and Harry Boland which called on people 'to support the existing Republic at the forthcoming Árd-Fheis of Sinn Féin'. O'Kelly replied that he took 'full responsibility' for the letter and again raised a matter of principle. He claimed that his 'freedom of political action in Ireland', which he had enjoyed as a diplomatic representative for three years, was being removed.[49]

The response of Gavan Duffy was firm and uncompromising. He informed O'Kelly on 7 February that the emergence of two parties after the Treaty had 'radically changed' the political scene, and suggested that he consider resigning his position.[50] They met on the evening of 20 February and O'Kelly told Duffy that he was not going to resign. He was, therefore, dismissed and it was agreed that he would end his appointment to Paris on about 11 March.[51] The Sinn Féin Árd-Fheis that had led to O'Kelly's letter was held on the following two days, 21 and 22 February. It was marked by a surprising degree of support for the anti-Treaty party, and a three-month period of relative co-operation in both the Sinn Féin organisation and in the Dáil ensued. During this time a new constitution was to be drawn up and an election agreed. The change in O'Kelly's situation, however, was to have repercussions for Chartres, although he still had his own problems in Berlin. These involved the continuing saga of the Bewley story.

When the Paris Congress was ending, Bewley had submitted not only a statement of his case to Chartres, but also a fuller statement to Michael Hayes which was to be presented to the Ministry of Trade and Commerce under Ernest Blythe. This statement was sent by Blythe to Michael Collins on 20 February.[52] Bewley knew that he could expect more sympathy from the department of Trade and Commerce, which had been responsible for his appointment in the first place. Moreover, it was evident that the department was more committed to a future with the Free State than looking back, as Gavan Duffy was, to the Republic.

Bewley's memorandum was couched in terms that played upon these sensitivities. He maintained that Chartres had not acted strongly enough to correct Briscoe when informed that letters addressed to 'Mr Consul Briscoe' had been received in Bewley's office. Then, having related his confrontation with Briscoe and McGuinness, Bewley claimed that they had denied his credentials to be consul, and narrated the following exchange:

> I said that I was the accredited consul of the Irish Government, whereupon Briscoe and 'Thompson' [McGuinness] stated that they did not recognise the 'so-called Free State' and talked about 'Michael Collins and his dupes.' Briscoe then said he had heard that I had denied that he [Briscoe] was consul. I said that I had denied it, because he was not consul. He said, 'I have been doing the work of a consul and consider myself the consul for the republic'.[53]

By associating Briscoe's claim to be consul with the republican cause that was hostile to Michael Collins, Bewley was acting shrewdly to protect his position. He did more. He claimed that Briscoe's purchase of the ship *City of Dortmund* was linked with Cathal Brugha, Liam Mellowes [*sic*] and 'a number of members of the IRA'.

He also claimed that Briscoe's dispute with Jurgens was, in part, caused by rivalry over running a shipping line from Hamburg to Ireland. Despite the well attested evidence that the issue with Jurgens was based on his deception of the Irish over the provision of armaments, Bewley's letter proved eminently successful. Blythe sent copies of the letter to Michael Collins and to Gavan Duffy, informing the latter that Briscoe 'is decidedly a shady character.' On 13 February 1922 Blythe had promised Bewley that he would help him to strengthen his position as consul, and advised him to forget about his admission to Chartres: 'I think you cannot take too great trouble to cause the matter to be forgotten', was the recommendation of Blythe.[54] When Collins replied to Blythe on 27 February, remarking from his experience that Briscoe was 'out on the make,' this reply was forwarded to Bewley, leaving him in no doubt that he was on the inner track and viewed more favourably than Briscoe.[55]

This endorsement of Bewley threatened the position of Chartres. On an official level it was clear that the consul's position was to be strengthened in a manner that might diminish the initiative and responsibility of the envoy; but there were more serious political implications. If Chartres was to continue to support Briscoe, he was likely to be branded as in the same camp as Brugha, Mellows and the extreme republicans. He had to tread very carefully, if he wished to be regarded as a supporter of the Treaty and a friend of Michael Collins.

Despite the delicacy of the situation Chartres sent a further report to Gavan Duffy which strongly supported Briscoe:

Mr Briscoe tells me, that he has never described himself as Irish Consul, but that he has been so described by others. He has credentials and in conducting his transactions always stated that he was authorised to act for Ireland. He tells me that when specifically asked—on one occasion in the course of legal proceedings—whether he was the Irish Consul he replied that he was not, as at that time no regular Consular representation had been established, but that he was authorised to act on Ireland's behalf. These legal proceedings took place last Autumn and were the outcome of transactions which Mr Briscoe was sent here to carry out. He assures me in positive terms that there is no foundation for the allegation referred to.[56]

If Chartres felt that he held the initiative in his conflict with Bewley, he was mistaken. Gavan Duffy passed on his letter to Blythe who, in turn, passed it on to Bewley with the comment that 'Mr Briscoe's "explanation" does not seem exactly satisfactory'.[57]

By this time the charge of anti-Semitism had faded into the background, and the observation of Chartres that Bewley should be removed on the grounds of 'decorum, national dignity and commercial prudence' counted for nothing. Moral values gave way to practical politics as Blythe endorsed Bewley; and Bewley, in his conflict with Chartres, was able to receive confidential memoranda about himself. This clearly placed Bewley in a strong position. In the midst of these developments there are indications that Chartres was unwell in the last days of February.

On 27 February Gavan Duffy wrote two letters to Nancy Power and inquired why there had been no acknowledgement of his recent letters. He asked whether Chartres was ill or whether he could he 'still be in the clinic'.[58] The next day Chartres sent a telegram to Duffy which confirmed the reception of the letters but which made no reference to illness. Back in his post Chartres prepared his report for the month of February.

The report for February 1922, despatched to Gavan Duffy on 7 March, was a long and informative account of the situation in Germany with particular reference to Ireland.[59] Chartres still badly wanted news from the Government that he could use in the Bulletin. It was clear that Desmond FitzGerald had not yet responded to the requests for specific forms of publicity.[60] As a result Chartres suggested to Gavan Duffy that:

a special officer should be attached to your own staff whose duty it would be to see that the foreign envoys were kept fully and properly posted ... the need is more acute than ever now that the situation has been transformed by the conclusion of the treaty and the old Dublin Bulletin is no longer issued.[61]

Chartres wanted exclusive information for his Bulletin which would give the Government view on matters of importance. He mentioned that an interview by de Valera had made a significant impact in the *Kolnische Volkszeitung* and enclosed a copy as an example of what was needed. He also urged the sending of short telegrams 'in cases where circumstances are being misrepresented to the detriment of the national interest'.

The incident at Clones railway station in which the IRA had shot some 'A' Specials attached to the RUC, Chartres maintained, called for immediate explanation. As it was 'the official statement of the Provisional Government was circulated through the Bulletin long after the question had grown stale,' and a bad impression had been given of the Government's action. Chartres's account of the matter reflected the anomaly of his, and every envoy's situation: he was being asked as envoy for the department of Foreign Affairs of the Government of the Republic to publicise pronouncements of the Provisional Government which was designed to produce a new constitution to replace the Republic! The quandary produced by the signing of the Treaty could not be better illustrated.

The report of Chartres also contained interesting observations concerning Germany's relationship with England. Chartres had spent an evening with Dr Knecht, the editor of *Germania*, formerly a paper under the control of Erzberger and friendly to the Irish cause, but now the mouthpiece of Dr Wirth, the head of the Weimar Republic. Knecht related that:

> he was full of sympathy with the Irish nation and would do all he could to promote its interests, but that the exigencies of the German situation precluded him from ever printing anything which might look like an attack upon Mr Lloyd George.[62]

This view of German dependence on England confirmed earlier impressions recorded by Chartres. Such a dependence made it difficult for the Irish to establish a relationship with the German government, a difficulty made more acute by the instability of the various Weimar administrations. For the month of February 1922 Chartres reported that the 'principal political event ... was the survival of the Wirth Government notwithstanding the attacks made upon it'. In a detailed analysis, which was typical of his reports, Chartres identified the abstention of the Independent Socialists under Breitscheid, as a key factor in the Wirth Government retaining power.[63]

Walter Rathenau, the minister of Foreign Affairs since 29 January, figured prominently in Chartres' analysis of the German political scene. He was seen as a key figure, but a controversial one. Having written against the London ultimatum in May 1921, Rathenau had accepted the post of Minister of Reconstruction in Wirth's first ministry to carry out the terms of the ultimatum. This inconsistency, Chartres maintained, was the origin of a campaign against him. Even his greatest political triumph, the Wiesbaden Agreement with the French, which marked the first accord of the combatants in the war, had been criticised by the right and by industrialists such as Stinnes. On the collapse of the first Wirth ministry in December 1921 Rathenau had stated that he would not accept office again, but he had contacted the British and French as a private individual in order to improve Germany's financial position. This had led to his appointment as leader of the German delegation to the Cannes conference in January 1922 and then to his appointment as Foreign Minister. Chartres concluded by stating that Rathenau, as a member of the Democratic Party, was a republican but not a socialist; and was 'regarded by large masses of the people as the one man who can save Germany economically'.[64]

Despite the obvious value of these reports and despite the concern of Chartres to convey the view of the Provisional Government, it became necessary to move him from Berlin to Paris. The move was not occasioned by the intrigues of Bewley, although these were not helpful to Chartres, but by the position of Sean T. O'Kelly.

Berlin and Paris

The private decision of Gavan Duffy to dismiss Sean T. O'Kelly from his post in Paris received a public airing at a meeting of Dáil Éireann on 1 March 1922. The atmosphere in the Dáil was tense: MacNéill, the Speaker and one of the interested parties, should have occupied the chair, but he was absent - insomnia was given as the reason; and Sean T. O'Kelly, although he did not speak, was present in the chamber for some of the days work.[1]

Several questions were addressed to Gavan Duffy concerning the ministerial visit made to the French Prime Minister in January. He replied that he had not arranged the meeting; that Eoin MacNéill had not made the visit as Speaker of the Dáil; that MacWhite had not made the visit on his instructions; and that he had not received any reports from those who were said to have made the visit. At face value the questions appear reasonably harmless, but underlying the questions was the essential issue posed by Sean T. O'Kelly—did Gavan Duffy, as Foreign Minister of the Republican Dáil, sanction a visit from members of a Provisional Government that was designed to end the Republican Dáil? The replies of Gavan Duffy were carefully constructed to avoid any questioning on that level. Indeed, his answers were rather disingenuous to say the least: MacWhite had visited Poincare and had written two reports of the meeting; MacNéill and Hayes had also submitted their version of events.[2]

Further questions were put to Duffy which generally referred to the dismissal of staff, but in particular related to the positions of O'Kelly and Boland. Mary MacSwiney asked Gavan Duffy 'whether he can give an undertaking to An Dáil that he will not dismiss from his Department any servants of the Republic for political reasons, nor in any way hamper their activities on behalf of the Republic to the service of which they pledged themselves?' A further point was made by Countess Markievicz who asked 'what instructions, if any, were issued by him calculated to restrain the Republican activities of representatives?'.[3] To these charges that he had instructed his officials not to support the Republic, Gavan Duffy replied with confidence and with clarity. He read out in its entirety the memorandum to foreign representatives that he had drawn up on 25 January. 'This Government,' he declared, 'has undertaken the duty of maintaining the existing Republic.'

As has been noted the memorandum could not be criticised for betraying the Republic—not even by MacSwiney or Markievicz; but the very nature of the division over the Treaty created inherent and inescapable difficulties for those who were prepared to work for the government in a post Treaty atmosphere—even though Duffy might call it 'the new Govenment of the Republic.' This underlying ambiguity found expression in Gavan Duffy's instruction to the representatives abroad. Strong opposition was voiced after he read out the directive to envoys that:

> as national unity is now broken by the emergence of two political parties in the Republican State, members of the diplomatic service will be under the obligation of reflecting faithfully the policy of the Government, whatever their personal opinions on party politics.[4]

On reflection, the willingness of Gavan Duffy to speak of the Government as the 'new Government of the Republic' served rather to confuse than to conciliate. His own position, as one of the few pro-Treaty supporters who hoped to remove the King entirely from the new constitution, was anomalous, and possibly offered false hopes to the anti-treaty party. This had been true in January and the passing of time had only made the situation worse.

Before Sean T. O'Kelly left Paris he made further efforts to obtain an answer to the incident of the ministerial visit to the French Prime Minister. O'Kelly told Duffy that he was perpared to delay his departure to facilitate Chartres, but his co-operation was accompanied by a persistent request that an answer be given to his questions about the visit to the French President. Duffy replied on 16 March. He enclosed extracts from letters by MacNéill and Hayes, which, in the words of Hayes, claimed that O'Kelly was not approached because 'I formed the opinion that he was not at the disposal of those who believed in the policy of the present Cabinet.'[5] MacWhite, it was said, acted at the request of MacNéill and Hayes. Duffy concluded: 'you will understand that in view of your approaching departure on the one hand, and of the tenor of these replies on the other, I have not pursued the matter further.'[6]

O'Kelly was not content with this reply. He maintained that MacNéill and Hayes were guilty of a 'gross breach of etiquette', and he concluded rather enigmatically that:

for the present I add nothing more on this subject, except to say that if I had received your reply earlier, I would have acted differently with regard to relinquishing my post here, especially as I am left to infer that the action of Messrs MacNéill and Hayes, as well as that of Mr MacWhite, is approved by you.[7]

There the matter ended. In this unstable and volatile situation Charters survived in the diplomatic corps by maintaining the confidence of Gavan Duffy and by keeping his avenues open to Michael Collins. However, the difficulties created by the dismissal of Sean T. O'Kelly meant that he was requested to take over from him in Paris.

On 9 March Gavan Duffy had informed the department of Finance that Sean T. O'Kelly's term of office was to end on 18 March, and that Chartres, 'who relinquishes his office in Berlin', would succeed him at the same salary of £500 per annum.[8] At the same time Chartres received notification from Gavan Duffy that he was to transfer to Paris.[9] He sent a telegram to Gavan Duffy saying that he could leave by about the 18 March, and cabled Sean T. O'Kelly inquiring if he could see him in Paris on the 19 March. A special St Patrick's Day dinner and a reception of the German-Irish Society made it impossible to leave Berlin any earlier.

Chartres then gave Gavan Duffy his views, as requested, about his successor. The name of Bewley had been raised and, not surprisingly, Chartres stated that 'I cannot take the responsibility of recommending his appointment'. Publicity, Chartres said, would constitute the main work of the mission, and he felt that Nancy Power could carry that out effectively with some assistance from Michael O'Brien. Any intervention by Bewley, he felt sure, would 'almost certainly result in a deterioration of the work.'[10]

In these circumstances Chartres advised against appointing a successor to himself immediately. Then Chartres made a proposal that seemed to run counter to his previous suggestion. He told Gavan Duffy that Nancy Power did not wish to stay in Germany indefinitely, and he suggested that she should:

> be transferred to Paris to act as my personal assistant during the balance of the time that she is willing to remain abroad. Of her efficiency, intelligence, quickness and sound judgment in dealing with matters as they arise I cannot speak too highly.

She knew his methods, Chartres added, and expertise like hers would be needed in Paris 'owing to the changes that have taken place there'.[11] Gavan Duffy did not act on the request to have Nancy Power transferred to Paris. Her experience was needed in Berlin, and there the clash between Chartres and Bewley was still simmering. Bewley wrote to Blythe on 11 March re-peating his charge that Briscoe and Chartres were co-operating together, and that Briscoe was the main source of the information that Chartres was providing.[12]

Faced by this continuing acrimony Gavan Duffy wrote to Blythe on 16 March advising that the issue between Chartres and Bewley should not be pressed, as Chartres was leaving Berlin.[13] Before Chartres departed, how-ever, two further incidents occurred: Bewley complained that Chartres was interfering in his department; and Chartres complained that Bewley had failed to appear at the St Patrick's Day celebration.[14]

The complaint of Chartres, related to Bewley's failure to attend the spe-cial St Patrick's Day dinner at the Eden Hotel on 17 March which was 'a national and official occasion'. A confidential report on the function by British Intelligence not only provides evidence that the fears of such surveil-lance by Chartres and Ryan were warranted, but also provides information about the meeting itself. Only eleven people attended—Chartres, Nancy Power, Michael O'Brien, and a few invited guests, Professor Pokorny being the only person present who was not of Irish descent.[15] 'As a social func-tion,' the informant noted, 'the meeting was a great success. As a political event it was of no account.'

It was also remarked that Muriel MacSwiney, the widow of Terence MacSwiney, had been invited to attend but could not travel from Wiesbaden. Bewley's absence was noted and was put down to disaffection because 'the post of envoy to Germany was originally promised to him'.[16] Chartres, it was reported, delivered a brief but spirited defence of the Treaty. He in-sisted that 'the Treaty must be carried out' and reminded his hearers that 'in unity alone is strength'. After the dinner the guests adjourned to the Landwehr Kasino for the annual meeting of the German-Irish Society, which was attended by a small gathering of friends.

The complaint of Bewley focused on an interview with Chartres that appeared in the *Irish Times* on 18 March. The article was headed 'Trade with Germany' and, although it mentioned Bewley as 'Irish Trade Commissioner' and praised his work at the Leipsig Fair, it gave prominence to the views of Chartres on commercial matters. 'Mr Chartres,' it reported,

> gives the impression of being a man of affairs, and one who has con-sidered the task before Ireland in building up its international commerce ... he is of the opinion that international trade would be most successfully carried out through the formation of a body acting very much in the same way as the department of Home Affairs in Ireland to handle trade enquiries and questions. He believes that the department should be a kind of co-operative society, a limited com-

pany, or a kind of private Chamber of Trade ... it might even dispense with the risk to the Irish merchant and importer by negotiating deals on the spot.[17]

However enlightened and enterprising these ideas might appear, it was understandable that Bewley should find them inimical to his standing as Trade representative, and he made his complaint to the Minister of Trade and Commerce. Gavan Duffy wrote to Charters on 27 March and urged him to resolve the friction that existed between himself and Bewley. On the same day he wrote to Ernest Blythe requesting that he put the same request to Bewley. The whole affair was, according to Duffy, 'becoming ridiculous', and it was time for the two men 'to have a thorough understanding and a truce to the constant bickering'.[18]

It might have been expected that the transfer would terminate the conflict between Chartres and Bewley. However, Duffy had noted in his letter to Blythe on 27 March that Chartres 'will be in close touch with Berlin and will no doubt go there frequently'. This information from Gavan Duffy indicated that the Paris appointment might not be as permanent and full time as first envisaged. That certainly was the impression given to both Chartres and Bewley for on 21 March both wrote letters applying for the post of envoy to Berlin. Chartres wrote:

> I leave Berlin, with a good deal of regret. It will, I think, be in the future an important centre for us, and it is a deeply interesting task to build up an organisation *ab initio*. I am, of course, at the disposal of the Government, but if it should be decided to have an Envoy permanently at Berlin and it was deemed desirable to send me back there, such a course would not be unwelcome to me.[19]

On the same day Bewley wrote:

> before I first came out here, I told you that my intention was to offer myself for the post of political envoy in Germany whenever an opportunity presented itself, and you told me that there was no reason why I should not do so. I understand that the position is now vacant, as Mr Chartres is going to Paris, I would therefore wish to offer myself for the post.[20]

Bewley made a formal request for the post to Gavan Duffy on 26 March and was informed on 31 March that he would not be appointed.[21] Daniel Binchy appeared in Berlin at the end of March but, although viewed favourably, his academic work precluded his appointment as an assistant at that time.

Considerable confusion, therefore, existed in Berlin as Chartres prepared to leave. He had suggested that Nancy Power should run the envoy's office in his absence, but he had then proposed that she might transfer to Paris. His own appointment to Paris did not exclude him from functioning in Berlin, nor did it exclude him from applying for the post of envoy, if it was restored.

Faced by these difficulties Gavan Duffy, acting on the original advice of Chartres, left Nancy Power and Michael O'Brien in charge at Berlin.[22] Nancy Power made it clear immediately that such an arrangement was only acceptable as a short term solution. She wrote to Gavan Duffy on 29 March that she did not wish 'to remain abroad permanently'. In fact she stated that she would prefer to be transferred 'in accordance with Mr Chartres' wishes'. This transfer to assist Chartres in Paris could, she felt, be made within a few weeks. She based her request for a move on the grounds that she had been appointed originally as 'personal assistant' to Chartres, and she maintained that Michael O'Brien was well able to take over the duties of the office without her supervising him for another two months.

However, Nancy Power, having stated her own personal preference, did leave the matter in Gavan Duffy's hands. 'Neither I nor, I am sure, Mr Chartres,' she wrote, 'would do anything, which might damage the work of the Berlin office.'[23] She then complied with Gavan Duffy's request to remain in her post for a little longer. The failure to appoint an envoy to Berlin, however, left a vacuum which provided Chartres with an opportunity, indeed it would appear an obligation, to return to Berlin to keep an eye on German affairs. It was also clear that the appointment to Paris, which initially appeared to be a permanent one, was to be of a temporary nature. This was later clarified in Gavan Duffy's announcement to the Dáil that Chartres 'has been appointed temporarily to Paris'.[24]

Chartres was not the only influential figure in Irish circles to leave Berlin at this time. On 28 March John T. Ryan travelled from Berlin to Munich to see St John Gaffney. He informed Joe McGarrity that he had plans for a new organisation in Ireland and America.[25] One can only surmise what the plans were, but about this time Ryan had sent a report to de Valera suggesting that contacts be built up with France through their Military Attaché in America and that efforts should be made to occupy the English in Egypt, thus removing their presence from Ireland.[26] Possibly to enable him to respond to this proposal, de Valera had written to Sean T. O'Kelly in Paris on 10 March 1922 asking for an address for Ryan—'Professor Jetter, or as I call him Mr Bisonkind.'[27] According to Ryan, the removal of O'Kelly from Paris prevented de Valera from pursuing this project. Other projects, however, were in hand.

On 24 March a two-masted steel schooner, the *Hanna*, carrying armaments for Ireland departed from Bremen. Those involved in the earlier
successful voyage of the *Anita* were once again involved: Charlie McGuinness
was the captain of the ship; Briscoe had assisted him in the buying of arms;
and Ryan had made funds available.[28] The *Hanna* berthed at Ballynagaul,
near Helvick, county Waterford on 2 April. The cargo of arms, about six
tons in all, composed mainly of ammunition, Mauser rifles and Parabellums
was unloaded under the supervision of Dick Barrett and transferred to Sean
Traynor of the Tipperary No. 1 brigade.[29] The arms were then transported
to the north. None were kept in the hands of the Southern Command.
Although tensions and divisions had manifested themselves in the IRA, most
immediately at the Army Convention of 26 March in Dublin, these arms
were not used for party purposes. Their arrival marked the last consign-
ment of arms from Germany for a unified IRA before the outbreak of the
Civil War. The fragmentation of the nationalist armed struggle also brought
to an end John T. Ryan's interest in Germany for the time being. He returned to Berlin from Munich on 4 April, and finally left Germany on 7
April making his way to America via Mexico.[30]

Chartres was already in Paris as the arms ship left Bremen. On 24 March
he wrote from the Grand Hotel, Paris, to Gavan Duffy informing him that
Sean T. O'Kelly had left for Rome that morning and would return via Paris.
He received his credentials on 29 March as representative for France.[31] Significantly O'Kelly left Paris on a mission to gather support for the anti-Treaty
party. His task was to visit his friends Fr Curran and Mgr Hagan at the Irish
College in Rome because, as his wife put it, they 'are so in need of the truth'.[32]
Both these priests had supported O'Kelly and the Irish cause during the War
of Independence. Their help was needed now and they were to prove equally
loyal supporters of de Valera.

As O'Kelly departed for Rome, Chartres began his term of office in Paris,
but he also put in a request for a fortnight's leave in which he could meet his
wife in Germany and complete his packing in Berlin. His heart was clearly
elsewhere. He gave expression to his feelings in a personal letter to Gavan
Duffy on 27 March seeking guidance. He asked:

> Can you give me any intimation, I do not mean anything official, but
> a private personal hint—whether I am likely to return to Berlin? ...
> As, I think, you gathered from our conversation in London, and as I
> have since indicated in our official correspondence, I am deeply inter-
> ested in the work of which I have laid the foundations in Berlin, and
> as you might find it easier to appoint to Paris, it is possible that my
> return eventually to Berlin might not be disagreeable to yourself. Of
> the increasing importance of Germany for our purposes, I have very

little doubt, and I should be glad to carry further what I have begun there.[33]

Duffy gave an encouraging reply on 29 March stating that 'so far as I am concerned, I should welcome your return to Berlin'. However, he called upon Chartres to nominate a really suitable person to replace him at Paris. Duffy also made it clear that he would have appointed Bewley in charge at Berlin until Chartres returned, if Chartres had not voiced a strong objection to his promotion. As for Bewley, Duffy regretted that Chartres and he could not see eye to eye, and he declared that he had known Bewley for several years and had a high regard for him, not withstanding the fact that he was 'mad on the Jewish question'. In conclusion, Duffy, without being explicit, made mention of a personal matter of some gravity which urgently called for an explanation or 'public denunciation of the person concerned.'[34] It is not apparent what this issue was, but another personal issue of grave moment did arise before Chartres left the foreign service. It was evident, therefore, that Chartres was not happy with his posting to Paris, and his actions accorded with his sentiments.

On 17 April he departed for a two-week break to Berlin, where he was resident for some time in the Eden Hotel, and he only returned to Paris on about 9 May. He left Paris a few days later on his way to Dublin, only returning to Paris in the first days of June. He finally left Paris to return to his Berlin post on 8 June, and the decision that he should return to Berlin was made on 27 May.[35] All in all, therefore, he only spent about four weeks in Paris during the time of his appointment, and for some of that time Chartres knew for certain that he was to be transferred again.

The brevity of his stay and its temporary character resulted in little of consequence taking place. Chartres regularly returned to his request that he should return to Berlin, or that Nancy Power should be sent as his assistance in Paris; and the small matters that did arise tell us more about Gavan Duffy than of Chartres.

On 1 April Duffy began a correspondence with Chartres in which he insisted that the Bulletin issued by the Paris office should make it absolutely clear that Sean T. O'Kelly had been dismissed and not merely resigned.[36] This hardline approach may well be ascribed to a commitment to principle; but Duffy's reaction to Chartres' comments on publicity indicated that he was not satisfied with O'Kelly's conduct of his mission. Chartres wrote to Duffy on 3 April stating that:

> publicity in any real sense I find here practically at a standstill. The bulletin seems never to have been noticed by the press for some time past ... there has never been kept in this office, as far as I am able to

discover, a single Irish cutting, a single record, a single quotation, a single index or register. There is here in my opinion a real national need which I have attempted to express and meet in this letter.[37]

Duffy's reply was brief and to the point: 'I am too well aware of the conditions which you found in Paris. That is why I was so anxious that you should take charge there.'[38] Unhappy memories of his time with O'Kelly in Paris in 1919 and 1920 probably coloured Duffy's judgement of O'Kelly's methods, but they should not be taken as a yardstick against which to measure O'Kelly's effectiveness as a representative. O'Kelly's many long and detailed letters as Paris envoy not only reveal an acute awareness of political realities, but also indicate that he used the press and other forms of publicity to good effect. His methods may have lacked the logical ordering so desired by Duffy and Chartres, but his approach had many positive advantages. Gavan Duffy also manifested a surprising degree of antipathy towards France. His expulsion from his post in Paris in 1920 appears to have shaped his opinion more than his upbringing in the country.

He informed Chartres on 4 April that the Bulletin was 'inclined to put Ireland in the position of a suppliant for the favours of her patron, France, as the leading celtic nation'. 'This kind of thing,' said Duffy, 'is rather humiliating and the premises are not sound.'[39] This perspective of France was to find expression in a major review of Foreign Affairs which Gavan Duffy drew up in June before he left office, but he was called upon to present a more basic report on Foreign Affairs when the Dáil met on 26 April 1922.

By the end of April the divisions in Ireland after the Treaty were assuming more serious dimensions, especially after the seizure of the Four Courts by members of the IRA opposed to the Treaty on 14 April. These divisions had already manifested themselves in the Foreign Affairs department with the dismissal of Harry Boland and of Sean T. O'Kelly. They were further accentuated on 18 April when Gavan Duffy attempted to dismiss Art O'Brien as Ireland's representative in London.[40]

The problem of reconciling action on behalf of the Republican Dáil Government with that of the Provisional Government, as aspired to by Gavan Duffy, was evidently proving extremely difficult. Faced by these problems Gavan Duffy simply noted in his report the new appointments on the diplomatic staff but made no reference to the dismissals. His treatment of such matters as publicity and the co-ordination of work abroad was equally brief.

In his conclusion, however, Duffy did not attempt to conceal the gravity of the situation that faced both his department and the country. He declared that 'Ireland had every reason to expect rapidly to become recognised as the First of the Small Nations. It would, however, be idle,' he said, to gloss over the fact that we have lost our prestige in recent months. The spectacle of fierce disunion at home, its manifestations abroad, particularly in the United States of America and at the time of the Irish Race Congress in Paris, the publicity given by the foreign press to reports, true and false, of violence in Ireland, have deeply shocked many friends of this country abroad and have given an appearance of justification to the persistent propaganda done by England during the War. If we are to retrieve the splendid position we held, we must take steps at home without delay to prove that we are a Nation and not a rabble.[41]

Gavan Duffy's words of warning were well merited, but they were not welcome. When the report was debated in the Dáil on the following day, 27 April, de Valera and Count Plunkett made critical rejoinders. De Valera denied that his party, the Republican Party, were to blame for the disunity, and he maintained that the Irish Race Congress was conducted 'in every way worthy of the nation.'[42]

Count Plunkett bitterly criticised the character of the report declaring that 'it was an insolent attack on the Irish people,' and would lead the world to believe that 'the Irish people themselves have to admit that they deserve the slanderous stigma that they are not a nation but a rabble'.[43] He concluded by stating that Gavan Duffy should be ashamed of himself. In reply Duffy retorted that he was simply reflecting the sentiments expressed to him by the representatives abroad, namely 'that it is positively painful to have to discuss Irish affairs with foreigners'.

However much one attempted to ensure that foreign affairs were not 'made a question of Party politics', Duffy said, the consequences of Irish disunity could not be denied. It was a fact that 'the effect of the disorder in Ireland, in whatever country it is reported, is deplorable upon the good name of Ireland—absolutely deplorable'.[44] The brief debate ended with the report being adopted by 57 votes to 50. The vote mirrored the divisions that existed among the Dáil deputies over the Treaty and on other issues. It was against this background that Chartres, having visited Berlin, arrived in Dublin in mid-May.

Chartres took up residence in the Shelbourne Hotel and a letter, written to him by Michael Collins on 5 May, finally reached him there. Collins pulled no punches about the gravity of the situation. He stated frankly that 'it seems certain beyond a doubt that Civil War will result—indeed, civil war is already an accomplished fact'—a startling revelation about Collins's frame of mind at the time.[45] Collins recorded his feelings with sadness because he believed that 'we have got one of the finest chances we ever got in our history', and he was convinced that the chance should be taken.

By the time the letter reached Chartres on 23 May attempts had been made to give that chance a further opportunity: a Pact between Collins and de Valera to co-operate over the coming election had been agreed on 20 May; and desperate efforts were being made to draft a Constitution for the new Free State that would reconcile the anti-Treaty party to the terms of the Treaty. Fragile hopes still existed that full-blown Civil War might be averted, but the military situation, as noted by Collins on 5 May, served as a warning that battle lines were being drawn up.

Despite all the talking, sides were being taken and divisions hardening since the signing of the Treaty. Chartres met Collins several times during his stay in Dublin and when, on 23 May, he replied to his letter, he left no doubt as to whose side he was on. He told Collins that

> the conversations I have had with you send me back to my work abroad with fresh courage. You may count upon me to the limit of my powers, and I wish you all success in the great task to which you have set your hand.[46]

He signed himself Eoin macSeartarris. His conversion to the Irish cause and his commitment to Collins appeared beyond question.

Chartres also saw Gavan Duffy and Griffith. He talked to Griffith concerning 'details of facts bearing on Irish prestige in Germany, and also to place before him suggestions on our future economic relations with that country.'[47] Chartres certainly did not feel that the position of Bewley should inhibit his proposals.

Following these conversations there was a meeting of the Foreign Appointments Committee on 26 May and Griffith was asked to sanction the immediate return of Chartres to Berlin. It was further proposed that Colonel Maurice Moore should go to Paris as temporary envoy for two months.[48] Presumably content with this decision Chartres returned to Paris and prepared to leave for Berlin. He wrote a report on the Paris mission on 8 June. He stressed the work that he had done in setting up a scheme for the preservation of records, and the general principles that he had inculcated for the conduct of publicity work.[49] He praised the interest shown by Sean Murphy and Vaughan Dempsey in his proposals. Murphy who, as first assistant had shown a lot of initiative during the absence of Chartres, and Vaughan Dempsey, who had been appointed as second assistant in early March, were to be the mainstays of the Paris office in the months ahead. Chartres, having completed his report, left on the evening of 8 June for Berlin. He had come to Paris with reluctance; he now returned to Berlin with alacrity.

Berlin: the Dismissal of John Chartres and Nancy Power

Chartres felt that his troubles were over when he resumed his position in Berlin and rejoined Nancy Power at the Irish headquarters in the Eden Hotel. He wrote confidently to Gavan Duffy on 14 June 1922 that he would soon look into the new initiatives which he had discussed with Michael Collins, Arthur Griffith and Duffy, himself, during his visit to Ireland in May. However, Chartres insisted that it was useless to begin any new project 'until I am in complete control here', and he asked for some idea as to when Bewley would be departing.[1] A Confidential Memorandum on the position of Ireland's Foreign Affairs, drawn up by Gavan Duffy at the date of the General Election, 16 June, further strengthened the position of Chartres by recommending special status for the Berlin mission.[2]

Duffy proposed that the principal Irish foreign offices abroad would be at Washington, Berlin and Geneva. Of Berlin he wrote that it 'is likely to become very rapidly the most active centre in Europe of international ambition, political and economic, and will be far more important to us than Paris'.[3] In large part, as Duffy made clear to Colonel Maurice Moore, his low estimation of French influence was occasioned by his feeling that France had not helped Ireland sufficiently at the Peace conference and by his own expulsion from Paris in 1920.[4]

If Duffy's analysis of the status of Berlin may have served to encourage the aspirations of Chartres, his further observations on the status of foreign affairs itself introduced a cold note of realism. While envisaging a potentially important role for Ireland as linking Europe with the Americas, both North and South, Duffy noted that 'there is increasing evidence of the fact that Ireland has lost heavily in prestige as a result of the violence and excesses of recent months'.[5] Duffy was concerned at 'the ignorance of Foreign Affairs in this country and the apathy concerning them', and he stressed that the 'money and trouble spent by the Irish Government upon foreign development will be amply repaid'.[6] He also made many enlightened suggestions for reform of the Foreign Affairs department.

Reading between the lines it appears that Duffy was making a case to doubting colleagues. In particular he attempted to counter the view expressed in Cabinet by William Cosgrave that 'our Foreign Affairs, other than commercial, would be a matter of no importance'.[7] Duffy hoped that his wide-ranging memorandum might modify Cosgrave's opinion. Events in Ireland, however, conspired to remove Duffy from office and to place others in charge of Foreign Affairs. These changes were bound to affect the position of Chartres at Berlin.

Duffy, for his part, had always based his support on the Treaty on the assumption that it might be possible to limit the powers of the British Crown in the forthcoming constitution. He had even drafted proposals to that effect in his latest memorandum on foreign affairs, suggesting, for example, that Ireland should work within the Commonwealth to secure 'the definite abolition of the Royal Veto', and 'the unqualified right of every member of the British Commonwealth to have its own foreign representatives'.[8] As he was formulating such aspirations, decisions were being made that rendered such thinking obsolete.

On 14 June Michael Collins told the voters in Cork to vote for the candidate of their choice in a manner that rendered the electoral Pact between himself and de Valera null and void. On the morning of the election the proposed new constitution was presented to the Irish people. It allowed the British King a prominent part in the constitution, including mention of his name in the oath for members of the Oireachtas. Moreover, the Second Republican Dáil that had continued to meet after the Treaty did not dissolve itself prior to the election of a new Parliament. It was legislative directives from England that brought about the dissolution of the Dáil. The Anti-Treaty members of the Dáil claimed that by co-operating with English legislation the legitimacy of the Irish Republican Dáil had been lost.

These three events—the ending of the Pact, the proposed Constitution, the dissolution of the Dáil—removed from the scene the constitutional forum to which both sides in the conflict could come together to resolve their differences. Men were already on the barricades, most notably in the Four Courts under Rory O'Connor, and the breakdown of the constitutional process made it almost certain that it was on the barricades that the struggle would be decided. Many were faced with challenging decisions in the light of these events, especially those involved in the drawing up of the Treaty. They had to ask themselves if the new Constitution accorded with their understanding of the terms of the Treaty. Both Chartres and Gavan Duffy had to pass their own judgements on the Constitution.

Chartres was quite happy to accept it. On 18 June he wrote to Collins saying that he had just read the constitution and congratulated him 'on this further great stride towards our national freedom'.[9] On the same day Char-

tres also wrote to Arthur Griffith. In both letters he was clearly content
with the actions of the Government and reported favourable progress with
persons in high authority in Germany on the plans that they had discussed
together in Dublin. The Constitution was not a problem for him. On 18
June he also sent a telegram to Gavan Duffy asking for an official view on
the Constitution as he wished to publicise the Government's policy. His
cable read: 'embarrassed by the want of instructions shall I give official interview about constitution'. Duffy replied in the negative and stated that he
was writing on the matter.[10]

This response concealed the acute personal difficulty that Duffy was having with the Constitution. He was so unhappy with it that he was contemplating resignation. So upset was Duffy that he wrote to Griffith on 19 June
1922 placing his resignation 'unreservedly' in Griffith's hands.[11] He made it
clear that, as a signatory of the Treaty, he could not support the new Constitution in its entirety as 'parts of it concede more than we are compelled to
concede to England by our obligations under the Treaty'.[12] His letter further illustrated the confusion at the centre of Government.

He proposed that he might remain as a minister of the Dáil cabinet as
long as he was quite free to take an independent line on the Constitution;
but he acknowledged that as the Provisional Government, which was responsible for the constitution, and the Dáil cabinet had been meeting in
joint sessions his singular attitude might prove unsatisfactory to his colleagues.
In these circumstances Duffy was prepared to remain in office until the new
Parliament met on 1 July, or to accept Griffith's verdict on his position.[13]
Griffith replied immediately indicating that he saw no reason for Duffy to
consider resignation until the Dáil met.[14]

Duffy informed Michael Collins of these transactions and expressed the
view that he wished to be free to publish 'reasonable criticism' of the new
constitution 'as distinct from the criticism which we are promised in the
papers from the anti-treaty party'.[15] Collins advised caution as the Government's attitude on the Constitution was not yet finalised. Like Griffith he
felt that the next meeting of the Dáil might provide a forum in which these
issues might be raised.

Plans, however, to resolve the problem at the meeting of the Dáil became impossible when, following the assassination of Sir Henry Wilson, the
forces of the Provisional Government attacked the anti-Treaty forces in the
Four Courts on 28 June. The Civil War had begun. One of the casualties of
the War was the department of Foreign Affairs.

The course of the war and the actions of the Provisional Government
greatly affected Gavan Duffy and John Chartres. Military action in Dublin
led to many deaths, including that of Cathal Brugha on 7 July. As a result of
the armed threat to the Provisional Government, Michael Collins announced

to a ministry meeting on 12 July that 'he had arranged to take up duty as Commander-in-Chief of the Army'.[16] It was agreed that Cosgrave should take over from Collins as Chairman of the Provisional Government during 'the absence of Mr Collins on military duties'. Griffith also attended this meeting and it was agreed that further public statements regarding the general situation and the prorogation of Parliament would be made by order of the Provisional Government and the Dáil Cabinet.

However, real power lay with the Provisional Government, and in that Government Cosgrave was the dominant figure—he was Acting Chairman, Acting Minister of Finance, and Minister of Local Government. Initiatives in Foreign Affairs, even if there had been peace, could not be expected from Cosgrave. Before issues could develop in the arena of Foreign Affairs, Gavan Duffy found himself at odds with the general policy of the Provisional Government. He wrote to Cosgrave on 16 July complaining that his name had been attached to a public announcement concerning censorship, propaganda, the treatment of prisoners, and the prorogation of Parliament. Duffy maintained that he was at variance with policy decisions on these matters, and stated that 'if the same thing happens again, I shall be compelled to resign'.[17] Matters of principle, therefore, were affecting Duffy personally and weakening his effectiveness as Minister for Foreign Affairs at a time when direction was badly needed. Ironically there were no signs of doubts or lack of resolution in a report from Berlin sent by Chartres on 17 July.

Chartres reported to Duffy that 12,000 copies of the Bulletin were being printed for each issue, and that its influence in the German press 'has been increasingly marked and the demand for it has grown'.[18] He also related that he had devoted a copy of the Bulletin to the draft Constitution in which he had omitted 'controversial points', and focused on the positive features of Irish sovereignty, democratic institutions and personal freedom. These features obviously made the Constitution acceptable to Chartres, even if they did not meet the full expectations of Gavan Duffy. Other Bulletins were published dealing with Ireland's international position and Ireland's mineral resources.

As well as the Bulletin Chartres reported that the brochure containing Michael Collins vision of the future role of the Irish Government had received a wide circulation. Many copies had been sent to MacWhite in Switzerland. Furthermore a statement by the Irish hierarchy on the treatment received by Cardinal Logue at the hands of the Royal Ulster Constabulary (RUC) had been circulated to the hierarchy in Germany and to the Catholic press. The impression created by the letter indicated that Chartres was personally committed to the policy of the Provisional Government, and was acting with great competence to further the aims of that Government.

Occupation with Irish matters prevented Chartres from giving his usual detailed analysis of the German scene. One finds, therefore, in his correspondence no mention of the assassination of Rathenau on 24 June 1922, but the previous memoranda of Chartres provided background information which made explicable the fall of the Wirth administration in November 1922, and the eventual accession to power of Stresemann.

For the present, as far as Chartres was concerned, everything was going smoothly, and he made plans for the future. Writing to Joseph Walshe on the same day, 17 July, he suggested that both himself and Nancy Power should take their holidays in August—she in Dublin, he in southern Germany—and that Michael O'Brien be left in charge of the Berlin office which was normally quiet during that month. He made that recommendation on the understanding that he would 'require all the expert assistance I can have in September and the immediately subsequent months'.[19] He fully expected to return to Berlin and to develop, with the help of Nancy Power, the policy that had been agreed upon with Griffith, Collins and Duffy. His hopes were dashed by the intervention of Charles Bewley.

On the very same day, 17 July, as Chartres was writing with such assurance to Gavan Duffy, Bewley wrote to Ernest Blythe alleging that Chartres was not acting in the interests of the Provisional Government. He wrote out of his 'duty as a citizen of the Irish Free State', and was guided by Blythe's instruction of 29 June that 'the present is not a conflict between two opposing political parties', but rather the action of a Government against a section of the community that was prepared to overthrow it.[20]

Ironically, the main burden of Bewley's complaint was the Bulletin of which Chartres had written so proudly and with such conviction. Bewley maintained that the issues for 8 and 12 July, of which he enclosed copies, had treated the Civil War as if it were 'a conflict between two opposing political parties', and had devoted twice as much space 'to the career of the "irregular" leaders as is devoted to the heads of the Government'.[21] These observations, Bewley noted, had also been adverted to by Professor Pokorny and by some other Germans. He added that Michael O'Brien had expressed sympathy with the Irregular forces. Bewley frankly acknowledged that some might see his comments as personally motivated by his unhappy relations with Chartres, but he hoped that his criticisms would be viewed objectively. He concluded that:

> I have marked this letter private and confidential, as it does not arise out of the ordinary course of my official duties. I will however be glad if you will show it or communicate its contents to any member of the Government whom you may think proper. I would personally welcome the fullest inquiry into the charges I have made; and if

you think I should repeat the substance of this letter to any other member of the Government, I am ready to do so.[22]

In his autobiography Bewley claimed that 'without comment I sent the Minister a copy of the Bulletin with translation'.[23] He was, in fact, making very precise comment. Indeed it would be fair to say that Bewley was launching a calculated offensive against Chartres and was prepared to go to any lengths to support his charges.

Blythe, who had constantly supported Bewley, immediately took up his allegations and referred them to Gavan Duffy. Blythe maintained that the disloyalty of Chartres was proven and that he should be dismissed.[24] Duffy was clearly shocked by the contents of the Bulletin for 8 July, and wrote to Chartres that it was 'open to the most serious criticism; as it extols Mr de Valera and his friends at the moment when they are wrecking the country and gives them quite a disproportionate amount of space'.[25]

He also complained about the explanation that Chartres had given in the Bulletin for the divisions in the Army, and concluded by saying that 'I shall be glad to know what you have to say about the matter, which I have been requested to bring to the notice of the Cabinet.'[26] Before Chartres received this letter he had written a letter of his own on 23 July making a further complaint about Bewley.

The particular incident concerned Bewley's intervention at one of Berlin's leading newspapers over a matter of publicity which Chartres felt was not only unhelpful but also outside his province. The main burden of Chartres' complaint, however, was far more serious. Duffy had asked Chartres why relations with Germany were not being advanced. Chartres replied that:

the answer is that my hands are tied until Mr Bewley has left Germany. The *demarches* which I have in comtemplation and for which preliminaries have been settled, have specific purposes; other persons and influences will be drawn in; and there is a point at which contact with Mr Bewley would be inevitable. An influential friend, who has provided me with access to two Ministers, assures me that such contact would be prejudicial. My movements along the lines discussed in Dublin are therefore checked until the conditions under which it was arranged I should work have been realised. The delay may be inevitable, in consequence of Mr Bewley's actions, I am being compelled to lose time and miss opportunities, the English are not allowing the grass to grow under their feet ... my recommendation on grounds of public policy and national interest (is) that Mr Bewley should be recalled from Germany.[27]

Chartres had made similar observations about Bewley in the early months of 1922 and they had not been acted upon then. There was little chance that they would be acted upon in July, when Bewley was formulating his more serious charges that it was Chartres who was acting against the national interest by supporting the Government's opponents in the Civil War. Chartres addressed those allegations on 27 July after he had received Gavan Duffy's letter of criticism.

Chartres began his reply by observing that, as Gavan Duffy did not know German, he may well 'have been misled by mistranslation or misinformation', and he strongly asserted that 'the statement that I have extolled those who are wrecking the country is unfounded'.[28] In regard to the 8 July issue of the Bulletin, Chartres maintained that 'the only expressions of appreciation are to be found in the sketches of General Collins and Mr Griffith', and he claimed that the other paragraphs, dealing with de Valera and his supporters, were a simply chronological recital of facts.

His main defence, however, was based upon the general character of the Bulletin which he stressed should be viewed as 'a continuing publication'. Viewed in that context, Chartres maintained, 'the statement about disproportionate space is, in my opinion, unjustified'.[29] He reminded Duffy of the contents of past issues of the Bulletin which had included lengthy and favourable articles on Griffith, Collins and many other aspects of national life under the Provisional Government. Many of these, he repeated, had been produced as pamphlets and had enjoyed a wide circulation. Chartres concluded that 'the suggestion that we are extolling the opponents of the Government is really indefensible'.

He made several other points to justify his position. He stated that when the Bulletin was published on 8 July there was no expectation in Germany of extended Civil War, and he repeated his regular complaint that the Publicity department was still not providing him with official information. Chartres then declared that in no number of the Bulletin could there be found any endorsement of the party opposed to the Government; that, on the other hand, praise had been given to the Provisional Government for all its initiatives; and that he had concentrated on 'dwelling upon the greatness of the work that is being done by the Provisional Government'. He admitted that he had not accentuated the differences over the Treaty because 'to harp on Irish differences would not only have been ill-advised on broad, general grounds but would have prejudiced the prospects of the special tasks with which I was entrusted recently when in Dublin'.[30]

The last page of the letter contained specific objections by Chartres to complaints about the Bulletin from Gerald Hamilton, and veiled references to a correspondence between Hamilton and Duffy which was personally injurious to the character of Chartres. As soon as Chartres had arrived in

Berlin he had warned Duffy about Hamilton, but Duffy had continued to communicate with him. One of these letters had come into the possession of Chartres and he informed Duffy that one of the comments that Duffy had made concerning himself was 'contrary to fact'. Chartres informed Duffy that he would deal with this 'grave personal imputation' in due time. For the moment Chartres focused on the broader issue raised by Bewley. He stated that 'you are aware that I have frequently urged, both in writing and orally, a Cabinet enquiry into issues which have arisen between us in connection with my efforts to protect the national interests and safety'.[31]

Signs of differences between Chartres and Duffy may well have been provoked by the issue over Gerald Hamilton, as prior to the airing of that problem few signs of serious differences between them had emerged. Whatever the origin of the differences Chartres prepared for his defence with tenacity. He told Duffy that he welcomed an inquiry; that he was happy to attend it as soon as possible; and, in the meantime, he asked Duffy to transmit copies of his letter to each member of the Cabinet. In order to guarantee himself a fair hearing, Chartres wrote to Arthur Griffith on the same day, 27 July, enclosing a copy of his letter to Duffy. Chartres was very angry. He wrote:

> I hope and believe that you will consider me incapable of the conduct imputed to me without qualification by Mr Duffy. Nevertheless, I cannot refrain from sending you a formal expression of the deep resentment with which I have received the accusation that I have endeavoured to influence foreign opinion against the Government. The suggestion that, after meeting you and General Collins last May and conferring with you as I did, I returned abroad to assist those who are seeking your overthrow and his, stirs me more deeply than I can express. [32]

As Chartres was formulating his defence, the balance of power in the Foreign Affairs department was radically changed by Gavan Duffy's resignation.

The formal ratification of Duffy's resignation took place at a meeting of the Provisional Government on 26 July 1922.[33] Gavan Duffy had been unhappy with various aspects of Provisional Government policy for some time. The final incident that forced him to resign was the refusal of the Cabinet to recognise the legitimacy of the republican Dáil courts. Duffy made this and other issues clear when he wrote a private and confidential letter to Michael Collins as Commander-in-Chief on 24 July 1922. He stated that:

I am very sorry to say that I have had to resign. Since you and other ministers left the remant of the Cabinet has been dominated by a spirit of narrowness and intolerance that has made it daily harder to co-operate. As you know I am loyally with the Government on the War itself, but on most of the other important issues that arise I have found myself nearly always in a minority of one.

To-day we had the last straw, when the Cabinet solemnly decided against recognising the undoubted jurisdiction of our Judges (whether courts are sitting or not) to deal with Habeas Corpus cases. That to my mind is the limit and absolutely indefensible, as well as being foolish and unnecessary from the practical point of view and putting the Government hopelessly in the wrong.[34]

The particular incident that occasioned the Cabinet decision to suspend the courts was the arrest of George Plunkett and the subsequent application of Mr Justice Crowley to summon the Minister of Defence and the Governor of Mountjoy before the Supreme Court of the Dáil to justify the prisoner's detention.[35] The decision to abolish the courts not only had far-reaching implications for the future conduct of the war, especially the treatment of prisoners, but also it created another reason why people should take the anti-Treaty side. For some the Treaty had been bad enough; for others the monarchical character of the proposed Free State constitution and the questionable dissolution of the Republican Second Dáil were added reasons for opposing the Treaty. Some, following the abolition of the courts, also joined the opponents of the Treaty as they regretted the abandonment of the policy and ideals associated with the Republican Dáil in its pre-Treaty days.

Even as the war was being waged, therefore, clarification of the issues at stake was being made. That clarification of principle led to a more dedicated resolution on the battle field. At Government level the departure of Gavan Duffy from his post in Foreign Affairs led to appointments that were totally committed to the Provisional Government. Initially, on 26 July, it was decided that Arthur Griffith should act as Duffy's successor, and that Desmond FitzGerald 'should make enquiries regarding the staff in that Department'.[36] While Chartres might have drawn some comfort from the appointment of Griffith, the nomination of FitzGerald to enquire into the Foreign Affairs staff would have been a matter of concern to him. As Minister of Publicity FitzGerald had failed to respond to countless requests for help from the envoys abroad, thus indicating a lack of interest or commitment to the work of the Department.

Moreover, the main driving force of the Department, even before the sudden death of Griffith on 12 August, was Joseph Walshe. He was to show himself sympathetic to the case made by Bewley. The position of Chartres, therefore, was extremely vulnerable when Bewley repeated the earlier charges that he had made against him. This time, however, Blythe passsed on these allegations to the whole Ministry. His circular letter to each member of the Ministry, claiming that Chartres was 'not a proper person to represent us in Germany', was sent on 27 July, just after the departure of Duffy from the Foreign Office—ideal timing from Blythe's point of view.[37] Blythe also enclosed a copy of Bewley's letter to him of 17 July, and the two copies of the Bulletin which were central to Bewley's complaint. Fortunately for Chartres Michael Collins was still prepared to stand by him.

The support of Michael Collins was guarded, and as will be seen there was good reason that it should be guarded, but it was prompt. He replied to Blythe on 28 July saying that he had

> looked through the translations from the Bulletin, and I am inclined to agree with Mr Bewley that it is not strictly playing the game, but I think that the matter is so cleverly done that you would be rather in a unique position to take disciplinary action. I think, you can only note it, and note similar future things, and then deal with the accumulative effect.'[38]

Collins wrote as Commander-in-Chief. He had no position in the Ministry, and few, if any, in the Ministry were aware of the connection between Chartres and Collins. The suggestion of Collins that more time be given to Chartres was not heeded.

In these circumstances the position of Chartres became not only difficult, but also potentially dangerous. The danger was highlighted by the arrest of Sean T. O'Kelly on 28 July. Incriminating letters were found in his possession linking himself, de Valera, Harry Boland and Art O'Brien with Joe McGarrity. The letter from Boland to O'Kelly, written on 27 July, had a definite military purpose. He wrote of the need for money and guns; of the support of McGarrity and Luke Dillon for their fight; and of de Valera's order that 'someone must go' to the Clan Convention in America.[39] Michael Collins informed the Provisional Government of these letters and called upon the Director of Publicity to use them to show that all those involved were planning Civil War.[40]

The letters were published in the press. Within twenty-four hours Harry Boland was shot in mysterious circumstances, while supposedly resisting arrest, and he died on 2 August.[41] Art O'Brien was also arrested. In these circumstances it was remarkable that Collins should have endorsed Chartres at all in the light of the revolutionary intentions of the Dáil's former envoys and McGarrity, with whom Chartres had enjoyed some association. From the point of view of Chartres, the condition of his three former colleagues in the Foreign service must have been disturbing. He alone of the major republican Dáil envoys remained in office, and he was, therefore, particularly vulnerable to the charges that were brought against him by Joseph Walshe.

Walshe, as Under-Secretary for Foreign Affairs, had great scope to exercise his ability as Griffith, possibly affected by the illness that was soon to take his life, played little part in the department's work. He certainly acted with great authority. On 3 August 1922 he informed Chartres that Bewley was not under the department of Foreign Affairs and that there could be no interference with his actions. Of these actions Walshe commented that 'these latter seem to be dictated purely by motives of loyalty towards the Irish Government and by a zealous devotion to its interests'.[42] He added that they 'appear entirely praiseworthy and your attitude towards him very unreasonable.' This letter of Walshe was in reply to that of Chartres of 23 July in which he had requested the recall of Bewley so that he could implement the Government's plans for a new policy in Berlin. Walshe's response left Chartres in no doubt that he was not going to get his own way in Berlin.

Further confirmation of this fact, if any was needed, was provided by another letter from Walshe on 8 August. This letter was in reply to that of Chartres of 27 July in which he had attempted to defend himself against Bewley's allegations. Walshe complained about the tone of the letter. He informed Chartres that as a subordinate addressing his superior, Gavan Duffy, his manner was 'a grave and intolerable departure from ordinary usage'.[43] Walshe was equally scathing in regard to the case that Chartres had presented to justify his actions. Of Chartres explanation about the Army, Walshe stated that it was

> merely evasive and explains nothing. The same holds true, of your answer to the complaint about the disproportionate space given to the Irregular leaders. The 'chronologial order of facts' as selected is equivalent to approval.

Walshe concluded by asserting that the rest of Chartres' letter was 'entirely irrelevant' and that 'an explanation is still awaited'.[44] At the same time Walshe sent instructions that the Bulletin should cease publication.

There was no doubt as to whose side Walshe was on. It was clear that the views of Bewley were valued at the Foreign Office. Chartres made no reply at the time to these charges brought against him. He had left Berlin for his holidays in Austria on 1 August. While his vacation may have removed him from the firing line, it also left the field open to Bewley. He was not slow in grasping his opportunity, and he wrote further letters to Blythe on 8 and 11 August sustaining his attack upon Chartres and the Bulletin.

The burden of Bewley's letters was that Chartres, by being unduly critical of England in the Bulletin, was creating obstacles to German-Irish accord. The Germans, Bewley maintained, relied on England to counter the potential threat from France, and any criticism of England was, therefore, not welcomed. In order to substantiate his views Bewley quoted from the *Deutsche Allgemeine Zeitung* of 7 July which declared that 'England remains our only hope, and it is the task of our foreign policy to continue in close touch with that country.'[45] Bewley was specifically opposed to what he termed 'Beschimpfung' or 'scolding', which was characterised by dragging subjects into the Bulletin 'for the purpose of attacking England'. He quoted extracts from the Bulletin over the past few months to justify his claim.

He instanced, for example, the Bulletin's mention of a speech of Sir Charles Dilke which claimed that many of the English titled families were illegitimate in origin; and he gave the example of a reference to the forged letter of Pope Adrian consenting to Henry II's conquest of Ireland, when stating that English propaganda was based on the repetition of lies.[46] The whole of Bewley's letter of 11 August was devoted to showing that the last copy of the Bulletin, that of 9 August, provided examples of 'scolding' in regard to the Canadian cattle trade that were not helpful to Irish policy in Germany.

Blythe acted on this information as he had done previously and sent copies of Bewley's letters to various members of the Cabinet on 17 August. He called for a decision on 'the class of propaganda published by Mr Chartres in the German Bulletin'.[47] Before a decision could be taken, Michael Collins was assassinated on 22 August. The deaths of Collins and Griffith placed great pressures on the Provisional Government, and removed the two most influential supporters that Chartres had from public office. The office of Foreign Affairs was also affected. On the death of Griffith, Michael Hayes, formerly the Dáil Minister of Education, assumed the role of Acting Foreign Minister with Joseph Walshe retaining his post as Under Secretary.

When Chartres, therefore, returned to Dublin in early September to defend his actions, he did so to a Foreign Affairs Department that was unknown to him and which, in the person of Walshe, had been extremely hostile. He was not, however, completely isolated.

An unsigned and undated memorandum concerning the Chartres issue with Bewley was submitted to the Government at this time. The author had visited Berlin in 1922, and had read Bewley's letter to Blythe on 17 July and Blythe's to the members of the ministry on 17 August. Referring to this letter from Blythe, the author declared that:

I consider it remarkable that an official of one Department should
criticise the manner in which the official of another carries out his
work, and in my opinion it is the Minister of Foreign Affairs should
direct the policy of the foreign bulletins.[48]

He considered Bewley's criticism of the Bulletin's English policy 'very trivial'.
Furthermore, he noted that while he was in Berlin and in contact with
Michael O'Brien he had received no indication from him that he was an
Irregular supporter as claimed by Bewley. Writing with obvious experience
of the Berlin scene, he mentioned that Professor Pokorny, one of the critics
of the Bulletin's standard of German, had lost his job as translator for the
Bulletin and badly wanted it back again. The implications were obvious: the
Professor was not an unbiased critic. The author concluded that

> from what I know of Mr Chartres, I do not think he would remain in
> the service of the Irish Government if he had the slightest idea that
> his conduct of his office was referred to Mr. Bewley 'for frank com-
> ments.' Now that Mr Chartres is here, no useful purpose would be
> served by allowing this fact to come to his knowledge. To sum up, it
> appears quite plain to me that the present Government arrangements
> in Berlin cannot continue with advantage ... judging from the ques-
> tions you asked me to day re. Mr Chartres's connexion with Barton,
> Masonry etc., it strikes me that there is a campaign to push him out
> of your service. Before that culminates I would like to impress upon
> you the confidence that A.G. (Arthur Griffith) and Mick (Michael
> Collins) reposed in him.[49]

The author wrote from a position of knowledge of both Berlin and of
Chartres, and was in contact with officials at Government level. The favourable verdict that he passed on Chartres would appear justified. Ironically the basic principle which Bewley maintained should govern Irish policy
in Germany—that recognition must be made for the fact that the Germans
looked to England to protect them against France—had been the corner-
stone of the policy of Chartres since he had taken up office in July 1921.
Chartres had shown himself acutely aware that the Weimar regime was dependent on England, and he had regularly reported on that fact in his memoranda. In the light of that consideration the examples of anti-English 'scolding'
gleaned by Bewley from the pages of the Bulletin appear, as the author of
the unsigned memorandum suggested, 'very trivial'. The charges made by
Bewley that the 8 and 12 July copies of the Bulletin (issues 123 and 124),
supported the Irregulars also lack substance.

Although Duffy was not happy with these copies and Walshe was not satisfied with the explanation of Chartres, the reply of Chartres made on 27 July did answer many of the objections made against him. Above all, he could claim that since the establishment of the Provisional Government he had given great prominence to the achievements of the Government, and had published the statements of Michael Collins as pamphlets as well as in the Bulletin. Moreover the British Intelligence report of Chartres' speech on St Patrick's day showed that he was solidly committed to the Treaty, and this public statement may well be taken as a genuine expression of everything that he was stating privately to Michael Collins and to Arthur Griffith.

The excuse of Chartres for not accentuating differences over the Treaty was also justified. Chartres had, as will be recalled, claimed that to 'harp on Irish differences would not only have been ill-advised on broad, general grounds but would have prejudiced the prospects of the special tasks with which I was entrusted recently when in Dublin'.[50] Those tasks were to foster trade between the two countries, and Germany was not likely to engage in trade with a bitterly divided Ireland. Important support for the policy of Chartres on this matter was provided by the example of Colonel Maurice Moore, the envoy in Paris.

Writing to Gavan Duffy on 18 July 1922, Moore complained of the official propaganda, presumably under the direction of Desmond FitzGerald, which was contained in the *Free Press* and the *War News*. He maintained that it was a 'disgrace to the Free State party', and would give the impression that Ireland was full of burglars and robbers.[51] Chartres, like Moore, even when the Civil War was underway, was still trying to project an image of Ireland that was positive and would be helpful for the purposes of trade. Neither Bewley, the trade representative, nor Blythe, the Minister of Trade and Commerce, made allowance for this, nor, apparently, did Desmond FitzGerald when devising his publicity campaign.

While the pen pictures of the Irregular leaders were non-condemnatory and even laudatory, they were written, according to Chartres, when there was no 'expectation of extended civil war'.[52] On this particular point Chartres, it will be recalled again, had complained of inadequate information from the Government Publicity office. At the very least Chartres might have expected that the wait and see policy which Michael Collins had enjoined would have been adopted by the Government.

The balance of influence, however, was swinging towards those who, as the anonymous author put it, were waging 'a campaign to push him out of' the Foreign service. That author remarked that, as his correspondent was to meet Chartres, they should discuss a more suitable arrangement for the Berlin office. Clearly the correspondent was a Government official. Two such officials, at least, met Chartres, who was resident in the Shelbourne Hotel, early in September.

On Tuesday 5 September Chartres met William Cosgrave, Chairman of the Provisional Government, and Michael Hayes, the Acting Minister for Foreign Affairs, in separate meetings. A one-page handwritten memorandum, half of it in code, recounts some of his conversation with Hayes, presumably a report of their meeting. Replies by Chartres in note form indicate that he was responding to questions put to him: he 'knew German very well'; Pokorny used to translate for the Bulletin and would like to be back again; he had been instructed to make a fresh start in Berlin; and so on.[53] The evidence is fragmentary, and the report places Chartres on the defensive.

Ensuing correspondence reveals that a proposal was put to Chartres that the ministry of 'foreign affairs' should be transferred to 'economic affairs'.[54] A clear indication that the representations made by Bewley and Blythe had had some effect, and that Cosgrave's own predilection for a more practical type of foreign service was to be implemented. Chartres suggested to Hayes that if such a policy was embarked upon, then it would be desirable to call the new Ministry that of Economic and Foreign Affairs. He argued that such a title:

> would give the Foreign Representative, even in informal conversations, a locus standi which otherwise he would lack. This point is of significance in Germany, where designation is expected to correspond with function.[55]

Chartres made the further suggestion that such a representative might be termed 'Commissioner' and that all Irish activities should be co-ordinated through him. At this time, remarkably enough, Chartres still believed that he had some claim to be the new 'Commissioner' for Germany. He wrote to Cosgrave on 8 September stating that 'my experience and German connexions place me in a position to do good work in Germany'.[56]

Chartres wished to proceed with the implementation of the plan that he had agreed with Griffith and Collins in the previous May. He still entertained hopes and dreams that this project might be accomplished. 'What I have specially in view, as I think you know,' he wrote,

> is to investigate and attempt large constructive steps as distinguished from individual commercial transactions. It would be necessary, however, that information accumulating in the consular office should be at my disposal, and also that I should be in a position to avail myself of it for the purposes of commercial intelligence.

The vision of Chartres was on the grand scale, but Bewley and the consul's office was to be put in its place. In such a framework Chartres believed that great things could be done in Germany: the situation in Germany,

> is quite exceptional and requires exceptional treatment. Contained in it are possibilities capable of being used to Ireland's great economic advantage in ways already tested ... I am convinced that, notwithstanding present conditions in Ireland, preliminary work could be undertaken without delay.[57]

The very fact that Chartres could make such positive and hopeful proposals indicates that he was unaware of the level to which the odds were stacked against him. He concluded by asking Cosgrave whether 'in the situation that has arisen, I am returning to Germany with authority to pursue the necessary activities.' He evidently longed to be given the chance to participate in what he felt was a new and exciting enterprise in Germany. His hopes were to be dashed. The reply when it came was in the negative, but it took some time in coming.

There were several reasons why Chartres was not re-appointed. The principal reason was the ill-founded allegations of Bewley which had been promoted so assiduously by Blythe. As a result Chartres was viewed with suspicion by many and regarded with implacable hostility by Joseph Walshe, who remained as Under Secretary at the new department of External Affairs. There were other reasons, however, and some of these related to changes in the ministry of the new government.

On 9 September the new Dáil met and Cosgrave was elected President. He was also head of the Provisional Government and he retained his position as Minister of Finance. The ambiguity in his position manifested a wider ambiguity about the status of the Dáil itself. The anti-Treaty deputies were absent and refused to recognise the Dáil as the successor of the Republican Second Dáil. Indeed, one of the principles underlying the armed struggle of the anti-Treaty forces was their claim that they were fighting for the ideals of the Republican Second Dáil. In order to refute this claim and to resolve the tensions between the Dáil and Provisional Government Cosgrave established one single government ministry.

The composition of that ministry and the attitude of influential members of the ministry towards Foreign Affairs were important factors in the failure of Chartres to secure re-appointment. In that regard the appointment of Desmond FitzGerald as Minister of External Affairs was a vital blow to Chartres. While the very term 'External Affairs' indicated that the proposals for a move towards a wider and more business orientated brief for the former Ministry of Foreign Affairs were to be implemented, the naming of FitzGerald as its head meant that Chartres was unlikely to play any part in it. As Minister of Publicity, FitzGerald had been the subject of much indirect criticism from Chartres, and his vision of foreign affairs did not envisage any expansion in Germany. FitzGerald was not only in full agreement with the pragmatic view of Cosgrave in regard to foreign policy, but also he was inclined towards a policy that was aligned with Britain and the Commonwealth—a policy which, to a high degree, was made necessary by the Civil War.

The defence of the state required that its links with England, the main source of its military support, should be strengthened. Granted that FitzGerald was at the helm of Foreign Affairs and that Cosgrave, the head of the Government, shared many of his aspirations, it was not likely that there would be major developments in Germany or, indeed, in Europe. Even if Chartres had been *persona grata* with the new Ministry, it was unlikely that he would be re-appointed to conduct an expansionist programme. The wonder is that it took so long for his appointment to be terminated. Meanwhile he lived with the unreal hope that he would return to Berlin.

That Chartres still entertained hopes that he might return to Berlin is made clear from a three page memorandum which he submitted to the Minister of External Affairs on 21 September 1922.[58] He gave an account of the work of the Berlin office and of the staff which, while attempting to show that his work was valuable and thorough, it did not attempt to reply to Bewley's allegations. Indeed, he wrote of the Bulletin as if it had not been the subject of criticism. Having elaborated on the filing system that he had set up to classify all news relevant to Ireland for promotional purposes, Chartres then claimed that this information was used successfully in the Bulletin, and in contacts with news agencies and politicians. He then itemised other work done in the office, notably reports on the attitude of the German press towards Ireland and reports to the Minister on the political situation in Germany.

The staff of the delegation were considered next. Nancy Power, who was still in Dublin following her return from Berlin in August, was singled out for great praise. Chartres made the point that in the last calendar year he had been absent from Berlin for six months and during that time she had run the office without any assistance. 'I have seldom, if ever,' Chartres concluded, 'met anyone so quick of comprehension or so efficient in assimilating methods and carrying out general instructions in detail.'[59] He also praised Michael O'Brien claiming that he had 'the makings of an excellent official'.

The message was clear: the Berlin office was being run extremely competently by Chartres and his team, and they should be involved in the new administration in Germany. It was not to be. Bewley had written to Hayes early in September indicating that he had a wish to leave his Berlin posting in October because of differences and difficulties with Chartres.[60] He indicated that he was willing to work in another Germanic country. His hat, therefore, was in the ring for future work with the department.

The message was to dawn on Chartres that he could not presume that the Berlin post was his. On 25 September he informed External Affairs that he was anxious about Berlin and asked for a decision about his future.[61] His position became much clearer on 2 October, when Walshe sent a letter to him requesting that he stay in Ireland until Bewley had returned to Dublin. On the same day Walshe informed Nancy Power that she was transferred from the Foreign to the Home service.[62]

This decision was a crushing blow to Chartres. Power consulted with him over her transfer and Chartres wrote immediately to FitzGerald. Unbelievably he still held out hopes that he might go to Berlin. Chartres stated:

> if I am returning to Berlin to undertake work on the lines that I have discussed, it would handicap me very seriously to withdraw, during the period of transition and reorganisation, the only really valuable assistant I have.[63]

He even talked of a 'new start' in Berlin. The reply of Walshe on 5 October finally convinced him that all was lost. Walshe stated that the instructions of FitzGerald were that Nancy Power 'has been definitely transferred to the Home Service.' He added, by way of explanation, that

> as the work in Berlin until the end of the year will no longer be of very serious importance, and as the Bulletin will no longer be published, the Minister thinks that Miss Power's services will not be indispensable there.[64]

Walshe concluded by saying that Bewley would soon be in Dublin and that then 'the entire question of the Berlin trade representation will be finally settled'. Chartres immediately wrote to FitzGerald asking to see him about Bewley.[65] He must have realised that if Bewley was to be involved in discussions about the future of the Berlin office, then the chances of his own views counting for much were slim. Moreover, with little work of 'serious importance' planned for Berlin and with the closure of the Bulletin, the plans of Chartres for the Berlin office had already been effectively laid aside. In these circumstances, and with the transfer of Nancy Power as an added blow, Chartres offered his resignation.[66] FitzGerald was slow to see or to contact him. In the absence of dialogue Chartres addressed a damning memorandum about Bewley to Cosgrave on 12 October.

Chartres had evidently decided that his policy of refraining from comment about Bewley had not served his cause. Possibly he also realised that his silence over the Bewley allegations was seen as an admission of their veracity. His memorandum raised new and more damaging charges against Bewley. Chartres reported: firstly,

> I am informed that Mr Bewley has recently uttered malicious and cowardly slanders on Miss Nancy Power, stating that Miss Power caused grave scandal by living with me in the same hotel in Berlin.
>
> secondly, this statement, I am told, was made by Mr Bewley within the past month to Professor O'Brien, of Galway University, by whom it has been repeated in Dublin. Professor O'Brien also said that he was given to understand it was on this account that Miss Power was not returning to Berlin.
>
> thirdly, Mr Bewley's hostility to myself dates from last January when I forwarded to the Government a report on his disorderly conduct in public in Berlin. It is in furtherance of a series of attacks upon me that he has defamed Miss Power so unscrupulously.[67]

Chartres upbraided Bewley for his 'recklesness and malice', and stated that Nancy Power's residence in the hotel was 'a condition of her work' which was authorised by her official superiors. He defended her honour and recommended that Bewley 'should be required to retract his imputations in writing'. He concluded by saying of Nancy Power that

> she has done nothing to invite or justify Mr Bewley's cowardly attack, and she has been defamed by Mr Bewley for discharging her public duties in the only circumstances that were open to her. I beg respectfully and earnestly to commend the case to your consideration.[68]

The case did not help either Chartres or Power to return to Berlin. Indeed no evidence exists to show that the issue was dealt with at Government level. On the contrary, the department of External Affairs was slow to discuss the matter with Chartres, and it was not until 20 October that he finally met Desmond FitzGerald.[69]

The day after this meeting it was Bewley who was informed that he was to resume his duties in Berlin as Trade Commissioner, a title which, ironically, may well have had its origin in the earlier recommendation of Chartres.[70] Evidently the startling revelations and charges by Chartres against Bewley were not considered grave enough, or of sufficient credibility, to prevent his appointment.

The final decision about Chartres' appointment was made in the midst of decisive events which shaped the course of the Civil War. The Provisional Government announced the introduction of Military Courts on 15 October and completed its debate on the Free State constitution on 25 October. The anti-Treaty forces declared a united front on 16 October between the IRA executive and the politicians of the Second Dáil who opposed the Treaty. On 25 October, the same day as the new constitution was approved, the Second Dáil met in secret and announced that it was the real government of the country, and that de Valera was President of the Republic.

Both groups, therefore, claimed to have civil authority with an army to support it. FitzGerald was deeply involved with these events and it was understandable that the petitions of Chartres could not be met immediately. However, on 28 October he telephoned Chartres and requested him to go to Berlin in order to hand over his control of the office. Chartres wrote a letter of protest to Cosgrave. He complained that such an action was 'tantamount to an immediate dismissal', and he maintained that his credentials had still not been cancelled.[71]

Chartres asserted that FitzGerald had been influenced by the slanderous stories of Bewley, and stated that he felt 'entitled to an explanation and to a precise statement of how I stand.' He was not only unhappy with his dismissal but also unsure about a promised transfer to the department of Industry and Commerce.

Clarification was soon to come, but it was not such as to please Chartres. He saw FitzGerald and received from him formal notification that his appointment to Berlin had ended. FitzGerald informed him that 'we have decided to discontinue the work of your Information Bureau in Berlin, consequently your appointment with this Department will terminate as from the date of the closing of the Berlin office'.[72] He repeated his request that Chartres should go to Berlin to close the office down. He also reassured Chartres, in words that would have brought him little consolation, that 'I take this occasion of assuring you that the fact that the Bureau can serve no useful purpose during the present period in no way takes from our appreciation of the good work done in Berlin in the past.' The decision, it would appear, was taken by FitzGerald and Walshe alone: there was no discussion of Chartres at cabinet level.[73]

Writing from the National Liberal Club in London on 2 November, Chartres informed FitzGerald that that he would be in Berlin in a few days' time and that he would close down the office.[74] He also remarked that he had seen Gordon Campbell, Secretary to the Ministry of Industry and Commerce, about a transfer to that department.[75] The ministerial changes made in September, in which Blythe was moved to Local Government and was replaced by Joseph McGrath at Industry and Commerce, could only have helpful to Chartres' request for a transfer. It was not until he was in Berlin that Chartres received FitzGerald's letter terminating his appointment. Chartres briefly thanked him for his words of appreciation and proceeded to close down the delegation.[76]

He raised certain questions to FitzGerald about the staff, the office equipment and finances on 8 November, making the proposal that Michael O'Brien might be transferred to the staff of the trade representative. Walshe replied immediately stating that there would be no question of a transfer for Michael O'Brien.[77] Granted Bewley's critical attitude towards O'Brien, there was little likelihood of him receiving the post, but his rejection underlined the fact that there was to be a complete sweep of the previous Berlin administration. Walshe also made it clear that Gerard O'Loughlin, the trade consul in Denmark, would soon arrive in Berlin with 'full instructions' in regard to remaining staff, and 'full powers' in regard to office equipment. Chartres' freedom of action in closing the office was to be extremely limited.

He was not, however, without a certain freedom of initiative, and this enabled him to have a final dig at Bewley. On 17 November he informed FitzGerald that a representative of the Cabinet had come to him for assistance in a trading matter, having found the trade representative's advice 'not very helpful'.[78] With obvious satisfaction Chartres told FitzGerald that he was able to put the visitor in touch with 'the highest relevant German official', and as a result a very favourable commercial order was obtained for the Government. He also informed FitzGerald that Gordon Campbell had indicated that he could serve on a statistical committee in the department of Industry and Commerce under Mr Hooper when his transfer was complete. This letter marked a final flash of independence for Chartres.

On 24 November Gerard O'Loughlin arrived in Berlin and began the supervision of the office closure. The balance of power had swung in Bewley's favour. On 30 November FitzGerald appointed him Trade Commissioner on behalf of the Irish Government (previously he had held the position on behalf of the Provisional Government); and at the same time, almost as an ultimate mark of humiliation, the furniture in Chartres' office was transferred to Bewley's.[79] The severing of his links with Berlin was not a happy experience for Chartres. He departed on 4 December, having remained to complete the statement of accounts for the period of his responsibility.[80]

The Ireland that Chartres returned to in December 1922 had advanced a stage further on the path of Civil War. The constitutional divisions separating the two rival parties had been more finely drawn by the creation of the Irish Free State on 6 December. It marked, in a sense, a triumph for those who supported the Treaty: they had sustained the Provisional Government in power despite the attacks of the anti-Treaty forces; and they had formulated a constitution which enabled them to progress from a merely provisional government to that of a new Free State.

The divisions on the field of battle had also become more savage and ruthless. On 24 November Erskine Childers, having been found guilty by a military court, was executed; and a few days later Liam Lynch, chief of staff of the IRA, called for a policy of retaliation against all those who had in any way sanctioned such a policy of reprisal. As a result of Lynch's call for action, Tom Hales, a Free State deputy, was assassinated on 7 December. On the next day, the feast of the Immaculate Conception, four leading anti-Treaty prisoners, Rory O'Connor, Liam Mellows, Dick Barrett and Joe McKelvey, were executed in Mountjoy prison. The war had reached a new and gruesome stage of assassination and reprisal. It was against this background that Chartres returned to Dublin and to the department of Industry and Commerce.

In Germany Bewley was quick to take initiatives on his own account once Chartres had left. One of his first actions, which may be significant in the light of the rumours of his alliance with Pokorny, was to make a request to the department of External Affairs for £30 to assist Pokorny in the publication of a book. He did this on 4 December, the very day that Chartres departed. At a time when every item of expenditure was examined minutely £30 was a significant sum of money, but it was granted to Pokorny.[81]

Bewley, himself, did not last long in Berlin. Surprisingly after all his tireless scheming to obtain the dominant position in Berlin, he handed in his resignation on 10 February 1923.[82] In part he was upset that he was not appointed as an envoy, but he was also annoyed over a particular incident in which it emerged that he could not issue a passport to a German citizen who wished to visit Ireland. This restriction on his authority and the submission to the British authorities, which could issue a passport, impelled Bewley to say later that he was fed up acting as an 'unaccredited representative of a half-independent state.'[83] As Bewley was leaving Germany another man arrived who had been associated with Chartres and the Berlin mission from the very first—J. T. Ryan. Some mention of his activities is necessary as his return had some implications for Chartres, and his story completes the German gun-running enterprise which began in 1920.

From the start of the Civil War Joe McGarrity and Ryan had thrown in their lot with de Valera: at the end of July 1922 McGarrity had been involved in the message of armed support that had led to Harry Boland's death; and in September 1922 Ryan, from his base in Mexico, had advised McGarrity that 'Topman (de Valera) can win clear title and unite family by determined stand'.[84] McGarrity was determined to make the call for 'a determined stand' a reality. He had encouraged de Valera to set up his rival alternative government on 25 October, and when Ryan arrived in New York on 13 November he and McGarrity drew up an 'international proposition', which was put to Liam Lynch.[85] The proposition involved a revival of Ryan's German mission.

Lynch responded immediately by sending General Sean Moylan and Brigadier Michael Leahy to meet the Clan in America as representatives of the Army Council of the IRA. They arrived on 12 December.[86] An important meeting took place on 12 January 1923 at which Ryan and McGarrity met Moylan and Leahy with some other leading American activists present.[87] It was agreed that funds should be raised to meet the military requirements of Liam Lynch, and that Ryan and Moylan should go to Germany.

Ryan departed on 22 February and arrived in Hamburg on 3 March. Moylan joined him some time later.[88] He had $41,760 for his mission (the money was McGarrity's personal contribution to it), and £1,000 had been sent earlier to two officials for preliminary work, possibly Laurence Hoover and William Henry Pickford, who were 'professional Arms Dealers'. The latter had left America for Hamburg on 8 February, and both men were known to be acting in the Irregulars' interest.[89] While these plans were being made, the British and Irish Free State Intelligence departments were acting in concert to avert the danger arising from any gun-running.

From the first moment of the arrival of Moylan and Leahy in the United States, their movements were monitored by British intelligence, and reports of their contacts with McGarrity, even of private meetings, were made to the Foreign Office in London. These reports were then forwarded to the Free State government.[90] A letter from General Diarmuid O'Hegarty, head of the Free State Intelligence department, to Colonel Carter at Scotland Yard on 3 April 1923 confirmed that for some time they had been able to monitor the correspondence between Lynch, Moylan and McGarrity.[91] Even Lynch's letter to Moylan of 6 February 1923, in which he made the strange suggestion that one large gun would be sufficient to turn the tide of battle, was in their hands. They also knew of the movements of Hoover and Pickford, and above all they knew that John T. Ryan was 'Jetter' and was in Germany. They did not, however, know his present location. The pressure was on the German mission.

It was also, in a different way, on Chartres. Unfortunately for him, O'Hegarty reported that 'someone, probably Chartres, wrote from Berlin to R. Brennan ... referring to "certain matters of a special character which were in the responsible charge of Professor Jetter"'.[92] The connecting of Chartres' January 1922 memorandum from Berlin with Ryan could not have been helpful to him, especially as a handwritten addition had commented that 'Brennan is an irregular'. Chartres was in danger of being found guilty by association. Ryan and Moylan, who had joined him in Germany, faced the more serious danger of being detected.

Despite becoming aware that the Free State knew of their plans, they persevered with their enterprise until Liam Lynch was mortally wounded on 10 April and the adverse course of the war made inevitable the order of Frank Aiken, the new Chief of Staff of the IRA, to dump arms. This occurred on 24 May. One of their last efforts, however, merits attention. Early in May 1923 contact was made with Hitler's Nazi organisation in Munich, and it was ascertained that the Nazis were prepared to sell arms for money. Ryan reported to McGarrity on 14 May that:

> it was stated that the business, if done would have to be concluded with great caution as [Hitler] had received a promise of [money] from [England], but as yet it had not come. Who spoke for [England] has not yet developed.[93]

Here is not the place to speculate on the promise of English money to finance Hitler in the months before the Munich *putsch*, although the implications are startling, but from Ryan's point of view the end of the road had been almost reached. It became impossible to meet Aiken's requirements that the arms should arrive before 1 June, and finally the funds for the German mission, in total $73,000, were transferred to de Valera on 17 July 1923.[94]

McGarrity advised Ryan on 25 July that the sooner he returned home the better, and certainly by December 1923 he had returned to Buffalo, New York, thus ending the Irish/American mission to Germany.[95] At the same time the Free State government made a decision to close down, at least temporarily, the Berlin mission.

After Bewley's departure Conor Duane, his assistant, had maintained the office open in desperate circumstances, often verging on starvation, until it was closed on 2 January 1924. As if to underline the failure of the Irish effort in Germany, it was announced that in future all business relating to Ireland would be 'handled through the British Consulate'.[96] The failure of the Berlin mission could not have been more dramatically illustrated and for that Bewley was mainly responsible. However, FitzGerald and Walshe must also shoulder some of the responsibility. They preferred Bewley to Chartres in Berlin as the instrument of their policy, and they had their way. Both on a personal level and on a broader level of policy, Chartres had reasons to be unhappy with developments at the Department of External Affairs, and these merit examination in a concluding assessment of his work.

The Last Days of Chartres

On a purely personal level Chartres had good grounds for complaint at his dismissal from Berlin. From the date of his appointment on 1 June 1921 he had, with the assistance and advice of Nancy Power, created an efficient Irish office in Germany. Together, and their tenure of the Berlin office should be seen as a joint effort, they had overcome the most difficult of circumstances to put Ireland on the map. The obstacles were many. The position of Chartres as an unofficial envoy was extremely precarious, and the condition of Weimar Germany was equally volatile and unstable.

Despite these difficulties information and insights into the factors governing the German situation were conveyed to the Irish Government in the memoranda which Chartres despatched regularly to Dublin. Indeed, produced as they were by one man and a small group of contacts, they compare favourably with the reports drawn up by D'Abernon, the British ambassador, with the assistance of a complete diplomatic organisation.

Moreover, the Irish Bulletin, despite the later criticism of Bewley, conveyed to the German press and people much important information on the state of Ireland, and the official reports by Chartres were enlightened and eminently practical. Regrettably, as in the matter of publicity, they were not always acted upon in a fitting manner. Such was the character of the work of Chartres and Nancy Power under both the political regimes under which they served. While acting for Dáil Éireann, with Count Plunkett and Arthur Griffith as Foreign Ministers, they upheld the interests of the republican Dáil. While acting for the Provisional Government, with Gavan Duffy of the Dáil cabinet acting as Foreign Minister, they attempted to uphold the policy which he enunciated in the complex times of transition from Dáil Éireann to the Free State. The entrance of Charles Bewley upon the Berlin scene in December 1921 ended the harmony that existed in the Irish delegation to Germany.

The seeds of division may well have been sown in the manner of Bewley's appointment by the department of Trade. Although the department of Foreign Affairs was aware of the appointment, it was made without any reference to Chartres. Prior to Bewley's appointment Chartres was, as part of his mission, attending to commercial matters, and the drawing of demarcation lines between their two areas of responsibility was bound to be difficult. However, it was the issue over Bewley's anti-Semitic remarks made publicly to Robert Briscoe in January 1922, rather than any specific conflict over work practices, that occasioned Bewley's hostility to Chartres.

The proposal of Chartres, made on 30 January 1922, that Bewley should be transferred 'in the interests of decorum, national dignity and commercial prudence' was the source of all future confrontation. Any evaluation of the rights and wrongs of the case between Chartres and Bewley will be determined by the opinion that one draws about this particular incident. If one considers that public anti-Semitic outbursts are unworthy of an Irish representative, one will support the stand taken by Chartres; if one considers that such outbursts are of minor importance, then one will be inclined to view Bewley with favour. That is what Ernest Blythe did in his capacity as Minister of Trade and Commerce. He not only backed Bewley over this particular incident, but also he transmitted to Bewley private correspondence on the matter written by Michael Collins and Gavan Duffy.

This endorsement of Bewley by Blythe did much to consolidate his position in Berlin and, at the same time, to undermine that of Chartres. The way was prepared for the major attack on Chartres in July and August 1922 when Blythe forwarded to the Cabinet Bewley's hostile criticisms of the Bulletin which Chartres edited. The picture of one Government department engaged in secret manoeuvres to disrupt the working of another department reflects adversely on the department initiating the attack—that is, the department of Trade and Commerce. Even allowing for the tense atmosphere of the Civil War the particular allegations that Bewley raised should have been viewed more objectively. In many instances they were found to be wanting and to a high degree answered by Chartres. The anonymous observer, it will be recalled, considered them 'very trivial'. Chartres, himself, claimed that these charges had their origin in the criticism that he had made of Bewley's anti-Semitism. It is hard to disagree with him. The tragedy is that so many members of the cabinet took the side of Bewley.

The role of Joseph Walshe was critical. As Under Secretary at Foreign Affairs he was fully aware of the anti-Semitic issue associated with Bewley, and yet, in the crucial month of August when he was the dominant figure in the Foreign Office, he accepted Bewley's allegations without question. Instead of a question-mark hanging over the head of Bewley, it was placed over the head of Chartres. As a result, FitzGerald and Walshe representing External Affairs, selected Bewley rather than Chartres for Berlin, and Cosgrave, who was also aware of Bewley's anti-Semitic background, failed to prevent his appointment. There were to be further repercussions over Charles Bewley and Berlin.

Despite his record of anti-Semitism and of instability, and despite the fact that Walshe, who was well aware of these failings, was still in office with the enhanced status of Secretary of the department, Bewley was appointed as ambassador to Berlin in July 1933. True to his past record Bewley fully supported the regime of Hitler, attending his rallies and supporting the Nuremburg laws against the Jews, until in 1939, by which time he was in conflict with Walshe, he retired.[1] This later conduct of Bewley serves to confirm that Chartres was the more suitable candidate for Berlin in 1922.

The consequences of Bewley's appointment to Berlin both in the 1920s and 1930s were disastrous for Ireland. His first appointment was also a tragedy for Chartres. This was recognised by an adviser to President Cosgrave who, commenting on the closure of the Berlin office in January 1924, stated that 'I feel that it is a distinct loss to us in many ways ... that Chartres is not in Berlin. I strongly suggest his return.'[2]

By then it was too late. Chartres had taken steps in another direction, and those who had forced him to take those steps were not inclined to invite him back into the Foreign service. Bad as the consequences were for Chartres and Berlin, the attitude and actions of Cosgrave, FitzGerald and Walshe were equally damaging for the vision of the Foreign Affairs department that had been enunciated by Count Plunkett and Gavan Duffy.

Both Count Plunkett and Gavan Duffy, had adopted a positive approach to foreign policy and had advocated an expansion of Irish representation throughout the world. Even in 1920 when Dáil Éireann was an illegal assembly and the difficulty of establishing a base in Germany was great, Plunkett still aspired to create a centre in Berlin, and the Dáil was looking for thirty representatives to serve its interests abroad. In similar vein Gavan Duffy had submitted his plans for foreign policy development on 20 June 1922, when he had proposed major offices at Washington, Berlin and Geneva with lesser representation at Paris, Rome and Ottawa. Berlin, he had stressed, would become the most important centre in Europe.

The Free State administration turned their backs on this expansionist policy when they assumed office in December 1922. There were several extenuating circumstances for this change of policy. The most notable reason was the Civil War.[3] Not only was the Free State almost exclusively dependent upon England for the supply of armaments to defeat the Irregulars, but also the need to exchange Intelligence notes served to forge bonds of common purpose with England. There was one other side effect of the Civil War that contributed to the Free State's difficulty in maintaining foreign representation abroad: the representatives of de Valera's government abroad often set up offices to rival those of the Free State. In such circumstances it was reasonable for the department of External Affairs to seek to avoid confrontation and to proceed with caution.

Allied to these considerations deriving from the results of the Civil War, there was another reason militating against expansion in the foreign service, namely the matter of money. The department of Finance was the dominant force in the new administration of the Free State and was only prepared to sanction expenses that were of proven necessity. Taken in combination these considerations created a disposition favourable towards a foreign policy that was linked to England and was limited in its aspirations. Such a policy was developed by the Free State department of External Affairs, and was symbolised by participation in the Imperial Conference that took place in London between October and November 1923. In the words of a recent analyst 'the European Continent was ignored by the Department of External Affairs. Commonwealth and dominion status occupied the Irish Free State'.[4]

There was, however, one other striking additional feature to the Free State foreign policy—entry into the League of Nations. This was the major initiative taken by FitzGerald and Walshe and took place on 10 September 1923. Their policy was in accord with Gavan Duffy's proposals of June 1922 and with the recommendations regularly made by Michael MacWhite since his appointment to Geneva. If their implementation of Duffy's proposal to join the League of Nations, while not without its critics, may merit commendation, then their rejection of his other proposal to advance Ireland's diplomatic representation throughout the world merits criticism.

There were extenuating and excusing circumstances for this failure to expand, but there was also an unwillingness to act. It will be recalled that Cosgrave, who was President of the Executive Council, had expressed an extremely pragmatic view of foreign affairs in June 1922 when faced by Duffy's plan for the future, stating that 'our Foreign Affairs, other than commercial, would be a matter of no importance'.

FitzGerald was at one with these sentiments. On 25 June 1923 he declared in the Dáil that:

> we are not anxious to have elaborate Embassies in other countries where our representatives will spend money in entertaining people. We are only anxious to send a man abroad who will do valuable work so that we shall get value for our money.[5]

This attitude inevitably led to a new emphasis in foreign policy priorities, and it may reasonably be contended that this changed focus of policy was effectively symbolised by the departure of Chartres from Berlin. Whereas Dáil Éireann would have viewed the closure of the Berlin office and the subsequent transfer of its representation to a British consul as a major humiliation, the Free State accepted it as a minor accommodation. Two contrasting mentalities are revealed which reflect the deep underlying contradictions that led to the division in the Sinn Féin ranks over the 1921 Treaty. These divisions will be elaborated on in a conclusion on the last days of Chartres and on his contribution to the Treaty.

The return of Chartres to Dublin in December 1922 was made difficult by the actions of the department of External Affairs. Sadly the acrimony between Chartres and the department continued almost until the day of his death. There was a long running saga concerning his statement of accounts and his own personal expenses. Joseph Walshe was particularly exacting in his demand that Chartres should be responsible for the very last penny that was spent in Berlin. Despite a report from the Accountant General on 24 January 1923 that he was 'impressed with Mr Chartres' readiness to answer all queries', and that he had 'come to the conclusion that the unsatisfactory state of affairs was partly caused by Mr Chartres' absence from Berlin for three months'. Walshe was not prepared to let the matter rest.[6] Issues had been raised over Chartres' holiday in Austria in August 1922 and over his dress allowance, and these were pursued by Walshe. Chartres requested on 15 March 1923 that 'the points in issue should now be referred to President Cosgrave'. The saga ran on, however. As late as 8 February 1925 Chartres was asking the Accountant General for an 'impartial inquiry', and in November 1925 questions were still being asked about vouchers for his expenses.[7]

Possibly suspicion of Chartres may have been generated by his connection, however tenuous, with the 1923 mission to Germany of J.T. Ryan. Possibly too the pressure on Chartres was brought about by the stringement requirements of the department of Finance, but Walshe encouraged, rather than mollified, their demands. In the midst of the controversy FitzGerald remained aloof from Chartres who had no chance to explain his position to him in person. Petty and small-minded as this dispute was, it reveals an attitude towards Chartres by FitzGerald and Walshe that was unfriendly and dismissive. It certainly made it more difficult for Chartres to secure his appointment at the department of Industry and Commerce.

Chartres, as one of those involved in the Treaty negotiations, was in a delicate position. Of those who had attended the conferences in London as plenipotentiaries and had accepted the Treaty, only Duggan survived as a supporter of the Free State. Griffith and Collins were dead; Barton had sided with de Valera and had been appointed as a member of his alternative republican government in October 1922; and Gavan Duffy, having expressed scathing criticism of the execution of Childers, had moved even further away from official government policy.

In these circumstances it was seen as important by the government to be supported by those who were involved in the signing of the Treaty. Duggan had been appointed as a minister without portfolio in the new administration; so too had Fionan Lynch, who had also performed secretarial duties at the Treaty negotiations. Chartres remained outside the inner confidences of the new Free State administration. He was clearly viewed with suspicion. The question of payment for the month of December prompted Chartres to write to FitzGerald on 6 January 1923. When he sought information concerning the date of his transfer from External Affairs to his new department, he was curtly informed by Walshe that his contract had ended in December and that he had ample time to complete his work in Berlin before the end of November. Moreover, Walshe added that the department of Industry and Commerce was outside the brief of External Affairs.[8]

Despite this lack of assistance Chartres soon found a niche for himself at his new department. Initially he worked on a statistical committee and then became editor of the *Irish Trade Journal*. His past experience with *The Times* of London and his work at the British department of Munitions would have equipped him well for his task. His record showed that he could file away a vast amount of information and summarise his findings in a concise and readable form. The indications are that not only was he well qualified for the assignment, but also that the work was congenial to him. Moreover, Nancy Power, who had also been transferred to the same department, shared his office.[9] What more could he ask for? Granted that his grand design for Berlin had to be abandoned, then he could take considerable satisfaction from carrying out a task that he enjoyed doing and working with a companion whom he admired and respected.

With the Civil War being waged until the order to dump arms was made on 24 May 1923, his position could have been a lot worse. Little in known of his specific contribution to the work of the department of Industry and Commerce, but in 1925 the first edition of the *Irish Trade Journal* appeared. Details of any political involvement on the part of Chartres are also scarce. He did, however, take a significant political initiative on 26 March 1927.

On that day an article on 'The English Peril', written by Chartres, appeared in the very first issue of *The Nation*. It was the first of three articles signed Fear Faire—the Watcher; and it appeared on the first page of the journal alongside a trenchant editorial. Anonymity was certainly desirable because *The Nation* was a weekly journal devoted to the Fianna Fáil party, which had been created by de Valera almost a year earlier on the 26 May 1926. The foundation of the party caused a split in the anti-Treaty republican movement and marked the first step towards de Valera and his followers participating in the institutions of the Free State. Not only did de Valera's action split Sinn Féin, but also it marked the abandonment by de Valera of his claim to be President of the Republic as head of the Second Dáil government which he had set up in October 1922. One of de Valera's helpers, indeed one of his most valuable supporters, was Sean T. O'Kelly. Chartres had known O'Kelly from his Paris days and it was to O'Kelly, as editor of *The Nation*, that Chartres submitted his articles. To align himself with de Valera and O'Kelly was a dangerous step for Chartres.

As the first editorial of *The Nation* made clear its policy was not sympathetic to the policy of the Free State. '*The Nation* stands for an Irish Republic,' it boldly declared.

> *The Nation* stands for the freedom for which the man and women of 1916 and the years succeeding fought and died. *The Nation* takes its stand with Wolfe Tone when he declares his objects to be 'to assert the independence of Ireland; to subvert its execrable Government, and to break the connection with England, the never failing source of all Ireland's political evils.' ... We believe that the majority of the Irish nationalists who followed the false prophets in 1914 and 1921 are as convinced as we are to-day that the path which they then chose (to free Ireland) has led not to success but to utter disaster.[10]

Association with such a policy was hard to reconcile with the holding of government office, as Chartres did, in an administration that had accepted a constitution with the British connection as an integral part of it. The implications for Chartres were potentially damaging, but he did not live long enough to find out just how damaging the consequences might be.

He died suddenly on 14 May 1927 at the age of sixty-five. The passing away of Chartres took place with very little publicity and equally little controversy. One small issue, however, did arise, an issue which has become central to the debate on his role in the Treaty negotiations. Following his death *The Nation* printed a short obituary tribute. The main events of his life were outlined and in regard to his role in the Treaty talks it was noted 'that Mr Chartres used all his endeavours during the negotiations to prevent such an agreement being reached'.[11]

Nancy Power made an immediate rejoinder which was published in *The Nation* of 28 May. She maintained that the efforts of Chartres

> during the negotiations were constructive, and were directed towards the strengthening and improving of the position which was emerging from the discussions. The part he played was certainly not the one of obstruction which your paragraph implies and he himself took considerable pride in his contributions to the Articles of Agreement.[12]

Nancy Power was in no doubt where Chartres stood on the Treaty, but questions concerning his attitude to it, and his responsibility for it, have been raised from the day of his death. It is fitting in conclusion to make some judgement on Chartres and the Treaty.

One thing is certain: the role of Chartres in the negotiations was both central and substantial. He had contributed five personal memoranda—on 14 October, 20 October, 28 October, 25 November (the minutes of the sub-conference meeting) and 29 November; and he had also made, in co-operation with Childers, a major contribution to the official Irish memoranda of 24 October, 29 October, 22 November and 28 November.

From first to last he had made every effort to implement the policy outlined by de Valera before the delegation left Dublin in October, namely that the claim for an Irish independent Republic should be maintained by only recognising the English King in some form of External Association. Not only his written work, but also his perceived alignment with Childers, Barton and Duffy, placed him in the ranks of those who sympathised with the aims of de Valera. At times Childers may have complained in his diary that he was a lone voice crying in the wilderness, but more often than not he portrays himself and Chartres as ploughing a lonely furrow together. Certainly when Chartres was recalled to Berlin in November, Childers, Barton and Gavan Duffy saw him as a loss to their side.

Although one may point to some signs of accord with Griffith and Collins—for example Chartres typed Griffith's private letter to Lloyd George on 2 November and he was nominated by Collins to be the lawyer at the 24 November sub-conference—these appear to be small signs of compatibility compared to the ties of sympathy and similarity of policy that placed him in the opposition camp. One would be inclined to conclude that Chartres had rejected the policy of Griffith and Collins, the two men who had brought him into the Irish national movement, and sided with de Valera. Fortunately a personal account of Chartres has survived to put the record straight. It makes surprising reading.

On the first anniversary of Griffith's death Chartres wrote an appreciation of him in the *Clonmel Nationalist*. Chartres recalled his first impressions of Griffith—his humanity, his kindness and his courage—and recorded that he had been telegraphed by Griffith in September 1921 to act as one of the secretaries to the conference. 'Here,' at the Conference, Chartres recalled, 'in days of trial and test, earlier and scattered impressions of him were rounded and made indelibly complete.' One impression was particularly striking. 'Arthur Griffith,' Chartres said,

> apart from one single occasion, remained outwardly calm, earnest, attentive, sure. The one exception was on a certain critical morning, the full history of which cannot be written yet, when he dealt swiftly with a mean man. It was a revelation of temperament, more illumi-

nating than twenty years of placid friendship, to see Griffith leave his
position on the hearth rug where he was talking with Childers, pace
rapidly round intervening tables to the opposite side of the room,
and, with shoulders advanced and hands clenched by his side lecture
the other man who had failed him, and who with almost feline gesture minced and shrunk. There was plenty of fire in Griffith, but he
reserved it, as a rule, for persons and conduct which a man of his
purity of life and aim must despise.[13]

One cannot be sure of the occasion but the precise incident is hardly important. The significant fact is that Chartres was in complete sympathy with
Griffith, and was so opposed to one of the delegates, presumably either Barton
or Duffy, that he could describe him as 'a mean man'. Chartres recalled one
other impression from the Conference meetings. 'I remember,' he wrote,

> sitting with him [Griffith] one night during the London negotiations
> until the very small hours discussing many points that had arisen,
> especially in connexion with a plan ultimately adopted by the Cabi-
> net, which I had proposed to himself and Michael Collins. When at
> last we went upstairs Griffith paused at the door of his room and said:
> 'I'd like to finish that last point. Just come in here', and the conversa-
> tion was continued for another half hour. Next morning at half-past
> seven he came into my room to ask for some notes I had made, in-
> sisted on running downstairs himself to get them, and wrote for an
> hour before breakfast.[14]

Again one cannot be sure of the occasion, but of Chartres respect for Griffith
and of his contact with Collins there can be no doubt. Granted his evident
admiration for Griffith, it was natural that Chartres should approve of his
life's work: 'he was a patriot in the true sense of the word ...' Chartres said,
'he loved his country with entire singleness of heart'. This article by Chartres provoked a private response from Robert Barton. Writing to Gavan
Duffy he said,

> If all he [Chartres] says here about his closeting and intimacy with
> A.G. [Arthur Griffith] is true then he played a very double game in
> London. I never felt at home with him and have often wondered since
> what role he really played.[15]

Barton was mystified. He had no knowledge of the earlier ties of Chartres
with Griffith and Collins. Gavan Duffy should have been less surprised. He
had met Chartres while on foreign service and had actually recommended

him to Collins; but the mystery remains—by identifying himself so closely with Childers, Chartres certainly laid himself open to the charge of playing a double game. He certainly concealed from his colleagues any signs of his sympathy for Griffith or of his co-operation with him.

Granted his admiration for Griffith, and his close ties with Collins, it is hardly surprising that Chartres supported the Treaty. To the charge that such support was incompatible with his memoranda on the Crown, Chartres could reply not only that he was a civil servant simply carrying out his brief faithfully by defending External Association, but also he could say that the final draft on the oath formulated by Collins did encapsulate some of the principles for which he had argued.

The emphasis was on swearing 'true faith and allegiance to the Constitution of the Irish Free State', rather than an oath directly to the King; and faithfulness to the King was based on the 'common citizensip' of Ireland and Britain based on Irish 'adherence' to the British Commonwealth of Nations. This formula was resonant of the Irish memorandum of 24 October, in which Chartres had played a leading part, and which declared that 'Ireland will consent to adhere for all purposes of agreed common concern, to the League of Sovereign States associated and known as the British Commonwealth of Nations'.

While accepting that the Irish had conceded much during the negotiations and acknowledging the claim of Tom Jones on behalf of the British that 'in essentials we have given nothing that was not in the July proposals', a case could be made that, if the Republic had not been secured, some vestige of the policy of recognition by External Association had been achieved.[16] Collins acted on that belief and claimed that 'Ireland had achieved the freedom to achieve freedom'. Chartres was happy to follow the same path. Nancy Power recorded that:

> when I saw him [Chartres] after the signing of the Treaty I gathered that he had fought hard for external association ... He did say to me at the time that while there was a real difference between the Treaty as signed and De Valera's proposals that difference was so fine that you could not expect people to go to war and give their lives for it ... Mr Chartres's devotion to Michael Collins was intense. He could easily have said 'what is good enough for Michael Collins is good enough for me.'[17]

That is what Chartres did. Bound by ties of personal loyalty to both Collins and Griffith and feeling that the principles for which he had argued had not been totally compromised, Chartres accepted the Treaty and retained his position as republican envoy to Berlin.

During his time in Berlin after the Treaty, Chartres manifested complete accord with the policies of Griffith and Collins, and was content with their acceptance of the proposed new Free State constitution. In his tribute to Griffith, Chartres had referred to him as 'a patriot in the true sense of the word,' and he admired him greatly. His commitment to Collins was, if possible, of even greater intensity. His protestations of loyalty to Collins are worth recalling: 'I congratulate you again and wish you all good fortune in your work for Ireland,' he had written on 21 January 1922; and on 23 May he had declared 'I wish you all success in the great task to which you have set your hand.'

The death of Collins and the loss of his contribution to the shaping of a post-Treaty Ireland was a blow to Chartres, and to others—witness the Army Mutiny of 1924 when former members of the IRB declared that the new Free State policy was not that promised by Collins. Moreover, his own dismissal from the foreign service provided a clear indication that his thinking was not compatible with that of the new men of influence who fashioned the policies of the Free State. Nothing is known of his attitude to the reprisal killings during the Civil War, but it would appear that Chartres, even while working in a government department, was out of sympathy with government policy. The failure of the Boundary Commission in 1925 to act in accordance with the hopes of the Irish delegates to the Treaty negotiations further alienated him from the policy of the Free State. Chartres was convinced that the Boundary Commission was part and parcel of the Treaty agreement.

When preliminary talks were underway about the Commission in early 1924, Chartres met Richard Mulcahy, the Minister of Defence, and made it clear that the setting up of the Boundary Commission to determine the status of the Six Counties was an integral part of the Treaty. 'The first point,' he wrote later,

> is that recognition of the Crown was expressly contingent upon the Six Counties agreement. -If the English government fail to honour that agreement the terms of the bargain made for the recognition of the Crown are destroyed.[18]

Chartres maintained that the British were well aware of these implications of the Boundary Commission, and referred in some detail to a meeting at which both he and Collins were present. 'At the conference at which the Boundary question in this particular aspect was discussed,' he said,

> I handed Mr Collins a quotation from one of Carson's speeches, dealing with the exclusion of Donegal and making it clear that the intention

was to include as much, and only as much of Nationalist Ulster as would enable the minority to continue in power. This point was strongly emphasised by Mr Collins who concluded by saying: 'That is what Carson said himself'. Mr Lloyd George smiled and answered with a little shrug: 'what else could he have said?'

Chartres added that:

> The English delegates were present in full force. The whole of the arguments of the Irish delegation, illustrated by a series of careful maps, went to show that there was no question of slight rectification and that the transfer of substantial areas was involved. This position was fully accepted by the English representatives ...[19]

The failure of the Boundary Commission in December 1925 to make even the slightest change to the boundary, let alone 'the transfer of substantial areas', must have come as a blow to Chartres. He not only hoped for change, but also he believed that such a change was part of the binding agreement made in December 1921. Disillusionment with the implementation of the terms of the Treaty may well have led him to write the articles in *The Nation* in the weeks before he died. These articles were certainly critical of some aspects of the Treaty and by implication of the policy of the Free State.

The main concern of Chartres was the danger of Ireland becoming involved in an English war as a result of the Treaty. He wrote that:

> under the Treaty one tie, overwhelming in its vital significance, remains between England and ourselves—our obligation to engage in war on England's behalf ... the Irish Free State, by the terms of the Treaty, automatically becomes a belligerent on the side of England when England goes to war.[20]

Chartres suggested that Desmond FitzGerald had recognised this danger when, speaking in the Dáil, he had said that 'it is practically inconceivable that any country would attack this country unless they were already in the act of attacking Great Britain'. The peril was real, Charters asserted, because of England's desire for Empire, which he condemned, in the words of Arthur Griffith, as 'Britain's sordid imperialism'.[21]

Chartres stated the problem as he saw it: 'Ireland desires independence and peace. England desires military security in the event of war.'[22] Faced by this dilemma Chartres proposed that Ireland should be free and independent, and at the same time be recognised internationally as a neutral state. In building up his case Chartres cited not only Kevin O'Higgins, which would have been politically acceptable, but also the testimony of de Valera that 'neutrality is the best thing for this country'—which would have been far less politically correct. He hoped that neutrality would bring about a national rebirth and a new vision which would restore the shattered unity of the country.

Although he did not explicitly say so, his new and neutral Ireland would repair the failure of the Bounday Commission. 'National unity,' he declared,

> would also come about and old divisions be healed and forgotten. For a preliminary international policy of this kind is one to which, on its merits, all Irishmen—Free Staters or Republicans, Catholics or Protestants, Business men, Labour men, Farmers—could give eager adherence and consecrate their combined energies ... as for political Ulster, she could still exercise her powers of self-government. Does not Switzerland, a state relieved from the needs of centralisation by reason of its neutral status, include 22 cantons, 3 distinct races, 3 languages and 2 principal creeds.[23]

His vision, therefore, of a united Ireland was based on a practical example as well as on hope, but it failed to grasp the lack of attraction that neutrality and a united Ireland would have for the Ulster Unionists. Chartres' wish for change, however, indicated that he was not happy with the status quo as embodied in the Free State administration. This had important implications for his attitude towards the Treaty.

While Nancy Power was correct in stating that he played a constructive part in the shaping of the Articles of Agreement in 1921, he was less happy with the subsequent developments. Power hinted at this when she concluded that

> he may have felt disappointment at more recent developments, but when the Treaty was signed he had no doubt that its acceptance was for the good of Ireland. Michael Collins' word to him that the Treaty was a necessity was sufficient.[24]

'His faith in Michael Collins never wavered,' Power concluded; that was most certainly true. But his faith in other Free State leaders had wavered by 1927, and the indications are that Chartres was moving towards support for de Valera and the Fianna Fáil party. Disillusionment with Free State policy over the Treaty allied to dissatisfaction over the foreign policy of the department of External Affairs were almost certainly major factors in forcing him to consider where his loyalty lay. His death removed the necessity of making any formal choice of allegiance.

He died alone at his home, Lisieux, in Dartry Road, Rathgar, county Dublin. The *Irish Independent* announced his death in Irish and English and he was buried in Mount Jerome cemetery on 17 May.[25] Representatives from President Cosgrave and the Minister of Industry and Commerce attended as did Nancy Power, her mother, Jennie Wyse Power, Sean T. O'Kelly, Denis McCullough T.D. and his wife, who was a sister of O'Kelly's wife. No family were present. Despite the newspaper claims that the attendance at his funeral was 'large and representative,' it would appear that only a few friends and his associates in the department of Industry and Commerce were present. The connection with Sean T. O'Kelly was underlined by the fact that his wife, Cáit, was nominated as administrator of the estate on behalf of the widow, Annie Vivanti, who was living in Turin.[26]

Annie survived Chartres until 1942 when, having been interned at Arrezzo during the Second World War because of her German-Jewish origins, she died at Turin soon after her release. Her daughter was killed in a bombing raid at the start of the war.[27] The family name associated with his line of descent, therefore, ended; but it has survived in other lines of lineal descent. The original connection of the Chartres family with France has been symbolically restored in the present generation by the appointment of Bishop Richard Chartres of Stepney, London, to the European Chapter of Notre Dame cathedral at Chartres in France.[28]

Most of those who were associated with Chartres at the end of his life benefited from participation in the life of the Free State after de Valera and Fianna Fáil came to power in 1932. Nancy Power transferred from the department of Industry and Commerce in 1933 to become the private secretary to Sean T. O'Kelly, who was Minister for Local Government and Health. She died in 1963, having enjoyed a distinguished career in the Civil Service and having made an effort to secure equal rights for women in the administration of the Service.[29]

Sean T. O'Kelly, of course, was a leading figure in several Fianna Fáil administrations before becoming President of Ireland in 1945. Others of Chartres' former colleagues in Foreign Affairs also attained public office. Several of them were appointed ambassadors under the de Valera government when de Valera, himself, acted as Minister for External Affairs—Robert Brennan to the United States, Art O'Brien to France, and Leopold Kerney to France and then to Spain.[30]

Some of those engaged in the military struggle also achieved government office: Sean Moylan and Frank Aiken both became ministers on several occasions in Fianna Fáil administrations; and Sean MacBride, having been Chief of Staff of the IRA in 1936, founded the party of Clann na Poblachta after the war and became Minister of External Affairs in the first Inter-Party Government in 1948. Robert Briscoe was elected as a Fianna Fáil deputy to the Dáil in 1927 and held office for thirty eight years. He also became Dublin's first Jewish Lord Mayor in 1956 and placed the Star of David on his coat of arms—a fitting symbol of his triumph over the machinations of Bewley.[31] Bewley, himself, having returned to Germany during the war, was interned by the victorious allies at the end of the war accused of complicity with the Nazi regime. He died in 1969.[32] Briscoe's former companion in arms, Charlie McGuinness, continued on his maverick course until the end of his days. He was interned in Ireland during the Second World War because of his involvement in IRA contacts with Germany, and died at sea in 1947.[33]

Others of Chartres' former associates were unwilling to accept the Fianna Fáil departure. Joe McGarrity and John T. Ryan refused to co-operate with de Valera's plans in America, and at the end of his days, McGarrity, who died on 5 August 1940, was assisting Sean Russell, the IRA chief of staff, to fight for the full republican ideal against that proposed by de Valera. Once again McGarrity's plans envisaged a German connection and Russell made contact with Frank Ryan in Berlin prior to an abortive landing in Ireland by submarine.[34] The death of McGarrity, who had christened his son Eamon de Valera McGarrity in the hope that de Valera was the man to fulfil his ambitions for Ireland, marked the end of an era in Irish-American politics.

Possibly Chartres was fortunate that he died before a formal decision regarding his loyalties was required. He had no difficulty in accepting the oath, but to change from the pro-Treaty to the anti-Treaty side might have proved a difficult decision, especially if it was seen as an abandonment of his commitment to Collins. There remains, however, a more basic question of loyalty compared to which his stance on the Treaty pales into insignificance: was he, it may still be asked, on the side of England or of Ireland? In that regard the details of his will may be significant.

Chartres died intestate and left a modest amount of money: c.£480 in Ireland of which £279 was in two current accounts at the Munster and Leinster, and Barclay's Bank in College Green, Dublin; c.£860 in England of which £800 was on current account with Barclay's Bank in London.[35] The financial record indicate that he had not received any extraordinary payments for special services. In short, and to be blunt, if he was receiving payments as a double agent, then these payments did not appear in the final bank accounts on the day of his death, or in the petty cash available in his house. The money, of course, could have been syphoned off to other places but, as a straw in the wind, the financial signs, at face value, indicate a normal life-style—a negative indication that Chartres did not enjoy the wealth usually associated with spying. Moreover, if one judges Chartres by his words and deeds, and accepts the opinions of most of his contemporaries, then he was acting for Ireland and not for England after 1916. To focus on the charges and queries made by Mangan serves to dispel some of the doubts surrounding Chartres.

Mangan questioned his family background and his career record: both have been found to be correct and accurate. Because Mangan was not aware that Chartres had helped Collins in his gun-running enterprises, he failed to discern the perfectly reasonable explanation for his entry into the Irish ranks. While associating Chartres with the formula on the Crown, Mangan failed to detect that his various memoranda were faithful attempts to secure the policy of External Association as propounded by de Valera. Having only a limited knowledge of the vital role that Chartres had played in the creation of the Irish republican mission to Berlin Mangan questioned, rather than praised his contribution to the department of Foreign Affairs. From this perspective of rumour and doubt, allied to a certain ignorance of basic information, Mangan endowed Chartres with an aura of suspicion. To some extent the responses by Nancy Power and Piaras Béaslaí, made in 1935, offered a partial, if incomplete, answer to the doubts of Mangan.

This study adds substance to their career outline of Chartres and to the interpretation which they have provided of his actions, namely that by his provision of arms to Collins, by his integrity over the Treaty, and by his commitment to Ireland in Berlin he showed himself to be on the Irish side. His writings, of whose contents Mangan was unaware, confirm that impression. The account in the *Clonmel Nationalist* of his actions for the Irish cause after the executions of the Easter Rising manifests a clear hostility to English rule in Ireland as did his writing in *Nationality*. The same sentiments are to be found in his articles in the *Irish Press* of Philadelphia and in *The Nation*. Of course, it may be said that Chartres, as a skilful double agent, deliberately set out to deceive his Irish associates by writing in an anti-English vein. If deception was the guiding force of his career after 1916, then he was eminently successful.

However, most of the contemporaries of Chartres accepted him to be genuine and their testimony to his honest intentions must count for much. Arthur Griffith, Sean T. O'Kelly, Gavan Duffy, John T. Ryan, and de Valera, whatever their personal feelings about Chartres, had all met him and accepted him as sound and reliable. Nancy Power and Michael Collins, however, must rank as the two most important Irish witnesses on his behalf. Power, who knew him so well and who worked so closely with him, was convinced that Chartres was genuine in his commitment to Ireland. Moreover, her written accounts of his career accord accurately with the official papers. Her testimony may not simply be dismissed as fanciful musings: she supports her evidence with hard facts. If, however, her judgement may have been clouded by subjective considerations, the same could not be said of Michael Collins.

Collins was ruthless in the elimination of British spies, and employed a network of contacts both in England and Ireland to gather information about them. The murder of Jack Byrnes, alias Jameson, by Collins' Squad in 1920 illustrates most vividly the efficiency of his methods. Byrnes, 'the best Secret Service man we had' according to Sir Walter Long, was instructed to infiltrate the Collins organisation and was dead within months.[36] Chartres, like Byrnes, must have undergone the most detailed examination before being accepted into such a sensitive area as gun-running. No subjective considerations clouded the judgement of Collins. That Chartres survived and that Collins was still prepared to support him in a special way until he, himself, was assassinated says much for the bona fides of Chartres.

Possibly, however, the most significant piece of evidence in Chartres' favour comes not from an Irish but from an English, or more precisely a Welsh, voice. The private meeting in the Cabinet Office of 10 Downing Street between Tom Jones and Chartres during the crucial negotiations of November 1921 made dissimulation unnecessary. Chartres had no need to play a part with Jones. He could be himself or, at least, he could adopt a relatively neutral position.

The words of Jones are worth recalling. He found Chartres to be:

> utterly irreconcilable on allegiance to the King in Ireland. He had seen such things done in the King's name by the King's servants in the last two years that he would rather, as he put it, go underground tomorrow than consent to any intervention ever again by this country in the domestic affairs of Ireland. He spoke with great earnestness and there was no misunderstanding the depth of his conviction.[37]

Despite this acknowledgment of Chartres' commitment to the Irish cause by an informed and impartial observer, and despite the wealth of other evidence, the sceptical voices of the surviving anti-Treaty republicans are still to be heard. Surely, they ask, Maire Comerford was right to see Chartres as 'a plant' of British Intelligence? and surely his visits to Egypt indicate some connection with the Cairo gang of British agents who threatened to undermine the operations of Michael Collins in 1920? The tenor of the accumulated evidence lessens the strength of such questions. Moreover, particular points may be made in relation to the specific issues raised. In regard to the doubts of Máire Comerford, it is of significance that she was the first choice of Chartres as his assistant in Berlin: in other words he was prepared to work under her surveillance, thus indicating a degree of openness on his part. In regard to the Cairo gang, it has to be noted that as well as a British connection with Egypt of a military nature, there was also an Italian one with which Chartres was connected through D'Annunzio and the possibility of acquiring guns from him via the port of Fiume.

Conclusive evidence on any matter is hard to come by, especially in the world of spying where the dissemination of misinformation is part of the game, but the balance of evidence indicates that Chartres had returned to the inspiration of his Irish roots after 1916. Mangan's concluding observation about Chartres located him in the Dublin milieu in which he passed his last years. 'I saw him last,' Mangan wrote,

> in Dame Street, Dublin, opposite the corner of George's Street, solitary, waiting for something or somebody; an elderly professional man, of middle height, neatly dressed in dark grey, rather sallow, a little sad, stolid, apparently unobservant. A stockbrocker from the purlieus of nearby Anglesea Street, maybe, or a retired major.[38]

The vignette admirably conveys the outward persona projected by Chartres, and only time will tell whether the obscurity and inscrutability associated with his personality are justified. Possibly some papers of Annie Vivanti will be discovered, or some papers of restricted access in the Public Records Office in England will be released, that will confirm the doubts of Mangan and others and reverse the findings of this work. On the other hand fresh evidence may corroborate the findings of this study which indicate that when John Chartres signed himself Eoin mac Seartarris he was giving external expression to a genuine conversion to the Irish cause.

Notes

1 Frank Pakenham, *Peace by Ordeal* (London, 1935) p. 141.
2 Uinseann MacEoin, *Survivors* (Dublin, 1980) p. 400.
3 Pakenham, *Peace by Ordeal*, p. 141.
4 *Irish Independent*, 11 Oct. 1921.
5 *Irish Independent*, 25 Oct. 1935. Henry C. Mangan (1870–1961) was Dublin City accountant for over 25 years and a contributor to many journals. He became President of the Military History Society and a Governor of the National Gallery of Ireland.

CHAPTER 1: *Early Life: the British Connection*

1 Registry of Births, St Catherine's House; Burke's *Irish Family Records* (1976) p. 225; Official College and University Records, University of Dublin and George Burtchaell and Thomas Sadleir (ed.) *Alumni Dublinenses 1593–1860* (Dublin, 1935)
2 *Land Owners in Ireland c.1876* (Baltimore, 1988), and information from George Chartres, the family genealogist, who suggests that the family residence may have been Granite Hall, Dun Laoghaire, county Dublin.
3 Drew Rolls, Army Medical Service (5107); A. Peterkin and William Johnston (ed.), *Commissioned Officers in the Medical Services of the British Army 1660–1960* (London, 1968) p. 357; Register of Licentiates, Royal College of Surgeons, Ireland; Royal College of Surgeons, Ireland, *The Medical Register* (1861) p. 65; *Thom's Irish Almanac and Official Directory*.
4 Drew Rolls; Official College and University Records, University of Dublin.
5 Will of John Chartres, senior, PROE; *Irish Independent*, 10 Oct. 1921 and 4 Nov. 1935.
6 *Wellington College Register*, p. 102.
7 University of London General Register—he is not recorded as taking a degree at the University. King's Inn Admissions Register 1833–1991—he did not pursue his studies or fulfil any of the dining regulations.
8 Register of Admissions and financial records, Middle Temple, London.
9 *Instituto Della Enciclopedia Italiana*, Fondata Da Giovanni Treccani (1950) p. 526. No reference to their marriage having taken place in England could be found in the official English records.
10 Manager's Letter Files, News International for his career with *The Times*; *The Times*, 19 May 1927, p. 16.
11 PROE, MUN 5/27/263/2/3 for a list of officers to Aug. 1915.
12 Ibid. 5/11/200/28 memo on Origins of Ministry (Dec. 1916–July 1917)
13 Ibid. 5/27/263/2/11 for list of officers to Oct. 1918.

14 Ibid. 5/55/300/47 Weekly Report, 16 Nov. 1920 (number, 49); ibid. 5/55/300/105 for reports on the Shop Stewards movement; ibid. 5/55/300/108 for reports on Labour in Great Britain.
15 *Imperial Calendar*, 1918–19, p. 394; 1920, p. 394.

CHAPTER 2: *The Sinn Féin Connection*

1 *Clonmel Nationalist*, 11 Aug. 1923.
2 *Nationality*, 6 Oct. 1917.
3 Pádraig Ó Fiannachta (ed.), *Sean T.* Vol. II (Dublin, 1972) p. 155 translated from the Irish; *Irish Press*, 4 Aug. 1961 for the memoir of Sean T. O'Kelly in English.
4 Robert Brennan, *Allegiance* (Dublin, 1950) p. 270; the obituary of Chartres in the *Irish Independent*, 17 May 1927 also mentions the connection with *Nationality*.
5 Nancy Wyse Power, Statement to the Bureau of Military History, part 3, p. 11.
6 *Irish Independent*, 4 Nov. 1935.
7 T.P. Coogan, *Michael Collins* (London, 1990) p. 109. Coogan gives early 1919 for the meeting.
8 Brennan, *Allegiance*, pp. 270, 271.
9 *Irish Independent*, 28 Oct. 1935.
10 Ibid.
11 *The Times*, 19 May 1927, p. 16.

CHAPTER 3: *Paris and Foreign Affairs*

1 Two reports on Foreign Affairs, NA, DE 2/269, both undated but *c*.1919; *Irish Press*, 28 July 1961; G.M. Golding, *George Gavan Duffy 1882–1951* (Dublin, 1982) p. 20; Dermot Keogh, *Ireland and Europe 1919–1989* (Cork and Dublin, 1990) pp. 7, 8; Colm Gavan Duffy, 'George Gavan Duffy', *Dublin Historical Record* (Vol. 36, No. 30), June 1983 for an account of his father's life.
2 *Irish Press*, 27, 28 and 29 July 1961.
3 *Dáil Éireann, Minutes of Proceedings, 1919–21* (Dublin, nd.) 18 June 1919, p. 124; Keogh, *Ireland and Europe*, p. 8; Dermot Keogh, *The Vatican, the Bishops and Irish Politics 1919–1939* (Cambridge, 1986) for further background on this period of Foreign Affairs.
4 Ibid.
5 M. Collins to D. Hales, 15 Feb. 1919, Coogan, *Collins*, p. 239.
6 Sean T. O'Kelly to de Valera, 15. 16. 19 [*sic*] sent by hand 16 June 1919, NA, DFA Paris 1919–20.
7 O'Kelly to Mrs Chartres, 30 June 1919, NA, Gavan Duffy Papers (GD), 1125/13.
8 O'Kelly to Foreign Affairs, 7/9 July 1919, NA, DFA Paris 1919–20.
9 Ibid.
10 O'Kelly to Gavan Duffy, 3 Sept. 1919, NA, GD 1125/12 which contains an extract from an earlier letter of Gavan Duffy's.
11 De Valera to O'Kelly, 29 Jan. 1920, Killiney Archives, de Valera Papers (KDV), 1471/1; O'Kelly to Gavan Duffy, 10 March 1920, NA, GD 1125/12 for the same instruction; *Irish Press*, 29 July 1961.
12 Gavan Duffy to de Valera, 5 July 1920, KDV/1375.
13 Two Reports on Foreign Affairs, NA, DE 2/269, both are undated but appear to be *c*.1919. One records meetings on 11 Sept. and 9 Oct.; the other refers to two meetings with few attending. See Patrick Keatinge, *The Formulation of Irish Foreign Policy* (Dublin, 1973) pp. 72 f. for an account of ministerial policy and p. 74 for a table listing the first ten ministers with dates.
14 O'Kelly to D. O'Hegarty, 18 Sept. 1919, NA, DFA Paris 1919–20.

15 *Irish Press*, 29 July 1961; O'Kelly to Frank P. Walsh, 12 July 1920, KDV/1471/1 where O'Kelly states that he had been in bed for 14/15 weeks since 11 Feb.
16 O'Kelly to de Valera, 29 July 1920, KDV/1471/1.
17 O'Ceallaigh, *Sean T.*, pp. 89, 90.
18 O'Kelly to Griffith, 18 June 1920, NA, DFA Paris 1919-20.
19 Gavan Duffy to Collins, 8 March 1920, NA, DE 5/26.
20 O'Kelly to Gavan Duffy, 5 Aug. 1920, NA, GD 1125/12.
21 Gavan Duffy to de Valera, 9 Sept. 1920, NA, GD 1125/13.
22 Gavan Duffy to Frank P. Walsh, 3 Sept. 1920, KDV/1375; O'Kelly to de Valera, 10 Oct. 1920, KDV/1471/1; Ó Ceallaigh, *Sean T.*, p. 130.
23 *Dáil Éireann, Minutes*, 17 Sept. 1920, p. 216.
24 O'Kelly to Collins, 18 March 1921, NA, DE 5/26.
25 O'Kelly to Gavan Duffy, 18 April 1921, NA, GD 1123/12.

CHAPTER 4: *Berlin and Foreign Affairs*

1 O'Kelly to de Valera, 16 June 1919, NA, DFA Paris 1919-20; see also St John Gaffney, *Breaking the Silence. England, Ireland, Wilson and the War* (New York, 1930)
2 Gaffney, *Breaking the Silence*, p. 190; Memorandum on the German-Irish Society, NLI, Gavan Duffy Papers 15439(4)
3 G. von Berg to German-Irish Society, 19 March 1918 in *Documents Relative to the Sinn Féin Movement* (London, 1921) p. 42.
4 Gaffney, *Breaking the Silence*, p. 199.
5 Sean Ó Luing, *Kuno Meyer 1858-1919. A Biography* (Dublin, 1991)—see chapter 18 for his contacts with McGarrity.
6 Nancy Wyse Power, Statement, p. 1 where Duffy's companion and author of a report on Germany is Hamilton; and Gavan Duffy to Foreign Affairs, 10 Feb. and 11 March 1921, NA, DFA Berlin 1921-2 where his companion and author of a report on Germany is 'The Traveller'.
7 O'Kelly to Gavan Duffy, 2 Nov. 1919, NA, GD 1125/12.
8 Report on Foreign Affairs, June 1920, p. 2., NA, DE 2/269.
9 *Dáil Éireann*, Minutes, 29 June 1920, p. 173.
10 Ibid., 6 Aug. 1920, p. 195.
11 'Cousin' (Ryan) to 'Phil' (McGarrity), 16 Aug. 1920, NLI, McGarrity, 17486(1).
12 John T. Ryan, 'The Origin of the *Aud* Expedition,' *An Phoblacht*, 25 April 1931.
13 Wanted notice for John T. Ryan, NLI, Devoy, 18094.
14 Nancy Wyse Power, Statement, p. 1; Joseph Robins, *Custom House People* (Dublin, 1993) pp. 105-8; Marie O'Neill, *From Parnell to de Valera. A Biography of Jennie Wyse Power 1858-1941* (Dublin, 1991) for invaluable information on both mother and daughter.
15 'Cousin'[Ryan] to 'Phil' [McGarrity], 21 June 1921, NA, DFA Berlin 1921-2. One of two letters enclosed to Dublin on the same date.
16 Memorandum of Expenses for Special Tour, 11 March 1921, NA, DE 5/26.
17 Nancy Wyse Power, Statement, p. 5 and p. 15 where Power checked out Hamilton's claim to be related to the duke of Abercorn [family name Hamilton] and found it to be false.
18 Report on Foreign Affairs, Jan. 1921, p. 2, NA, DE 2/269.
19 Brennan to Presd., 10 Feb. 1921, NA, DE 2/97. (His salary was to be £100 per annum; he was given £200 to set up his office; a clerk was to be paid £4-6 per week; a typist £3 per week; and a messenger £1 per week.) Memorandum on Germany, 10 Feb. 1921, NA, DFA Berlin 1921-2 and NA, DE 2/270.
20 Memo on Germany, 10 Feb. 1921, NA, DFA Berlin 1921-2 and NA, DE 2/270.
21 Chatterton Hill to Duffy, 6 Feb. 1921, NA, DFA Berlin 1921-2.
22 Memo on Germany, 10 Feb. 1921, NA, DE 2/270; and Collins to Art O'Brien, 16 Aug. 1920, NA, DE 2/270.
23 Ministry meeting, 8 March 1921, NA, DE 2/270.

24 Gavan Duffy to Foreign Affairs, 11 March 1921, NA, DFA Berlin 1921–2.
25 De Valera to Collins, 2 April 1921, NA, DE 2/270.
26 Brennan to Collins, 6 April 1921, ibid.
27 For the Weimar Republic see John Hiden, *Germany and Europe 1919–39* (London, 1993; first edition 1977); Detlev J.K. Peukert, *The Weimar Republic* (London, 1993; first edition, 1987).

CHAPTER 5: *John Chartres and Nancy Power in Berlin*

1 Memorandum on Germany, 1 June 1921, NA, DFA Berlin 1921–2.
2 Nancy Wyse Power, Statement, p. 3.
3 De Valera to Collins, 24 April 1921, NA, DE 2/97; Brennan to Power, 29 April 1921, NA, DFA Berlin 1921–2; Collins to Power, 3 May 1921, NA, DE 5/27/1.
4 Brennan to Power, 29 April 1921, NA, DFA Berlin 1921–2.
5 Gaffney, *Breaking the Silence*, p. 275.
6 Ibid. p. 278; 'Spillane' [Gaffney] to de Valera, 14 May 1921, NA, DFA Berlin 1921–2.
7 Collins to de Valera, 29 April 1921, NA, DE 2/270.
8 De Valera to Collins, 16 May 1921, KDV/151.
9 Ibid.
10 Nancy Wyse Power, Statement, p. 6; Memo on Germany, 1 June 1921, NA, DFA Berlin 1921–2; Brennan to Collins, 29 April 1921, NA, DE 2/97.
11 Memo on Germany, 1 June 1921, NA, DFA Berlin 1921–2.
12 Ibid.
13 Nancy Wyse Power, Statement, p. 9.
14 Ibid. p. 6.
15 Ibid. p. 10.
16 Memo on Germany, 1 June 1921, NA, DFA Berlin 1921–2.
17 Ibid.
18 Nancy Wyse Power, Statement, p. 8.
19 *Irish Independent*, 4 Nov. 1935; Collins to de Valera, 4 June 1921, KDV/151.
20 O'Kelly to Collins, 7 June 1921, NA, DE 5/26.
21 Collins to de Valera, 4 June 1921, KDV/151.
22 De Valera to Collins, 7 June 1921, ibid.
23 John Chartres [Edward Seaton], 'The Bloody English', *Irish Press* (Philadelphia) 7 Jan. 1922. Later the articles, which ran almost every week until 15 April 1922, were attributed to a 'True Born Englishman'.
24 E.S. (Chartres) to Brennan, 11 June 1921; Brennan to Power, 5 and 13 Sept. 1921, NA, DFA Berlin 1921–2 for examples that give clarification of his code name.
25 Brennan to E.S. [Chartres], 9 June 1921, ibid.; Gaffney, *Breaking the Silence*, p. 278.
26 Gaffney to de Valera, 30 June 1921, Ibid.; Memo from Gaffney, 30 May 1921, ibid., which gives an account of his journey from America and of his arrest in Switzerland.
27 Collins to Chartres, 21 June 1921, NA, DE 5/27/1; MacEoin, *Survivors*, p. 407 has a reference to this cheque.
28 Report on Foreign Affairs, June 1921, p. 4, NA, DE 5/269; *Dáil Éireann, Official Report* (16 Aug.–26 Aug. 1921 and 28 Feb. 1922–8 June 1922) (Dublin, nd.) 17 Aug. 1921, p. 19.
29 MacEoin, *Survivors*, p. 42 for Comerford's view; Brennan to Chartres, 22 June and 25 Aug. 1921, NA, DFA Berlin 1921–2.
30 Chartres to Brennan, 4 July 1921, NA, DFA Berlin 1921–2.
31 Ibid.
32 Ibid.
33 Francis M. Carroll, *American Opinion and the Irish Question 1910–1923* (Dublin, 1978) pp. 169, 170.
34 Chartres to Brennan, 4 July 1921, NA, DFA Berlin 1921–2.

35 McCartan to Collins, 20 March 1922, NA, DE 5/57/13; McCartan to McGarrity, 2 June 1922, ibid., in which 'Roberts' is the code name for Ryan; *Intercourse between Bolshevism and Sinn Féin* (London, 1921) p. 4, available in NA, DE 2/303.
36 Nancy Wyse Power, Statement, pp. 6, 7.
37 Chartres to Brennan, 4 July 1921, NA, DFA Berlin 1921-2.
38 Chartres to Brennan, 9 and 12 July 1921, ibid.
39 Brennan to Chartres, 27 July 1921, ibid.
40 Chartres to Brennan, 4 July and 4/5 Aug. 1921, ibid.
41 Collins to Chartres, 6 Aug. 1921, NA, DE 5/27/1.
42 Chartres to Collins, 26 Aug. 1921, ibid.
43 Brennan to Chartres, 8 Aug. 1921, NA, DFA Berlin 1921-2.
44 Chartres to Brennan, 24 Aug. 1921, ibid.
45 *Dáil Éireann, Official Record*, 17 Aug. 1921, p. 16 and p. 21.
46 Ibid., 26 Aug. 1921, p. 82.
47 Brennan to Chartres, 25 Aug. 1921, NA, DFA Berlin 1921-2.
48 Chartres to Brennan, 5 and 18 Sept. 1921, ibid.
49 Ibid.
50 Ibid.
51 Brennan to Power, 5 and 13 Sept. 1921, ibid.
52 Nancy Wyse Power, Statement, p. 11.
53 Robert Briscoe (with Alden Hatch), *For the Life of Me* (London, 1958), pp. 79-81. See also C.J. McGuinness, *Nomad* (London, 1934); C. Desmond Greaves, *Liam Mellows and the Irish Revolution* (London, 1971); MacEoin, *Survivors*, p. 112 for Sean MacBride.
54 Greaves, *Mellows*, p. 258.
55 Briscoe, *For the Life of Me*, p. 82.
56 McGuinness, *Nomad*, p. 166; Briscoe, *For the Life of Me*, p. 96.
57 Collins to Chartres, 13 Sept. 1921, NA, DE 5/27/1.
58 Chartres to Collins, 18 Sept. 1921, ibid.
59 Ministry meeting, 30 Sept. 1921, KDV/141; Chartres to Brennan, 2 Jan. 1922, NA, DFA Berlin 1922-4.
60 Erskine Childers Diary, 14 and 16 Sept. and 6 Oct. 1921, Trinity College Dublin Manuscripts (TCDM), 7814/1 and 7814/2; Fionan Lynch Papers, NA, DE 4/5/21; J. Anthony Gaughan, *Alfred O'Rahilly. Volume II, Public Figure* (Dublin, 1989), pp. 104, 105 and pp. 127-9 for his claim to be secretary.
61 *Irish Independent*, 4 Nov. 1935.
62 Jennie Wyse Power to Nancy Power, 9 Oct. 1921, UCDA, Mulcahy Papers P7/D/7. The names of the individuals are in code: Charters (*sic*) is 'Mitchel'; Collins is 'House'; Griffith is 'Dazzler'. See Marie O'Neill, *Jennie Wyse Power*, p. 126.
63 Brennan to Power, 7 Oct. 1921, NA, DFA Berlin 1921-2.

CHAPTER 6: *The Plenary Conference Meetings*

1 Archive official to Secy. of Presd., 1 Feb. 1962, NA, DE 2/304(1).
2 Credentials and Instructions to Plenipotentiaries, 7 Oct. 1921, Barton Papers, p. 7 and p. 8, NA, Four Courts.
3 Kathleen Napoli McKenna, 'In London with the Treaty Delegates', *Capuchin Annual* (1971), p. 320; MacEoin, *Survivors*, p. 114.
4 Childers Diary, 10 Oct. 1921, TCDM, 7814/1.; Thomas Jones (Keith Middlemas ed.), *Whitehall Diary. Vol. III. Ireland 1918-1925* (London, 1971) p. 117.
5 Griffith to de Valera, 10 Oct. 1921, Barton, p. 18; Jones, *Whitehall Diary*, p. 117.
6 Seating of Plenipotentiaries, Barton, p. 20; Pakenham, *Peace by Ordeal*, p. 122. Other valuable works on the Treaty negotiations are Frank Gallagher (T.P. O'Neill ed.) *The Anglo-Irish Treaty* (London, 1965); Joseph M. Curran, *The Birth of the Irish Free State 1921-3* (Alabama, 1980); T. Ryle Dwyer, *Michael Collins and the Treaty* (Cork, 1981); Sheila Lawlor, *Britain*

and Ireland 1914–1923 (Dublin, 1983); Nicholas Mansergh, *The Unresolved Question. The Anglo-Irish Settlement and its Undoing 1912–72* (New Haven and London, 1991).

7   Anglo-Irish Treaty Negotiations, NA, DE 2/304(1) for list of meetings.
8   Note by Barton, Barton, p. 21.
9   Griffith to de Valera, 11 Oct. 1921, Barton, p. 22; Jones, *Whitehall Diary*, pp. 119–21.
10   Report of 4 p.m. meeting of 11 Oct. 1921, Barton, p. 33; Jones, *Whitehall Diary*, p. 123.
11   De Valera to Griffith, 14 Oct. 1921, Barton, p. 35.
12   Ibid.
13   Earl of Longford and Thomas P. O'Neill, *Eamon de Valera* (Dublin, 1970) p. 139; Robert Barton, *The Truth about the Treaty and Document No. 2* (Dublin, 1922), p. 9 states that de Valera had proposed the idea of External Association before the Truce of 11 July 1921.
14   Memorandum to Minister of Foreign Affairs, 14 Oct. 1921, Barton, p. 205.
15   Ibid.
16   Ibid.
17   Note by Barton, Barton, p. 201.
18   Memo to MFA, 14 Oct. 1921, ibid., p. 205.
19   De Valera to Griffith, 15 Oct. 1921, ibid., p. 44.
20   *Irish Independent,* 21 Oct. 1935.
21   Note by Barton on J.J. O'Connell and E. O'Duffy; Griffith to de Valera, 20 Oct. 1921, Barton, p. 55 and p. 56.
22   Maryann Gialanella Valiulis, *Portrait of a Revolutionary. General Richard Mulcahy and the Founding of the Irish Free State* (Dublin, 1992), pp. 101–4.
23   Note on the Crown, 20 Oct. 1921, NA, DE 2/304(5) and KDV/186 where the date 22 Oct. 1921 is given. See also Brendan Sexton, *Ireland and the Crown 1922–1936* (Dublin, 1989), pp. 30–1.
24   Ibid.
25   Ibid.
26   Ibid.
27   Irish Peace Conference, 21 Oct. 1921, Barton, p. 60.
28   Greaves, *Mellows*, p. 261; Briscoe, *For the Life of Me*, p. 99; McGuinness, *Nomad*, p. 170; Rex Taylor, *Michael Collins* (London, 1958), p. 137; and MacEoin, *Survivors*, p. 140 for the view of Pax O Faolain.
29   Irish Peace Conference, 21 Oct. 1921, Barton, pp. 64, 65.
30   Jones, *Whitehall Diary*, p. 139.
31   Childers Diary, 21 Oct. 1921, TCDM, 7814/2.
32   Jones, *Whitehall Diary,* p. 141.
33   Childers Diary, 24 Oct. 1921, TCDM, 7814/2.
34   Memo of Proposals of Irish Delegates, 24 Oct. 1921, Barton, pp. 71, 72.
35   Seventh Session of Peace Conference, 24 Oct. 1921, Barton, p. 73; Jones, *Whitehall Diary*, p. 142.
36   Childers Diary, 24 Oct. 1921, TCDM, 7814/2.

CHAPTER 7: *The Sub-conference Meetings*

1   Jones, *Whitehall Diary*, p. 141 and p. 144.
2   Brian P. Murphy, *Patrick Pearse and the Lost Republican Ideal* (Dublin, 1991), p. 124.
3   Ibid., p. 126.
4   Griffith to de Valera, 24 Oct. 1921, Barton, p. 76; Jones, *Whitehall Diary*, p. 144.
5   Kathleen O'Connell's Diary, 25 Oct. 1921, KDV/1473; de Valera to Griffith, 25 Oct. 1921, Barton, p. 78.
6   Delegates to de Valera, 26 Oct. 1921, Barton, p. 79 and Note by Barton, p. 77.
7   Ibid.
8   Note by Barton, ibid., p. 77.
9   De Valera to Griffith, 27 Oct. 1921, ibid., p. 82.

10 Childers Diary, 27 Oct. 1921, TCDM, 7814/2.
11 Ibid., 28 Oct. 1921.
12 Memo by His Majesty's Govt., 27 Oct. 1921, Barton, pp. 83, 84; Jones, *Whitehall Diary*, p. 147.
13 John Chartres Draft for Crown Clause, 28 Oct. 1921, Barton, p. 204 and KDV/186. The Barton Papers give the heading; the de Valera Papers give the date. Pakenham, *Peace by Ordeal*, p. 193.
14 Further Memo by Irish Delegates, 29 Oct. 1921, ibid., p. 87 and KDV/186.
15 De Valera to Griffith, 31 Oct. 1921, ibid., p. 88.
16 Jones, *Whitehall Diary*, p. 150; Childers Diary, 29 Oct. 1921, TCDM, 7814/2.
17 Childers to his wife, 31 Oct. 1921, TCDM, 7852–'5(1228).
18 Draft letter of Griffith to Lloyd George, 1 Nov. 1921, Barton, p. 93 and Barton Note on the letter, p. 92; Andrew Boyle, *The Riddle of Erskine Childers* (London, 1977), p. 284.
19 Jones, *Whitehall Diary*, p. 150.
20 Childers Diary, 1 Nov. 1921, TCDM, 7814/2.
21 Ibid., 2 Nov. 1921.
22 Gavan Duffy to Griffith, 2 Nov. 1921, Barton, pp. 94,95.
23 Childers Diary, 2 Nov. 1921, TCDM, 7814/2; Jones, *Whitehall Diary*, p. 153.
24 Ibid.
25 Griffith to Lloyd George, 2 Nov. 1921 (11 p.m.), Barton, p. 97; Jones, *Whitehall Diary*, pp. 153, 154.
26 Griffith to Lloyd George, 2 Nov. 1921 (noon), ibid., p. 96.
27 Ibid. p. 96 and p. 97 for the two letters.
28 Jones, *Whitehall Diary*, p. 153; Collins to O'Kane, 4 Nov. 1921, in Taylor, *Collins*, p. 132.
29 De Valera to Griffith, 9 Nov. 1921, Barton, p. 103.
30 Note by Barton, Barton, p. 92.
31 Childers Diary, 4 Nov. 1921, TCDM, 7814/3; Chartres to Brennan, 2 Jan. 1922, NA, DFA Berlin 1922–4.
32 Childers to his wife, 3 Nov. 1921, TCDM, 7852–5 (1232).
33 J.T. Ryan to McGarrity, 8 Nov. 1921, in Sean Cronin, *The McGarrity Papers* (Tralee, 1972), p. 105; Brennan, *Allegiance*, p. 329.
34 Jennie Wyse Power to Nancy Power, 15 Nov. 1921, UCDA, Mulcahy, P7/D/7.
35 Nancy Power to de Valera, 5 Nov. 1921, NA, DFA Berlin 1921–2.
36 De Valera to Power, 8 Nov. 1921, ibid.
37 Greaves, *Mellows*, p. 264; Briscoe, *For the Life of Me*, pp. 103–5; McGuinness, *Nomad*, pp. 172–9; MacEoin, *Survivors*, p. 141 for Pax O Faolain and pp. 113, 114 for Sean MacBride; letter to the *Irish Independent*, 18 Nov. 1924, and signed 'One of Them'; Quarter Master General to Minister of Defence, 19 Dec. 1921, KDV/148.
38 *Irish Independent*, 4 Nov. 1935.
39 Ibid.; Childers Diary, 15 and 18 Nov. 1921, TCDM, 7814/3 and 7814/4; Chartres to Brennan, 2 Jan. 1922, NA, DFA Berlin 1922–4.
40 Ibid.; the original letter, Chartres to Griffith, 8 Nov. 1921, was in Nancy Power's possession.
41 Ibid.
42 Childers Diary, 11 and 12 Nov. 1921, TCDM, 7814/3.
43 Sturgis Diary, 13 Nov. 1921, PROE, Sturgis 30/59/5.
44 Nancy Power Statement, p. 19; Coogan, *Collins*, pp. 284–7.
45 Childers Diary, 16 Nov. 1921, TCDM, 7814/4; Collins to O'Kane, 15 Nov. 1921, Taylor, *Collins*, p. 133.
46 Ibid., 18 Nov. 1921.
47 Lloyd George to Craig, 10 Nov. 1921, Barton, p. 109.
48 Ibid.
49 Griffith to de Valera, 11 Nov. 1921, ibid., p. 105.
50 Craig to Lloyd George, 11 Nov. 1921, ibid., pp. 111, 112.
51 Griffith to de Valera, 12 Nov. 1921, ibid. pp. 106, 107; Jones, *Whitehall Diary*, pp. 162, 163.
52 Ibid.

53 Jones, *Whitehall Diary*, p. 164; Pakenham, *Peace by Ordeal*, pp. 218–22.
54 Lloyd George to Craig, 14 Nov. 1921, Barton, p. 114.
55 Ibid., pp. 114, 115.
56 British Draft Treaty, 16 Nov. 1921, Barton, pp. 121, 122; Jones, *Whitehall Diary*, pp. 165, 166.
57 De Valera to Griffith, 17 Nov. 1921, Barton, p. 123.
58 Childers Diary, 21 Nov. 1921, TCDM, 7814/4.
59 Brennan to O'Kelly, 22 Nov. 1921, NA, DE 5/26.
60 Note by Barton on Heads of Agreement, Baron, p. 125.
61 Memo by Irish Representatives, 22 Nov. 1921, ibid., pp. 128, 129 and KDV/186 for same Memo; Jones, *Whitehall Diary*, pp. 169, 170.
62 Griffith to de Valera, 22 Nov. 1921, ibid., p. 134; Jones, *Whitehall Diary*, p. 170.
63 Jones, *Whitehall Diary*, p. 170.
64 Griffith to de Valera, 22 Nov. 1921, p. 134.
65 Cronin, *McGarrity*, pp. 107,108 and p. 110.
66 Griffith to de Valera, 22 Nov. 1921, Barton, p. 134.
67 Jones, *Whitehall Diary*, p. 171 and p. 172.
68 'Concessions contained in our proposals of 22 November', by Childers, Barton, pp. 131, 132.
69 Childers Diary, 23 Nov. 1921, TCDM, 7814/4.
70 Ibid.
71 Ibid., 24 Nov. 1921; Conference on Ireland, 24 Nov. 1921, Barton, pp. 142, 143; Jones, *Whitehall Diary*, p. 174.
72 Chartres to Mulcahy, 5 Feb. 1924, UCDA, Mulcahy, P35b/157.
73 Conference on Ireland, 24 Nov. 1921, Barton, p. 142.
74 Ibid.
75 Ibid., p. 142 and p. 143.
76 Ibid., p. 143.
77 Barton to editor of *Irish Independent*, 17 March 1922, Barton, pp. 190, 191.
78 Jones, *Whitehall Diary*, p. 174. His statement that Chartres was 'shut up brusquely by F.E.' (Birkenhead) does not accord with the recorded minutes.

CHAPTER 8: *The Final Round of Meetings*

1 Chartres to Griffith (MFA), 25 Nov. 1921, Barton, p. 146 and KDV/189.
2 Jones, *Whitehall Diary*, p. 175.
3 Jones to Chartres, 25 Nov. 1921, Barton, p. 147 and NA, DE 2/304/1 for the same letter.
4 Chartres to Jones, 28 Nov. 1921, NA, DE 2/304/1.
5 Childers Diary, 25 Nov. 1921, TCDM, 7814/5.
6 Chamberlain to F.E., 25 Nov. 1921, in Birkenhead (Earl of), *The Life of F.E. Smith, First Earl of Birkenhead* (London, 1959), pp. 382, 384; Pakenham, *Peace by Ordeal*, p. 281; Taylor, Collins, p. 130; Coogan, *Collins*, pp. 263, 264; Leon Ó Broin, *Michael Collins* (Dublin, 1980) pp. 99, 100.
7 Note by Barton, Barton, p. 196, and pp. 197–200 for extracts from the same letter, although there are some changes in the text.
8 Chamberlain to F.E., 25 Nov. 1921, in Birkenhead, *The Life of F.E. Smith*, p. 383.
9 D. O'Hegarty (Secy. to Cabinet) to Griffith, 22 Nov. 1921, KDV/144; Valiulis, *Mulcahy*, pp. 107, 108.
10 Draft by Minister of Defence, ibid.
11 Ibid.; Cabinet Meeting, 25 Nov. 1921, NA, DE 1/3.
12 Cabinet Meeting, 25 Nov. 1921, NA, DE 1/3. This extract from the minutes is also to be found in Barton, p. 162. See J. Anthony Gaughan, *Austin Stack: Portrait of a Separatist* (Dublin, 1977) p. 166 for Stack's account of this meeting which forms part of his memoir on the Treaty negotiations.

13 Childers Diary, 26 and 27 Nov. 1921, TCDM, 7814/5.
14 Ibid., 28 Nov. 1921.
15 Memo of Irish Delegates, 28 Nov. 1921, Barton, pp. 138, 139 and same document in KDV/186.
16 Jones, *Whitehall Diary*, p. 176.
17 Childers Diary, 28 Nov. 1921, TCDM, 7814/5.
18 Ibid.; Jones, *Whitehall Diary*, p. 176.
19 Ibid.; Jones, *Whitehall Diary*, p. 177.
20 Jones, *Whitehall Diary*, p. 177.
21 Childers Diary, 29 Nov. 1921, TCDM, 7814/5.
22 Griffith to de Valera, 29 Nov. 1921, Barton, p. 149.
23 Ibid.
24 Childers Diary, 29 Nov. 1921, TCDM, 7814/5: Barton, pp. 208-11 for the full paper on 'Law and Fact in Canada and Ireland'.
25 'Rough Notes' by Chartres, 29 Nov. 1921, NA, DE 2/304/1 and KDV/186.
26 Ibid.
27 Griffith to de Valera, 29 Nov. 1921, Barton, p. 149.
28 Ibid.; Childers Diary, 29 Nov. 1921, TCDM, 7814/5.
29 Childers Diary, 30 Nov. 1921, TCDM, 7814/5.
30 Collins to O'Kane, 29 and 30 Nov. 1921, in Taylor, *Collins*, p. 140.
31 Childers Diary, 1 Dec. 1921, TCDM, 7814/5.
32 Ibid.
33 Ibid., 2 Dec. 1921; Chartres to Brennan, 1 Dec. 1921, NA, DFA Berlin 1921-2; Chartres to Brennan, 2 Jan. 1922, NA, DFA Berlin 1922-4.
34 Conference on Ireland, Proposed Articles of Agreement, Barton, p. 153.
35 Meeting of Cabinet and Delegation, 3 Dec. 1921, NA, DE 1/3 and Barton, p. 162. See Barton pp. 159,160 for his critical view of the acting Cabinet secretary, Colm Ó Murchadha.
36 Ibid. and Barton, p. 163.
37 Ibid. and Barton, p. 164.
38 Ibid.
39 Ibid.; Taylor, *Collins*, p. 147.
40 Taylor, *Collins*, pp. 141 f.
41 Amendments by Irish Representatives to Proposed Articles of Agreement, 4 Dec. 1921, Barton, pp. 166, 167.
42 Ibid., p. 166; Barton to editor of *Phoblacht na h-Éireann*, 27 April 1922, Barton, p. 192.
43 Griffith to de Valera, 4 Dec. 1921, Barton, pp. 169, 170.
44 Ibid.
45 Jones, *Whitehall Diary*, p. 180; Jones to Lloyd George, 4 Dec. 1921, Lloyd George Papers, House of Lords Records Office, F/25/2/51.
46 Minute of Collins meeting with Lloyd George, 9.30 a.m. 5 Dec. 1921, Barton, pp. 171, 172.
47 Pakenham, *Peace by Ordeal*, p. 275; Coogan, *Collins*, p. 285; Ó Cuinneagáin, *On the Arm of Time*, pp. 46, 47, who also argues that Moya and Lady Lavery played a crucial part in persuading Collins to sign the Treaty.
48 Ó Murthuile memoir, UCDA, Mulcahy, P7a/209; John O'Beirne-Ranelagh, 'The IRB from the Treaty to 1924', *Irish Historical Studies*, vol. XX, no. 77, March 1976, p. 28; Coogan, *Collins*, p. 266 and p. 273; Ó Broin, *Revolutionary Underground* (Dublin, 1976) p. 196.
49 Proposed Articles of Agreement, 5 Dec. 1921, Barton, p. 175.
50 Articles of Agreement for a Treaty between Great Britain and Ireland, 6 Dec. 1921, in Arthur Mitchel and Pádraig Ó Snodaigh (eds.), *Irish Political Documents 1916–49* (Dublin, 1985), p. 117; Pakenham, *Peace by Ordeal*, p. 290.
51 Barton Note on Sub-conferences of 5 Dec. 1921, Barton, p. 184.
52 Dad (Stephen O'Mara, senior) to O'Mara (Stephen O'Mara, junior), 6 Dec. 1921, O'Mara private papers; KDV/127 for photograph of de Valera and others at Strand House on 5/6 Dec. 1921; Cronin, *McGarrity*, p. 108; Mansergh, *Unresolved Question*, pp. 188, 189.

CHAPTER 9: *Berlin: Charles Bewley and the Irish Race Congress*

1 Foreign Affairs to Bewley, 17 Oct. 1921, NA, DFA Berlin 1922–4; Charles Bewley, *Memoirs of a Wild Goose* (Dublin, 1989), foreword pp. ix–xii by John Duggan; D'Abernon to Curzon, 6 Jan. 1922, PROE, FO 371/7529 for British reports on Bewley's office at 7–8 Joachimstahler Strasse, Berlin.
2 Foreign Affairs to Bewley, 3 Nov. 1921, ibid.
3 Chatterton Hill to Bewley, 11 Oct. 1921, ibid., Berlin 1921–2; Chatterton Hill to de Valera, 23 Nov. 1921, ibid.
4 Bewley, *Memoirs*, pp. 77, 78.
5 E.S. [Chartres] to USFA [Brennan], 2 Jan. 1922, NA, DFA Berlin 1922–4.
6 Ibid.
7 Ibid.; Statement of Berlin Accounts, 1 Jan. 1922, NA, DE 5/27/1; Collins to Chartres, 3 Jan. 1922, ibid.; Chartres to Collins, 10 Jan. 1922, ibid.
8 Brennan to Chartres, 10 Jan. 1922, NA, DFA Berlin 1922–4.
9 *Official Report, Debate on the Treaty between Great Britain and Ireland* (Dublin, ND), 10 Jan. 1922, p. 411.
10 Ibid., 21 Dec. 1921, p. 85 and p. 87.
11 Ibid., 10 Jan. 1922, p. 406.
12 Ibid., 7 Jan. 1922, pp. 341, 342.
13 Ministry meeting, 11 Jan. 1922, NA, DE 1/4; O'Brien to Duffy, 13 Jan. 1922, NA, DFA London 1922–3.
14 *Irish Press* (Philadelphia), 7 Jan. 1922; *Irish Independent*, 4 Nov. 1935 for Nancy Power's statement that Chartres was the author.
15 Shane Reain [Ryan] to Phil [McGarrity], 1922, NLI, McGarrity, 17486(1). There is some doubt about the date, but the contents of the letter refer to events after the signing of the Treaty.
16 Ibid. Bewley is spelt as 'Buhlie.'
17 Dáil Cabinet meeting, 12 Jan. 1922, NA, DE 1/4.
18 Ibid., 16 Jan. 1922.
19 Brennan, *Allegiance*, p. 335.
20 Minutes of World Congress of the Irish Race (week ending 28 Jan. 1922), UCDA, MacSwiney, P48a/354(2), p.1. See Dermot Keogh, 'The Treaty Split and the Paris—Irish Race Convention', *Etudes Irlandaises*, No. 12, Dec. 1987.
21. Chartres to Collins, 21 Jan. 1922, NA, D/T S9242.
22 Minutes of the Irish Race Congres, UCDA, MacSwiney, P48a/354(2), p. 4.
23 Ibid., p. 5; *Irish Times*, 24 Jan. 1922, p. 6.
24 Foreign Office Memo number 1, 25 Jan. 1922, NA, DE 4/11/51.
25 Ibid.
26 Proceedings of the Irish Race Congress, Jan. 1922, UCDA, MacSwiney, P48a/351(1), p. 84; Minutes of the World Congress of the Irish Race, ibid., P48a/351(2) contain a shortened note of the proceedings.
27 Ibid., pp. 100, 101.
28 Ibid., p. 106.
29 Ibid., P48a/351(2); see Mark Tierney, 'Calendar of Irlande, vols. 1, 2, 3, in the collection Europe, 1918–29, in the Archives Diplomatiques, Paris', in *Collectanea Hibernica* (1979–80), pp. 212–14 for the French police reports of the Congress.
30 MacNéill, Report on the 'Irish Race Congress,' 2 Feb. 1922, NA, DFA Paris 1922–3; Ministry meeting, 3 Feb. 1922, NA, DE 1/4.
31 O'Kelly to Duffy, 2 Feb. 1922, ibid.
32 Memorandum, 28 Jan. 1922, NA, DFA Berlin 1922–4. There is no signature, but from the text it is clear that the author is Bewley. See also Secretary to Bewley, 13 Feb. 1922, ibid.
33 Chartres to Duffy, 30 Jan. 1922, ibid.; Briscoe to Chartres, 21 Jan. 1922, ibid.
34 Ibid.
35 Briscoe to Chartres, 21 Jan. 1922, ibid.

36 Chartres to Duffy, Report of 4 Feb. 1922, ibid.
37 Ibid.
38 Ibid.
39 Duffy to Chartres, 16 Feb. 1922, one of two letters, ibid.
40 Duffy to FitzGerald, 22 Feb. 1922, ibid.
41 MacWhite to Duffy, 3 Feb. 1922, Duffy private family papers.
42 MacWhite to Duffy, in Duffy's Memo on Foreign Affairs, 16 June 1922, p. 6, NA, DE 4/8/6.
43 O'Kelly to Duffy, 1 Feb. 1922, NA, DFA Paris 1922–3; Duffy to Accnt. Gen., 7 Feb. 1922, Ibid.; Keogh, *Ireland and Europe*, p. 11.
44 *Irish Press* (Philadelphia), 1 and 8 April 1922 for an account of the tour by McGarrity.
45 Ministry meetings 27 Feb. and 7 March 1922, NA, DE 1/4; for correspondence on Smiddy's appointment, NA, D/T S2011A; *Official Report, Dáil Éireann*, 3 May 1922, p. 355.
46 Gavan Duffy to Stephen O'Mara (junior), 27 Jan. 1922, O'Mara private family papers.
47 O'Kelly to Duffy, 1 Feb. 1922, NA, DFA Paris 1922–3.
48 Duffy to O'Kelly, 3 Feb. 1922, Ibid.; O'Kelly to Duffy, 6 Feb. 1922, ibid.
49 O'Kelly to Duffy, 1 Feb. 1922 (one of two letters), ibid.
50 Duffy to O'Kelly, 7 Feb. 1922, ibid.
51 Note for Paris file, confidential with reference to Sean T. O'Kelly, 20 Feb. 1922, signed Gavan Duffy, ibid.
52 Blythe to Collins, 20 Feb. 1922, enclosing a four page Memo by Bewley, NA, DFA Berlin 1922–4.
53 Ibid. from the enclosed memo.
54 Blythe to Bewley, 13 Feb. 1922; Blythe to Duffy, 16 Feb. 1922; and Blythe to Collins, 20 Feb. 1922, ibid.
55 Collins to Blythe, 27 Feb. 1922; Blythe to Bewley, 1 March 1922, ibid.
56 Duffy to Blythe, 4 March 1922, enclosing Chartres to Duffy, no date, ibid.
57 Blythe to Bewley, 7 March 1922, ibid.
58 Duffy to Power, 27 Feb. 1922, ibid.
59 Chartres to Duffy, 7 March 1922, ibid.
60 FitzGerald to Duffy, 9 March 1922, ibid., replying to Duffy's earlier letter of 22 Feb. and saying that he was sending some photographs of the present Government.
61 Chartres to Duffy, 7 March 1922, ibid.
62 Ibid.
63 Ibid.
64 Ibid.

CHAPTER 10: *Berlin and Paris*

1 *Dáil Éireann, Official Report*, 1 March 1922, p. 133.
2 MacWhite to Duffy, 2 and 24 Feb. 1922, NA, DFA Paris 1922–3; MacNéill to Duffy, 17 Feb. 1922, ibid.; Hayes to Duffy, 22 Feb. 1922, ibid.
3 *Dáil Éireann, Official Report*, 1 March 1922, p. 134.
4 Ibid. p. 135.
5 Duffy to O'Kelly, 16 March 1922, NA, DFA Paris 1922–3.
6 Ibid.
7 O'Kelly to Duffy, 23 March 1922, ibid.
8 Duffy to Accnt. Gen., 9 March 1922, NA, DE 5/26.
9 Chartres to Duffy, 11 March 1922, NA, DFA Berlin 1922–4.
10 Ibid.
11 Ibid.
12 Bewley to Blythe, 11 March 1922, ibid.
13 Duffy to Blythe, 16 March 1922, ibid.
14 Bewley to Blythe, 21 March 1922, ibid.; Chartres to Duffy, 24 March 1922, ibid.

15 D'Abernon to Curzon, 26 March 1922, PROE, FO 371/7529 submitting a report made on 20 March 1922. Professor Pokorny is named as 'Tokorny'.
16 Ibid.
17 *Irish Times*, 18 March 1922 giving a report made on 14 March.
18 Duffy to Blythe, 27 March 1922, NA, DFA Berlin 1922–4.
19 Chartres to Duffy, 21 March 1922, one of two letters, ibid.
20 Bewley to person not named, 21 March 1922, ibid.
21 Bewley to Hayes, 2 Sept. 1922, Ibid., where he gives an account of his application.
22 Chartres to Duffy, 21 and 24 March 1922, ibid.
23 Power to Duffy, 29 March 1922, ibid.
24 *Dáil Éireann, Official Report*, 26 April 1922, p. 238.
25 Reain (Ryan) to Phil. (McGarrity), 27 March 1922, NLI, McGarrity, 17486(1).
26 Ryan to McGarrity, 19 Sept. 1922, ibid. Ryan states that the report to de Valera was sent some 5/6 months earlier.
27 O'Hegarty to Carter, 3 April 1923, UCDA, FitzGerald, P80/385(45)—this letter contains extracts from the de Valera letter.
28 McGuinness, *Nomad*, pp. 199–206 for the log of the journey; Greaves, *Mellows*, p. 306; MacEoin, *Survivors*, pp. 141,142 for the account of Pax O Faolain; Briscoe, *For the Life of Me*, p. 147—he was recalled to Ireland for the Army Convention of 26 March.
29 MacEoin, *Survivors*, p. 141 states the ship berthed on 2 April and went to the Customs for clearance on 4 April; McGuinness, *Nomad*, states the ship berthed and went to Customs on the same day, 4 April.
30 Power to Duffy, 26 April 1922, NLI, McGarrity, 17458(4); Grabisch to Dr [McCartan], 15 April 1922, ibid.; 'Cousin' [Ryan] to Mrs McGarrity, 18 May 1922, NLI, McGarrity, 17486(1), from Chihuahua, Mexico.
31 Chartres to Duffy, 24 March 1922, NA, DFA Paris 1922–1923; Duffy to Chartres, 29 March 1922, ibid.; Berlin Accounts, NA, DE 5/57/2 for payment of salary from 26 March 1922.
32 Cait O'Kelly to Mary MacSwiney, 26 March 1922, UCDA, MacSwiney, P48a/135(1).
33 Chartres to Duffy, 27 March 1922, NA, DFA Paris 1922–3.
34 Duffy to Chartres, 29 March 1922, ibid.
35 Chartres to Duffy, 13 April 1922; Chartres to Duffy, 9 May 1922; Murphy to Duffy, 12 May 1922; Chartres to Duffy, 2 June 1922; Murphy to Duffy, 9 June 1922; Duffy to Griffith, 27 May 1922, NA, DFA, Paris 1922–3. These letters help to specify when Chartres was in Paris.
36 Duffy to Chartres, 1 April 1922; Chartres to Duffy, 4 April 1922; Duffy to Chartres, 6 April 1922, ibid.
37 Chartres to Duffy, 3 April 1922, ibid.
38 Duffy to Chartres, 10 April 1922, ibid.
39 Duffy to Chartres, 4 April 1922, ibid.
40 Duffy to Dutton, 18 April 1922, NA, DFA London 1922–3. Dutton refused to take over from O'Brien and this led to a delay in terminating O'Brien's appointment. See Duffy to Chartres, 14 June 1922, NA, DFA Berlin 1922–4; Keogh, *Ireland and Europe*, pp. 17, 18.
41 Report on Foreign Affairs, April 1922, NA, DE 2/269; *Dáil Éireann, Official Report*, 26 April 1922, pp. 237–9.
42 *Dáil Éireann, Official Report*, 27 April 1922, p. 312.
43 Ibid.
44 Ibid. pp. 312, 313.
45 Collins to Chartres, 5 May 1922, NA, D/T S9242.
46 Chartres to Collins, 23 May 1922, ibid.
47 *Clonmel Nationalist*, 11 Aug. 1923.
48 Duffy to Griffith, 27 May 1922, NA, DFA Paris 1922–3.
49 Chartres to Duffy, 8 June 1922, ibid.

CHAPTER 11: *Berlin: the Dismissal of John Chartres and Nancy Power*

1 Chartres to Duffy, 14 June 1922, NA, DFA Berlin 1921–2.
2 Confidential Memo on Position of Ireland's Foreign Affairs at date of General Election, June 1922, NA, DE 4/8/6; another copy in UCDA, FitzGerald, P80/395.
3 Ibid.
4 Duffy to Moore, 14 June 1922, NA, DFA Paris 1922–3.
5 Confidential Memo, June 1922, NA, DE 4/8/6, p. 3 and p. 4.
6 Ibid., p. 11 and p. 4.
7 Duffy to Cosgrave, 20 June 1922, NA, D/T S1393.
8 Confidential Memo, June 1922, NA, DE 4/8/6, p. 12.
9 Chartres to Collins, 18 June 1922, NA, DE 5/27/1.
10 Chartres to Duffy, 18 June 1922; Duffy to Chartres, 19 June 1922, NA, DFA Berlin 1922–4.
11 Duffy to Griffith, 19 June 1922, NA, D/T S1393.
12 Ibid.
13 Ibid.
14 Griffith to Duffy, 20 June 1922, ibid.
15 Duffy to Collins, 20 June 1922, ibid.
16 Minutes of Provs. Govt., 12 July 1922, NA, G 1/2. Collins's appointment was formally confirmed on 20 July 1922.
17 Duffy to Cosgrave, 16 July 1922, NA, D/T S1393.
18 Chartres to Duffy, 17 July 1922, NA, DFA Berlin 1922–4.
19 Chartres to Walshe, 17 July 1922, ibid.
20 Bewley to Blythe, 17 July 1922, NA, D/T S2305; Kennedy to Cosgrave, 9 June 1924, UCDA, Kennedy Papers, P4/1203(1) refers to 'a collection of papers' in his possession relating to unpleasantness among the Dáil's German representatives. He delivered them to Cosgrave.
21 Ibid.
22 Ibid.
23 Bewley, *Memoirs,* p. 87. Bewley also incorrectly states that the Bulletin appeared twice monthly—it appeared twice weekly.
24 Blythe to Duffy, 21 July 1922, NA, DFA Berlin 1922–4.
25 Duffy to Chartres, 21 July 1922, ibid.
26 Ibid.
27 Chartres to Duffy, 23 July 1922, ibid.
28 Chartres to Duffy, 27 July 1922, ibid.
29 Ibid.
30 Ibid.
31 Ibid.
32 Chartres to Griffith, 27 July 1922, ibid.
33 Extract from Provs. Govt. minutes, 26 July 1922, NA, D/T S1393; the minutes for 11 Aug. 1922 state that the resignation took effect from 25 July.
34 Duffy to Collins, 24 July 1922, ibid.
35 *Freeman's Journal,* 19 Aug. 1922, for letter of Gavan Duffy giving his reasons for his resignation; *Freeman's Journal,* 21 Aug. 1922 for the Government's rejection of his reasons. See Diarmaid O'Cruadhlaoich, *Step by Step From the Republic Back into the Empire* (Dublin, nd.) for an account of the incident by Judge Crowley, the judge at the centre of the dispute. See also Mary Kotsonouris, *Retreat from Revolution* (Dublin, 1994).
36 Extract from Provs. Govt. minutes, 26 July 1922, NA, D/T S1393.
37 Blythe to each member of the Ministry, 27 July 1922, NA, D/T S2305.
38 Collins to Blythe, 28 July 1922, NA, DFA Berlin 1921–2. See Macready to Collins, 28 July 1922, NA, DFA Paris 1922–1923 for an indication that some of this news of Irish Foreign Affairs was known in British circles because of confusion over their cable codes—the British Army code was EGERTO; the Department of Foreign Affairs was ESTERO.
39 Boland to O'Kelly, 27 July 1922, UCDA, Mulcahy, P7/B/29/162; and ibid., P7/B/4.

40 Collins to Provs. Govt., 29 July 1922, ibid., P/B/29/159; and NA, D/T S1394.
41 Statement by Joe Griffin, Military Archives, Cathal Brugha Barracks, CD, Lot 227; UCDA, Mulcahy, P7/B/4; Cronin, *McGarrity*, pp. 120, 121; *Irish Press*, 1 Aug. 1938 for statement by Anna Kelly.
42 Walshe to Chartres, 3 Aug. 1922, NA, DFA Berlin 1921-2.
43 Walshe to Chartres, 8 Aug. 1922, ibid.
44 Ibid.
45 Bewley to Blythe, 8 Aug. 1922, UCDA, Kennedy, P4/860 and NA, D/T S2305.
46 Ibid.
47 Blythe to Kennedy, 17 Aug. 1922, ibid.; Blythe to Cosgrave, 17 Aug. 1922, NA, D/T 2305.
48 Memo (unsigned and undated), NA, D/T S2305. It is written in note form with abbreviations—Dept. for Department; F for Foreign.
49 Ibid.—he writes Govt. for Government and C's for Chartres's.
50 Chartres to Duffy, 27 July 1922, NA, DFA Berlin 1921-2.
51 Moore to Duffy, 18 July 1922, NA, DFA Paris 1922-3; Duffy to Cosgrave (with extract from Moore), 20 July 1922, NA, D/T S1393.
52 Chartres to Duffy, 27 July 1922, NA, DFA Berlin 1921-2.
53 Interview of Chartres with Hayes (Professor Michael), no date given, NA, D/T S2305.
54 Chartres to Hayes, 6 Sept. 1922, NA, DFA Berlin 1922-4.
55 Ibid.
56 Chartres to Cosgrave, 8 Sept. 1922, I, ibid., 1921-2.
57 Ibid.
58 Note on Work and Staff of Berlin Delegation, 21 Sept. 1922, ibid., 1922-4.
59 Ibid.
60 Bewley to Hayes, 2 Sept. 1922, ibid.
61 Chartres to External Affairs, 25 Sept. 1922, ibid.
62 Walshe to Chartres, 2 Oct. 1922, ibid; Walshe to Power, 2 Oct. 1922, ibid.
63 Chartres to FitzGerald, 4 Oct. 1922, ibid.
64 Walshe to Chartres, 5 Oct. 1922, ibid.
65 Chartres to FitzGerald, 6 Oct. 1922, ibid.
66 Chartres to Cosgrave, 28 Oct. 1922, ibid., 1921-2 in which Chartres refers to offering his resignation some three weeks earlier.
67 Chartres to Cosgrave, 12 Oct. 1922, ibid.
68 ibid.
69 Walshe to Chartres, 19 Oct. 1922, ibid., 1922-4.
70 Memo for Bewley, 21 Oct. 1922, ibid.
71. Chartres to Cosgrave, 28 Oct. 1922, ibid., 1921-2.
72 FitzGerald to Chartres, 30 Oct. 1922, ibid., 1922-4.
73 Ibid. There are very few references to Foreign Affairs in the Provs. Govt. minutes for Aug.–Dec. 1922 (NA, G 1/3) and no mention of the Chartres/Bewley controversy.
74 Chartres to FitzGerald, 2 Nov. 1922, ibid.
75 Patrick Campbell, *Thirty Five Years on the Job* (London, 1976), pp. 21 f. for an account of his father, Gordon Campbell, who had worked in the Ministry of Munitions during the War, although there is no recorded connection between him and Chartres at that time. Gordon Campbell's father, Lord Glenavy, was chairman of the first Irish Free State Senate.
76 Chartres to FitzGerald, 8 Nov. 1922, NA, DFA Berlin 1922-4.
77 Chartres to FitzGerald, 8 Nov. 1922, ibid.; Walshe to Chartres, 15 Nov. 1922, ibid.
78 Chartres to FitzGerald, 17 Nov. 1922, ibid.
79 Ó Lochlainn [O'Loughlin] to Breathach [Walshe], 25 and 28 Nov. 1922, ibid.—translated from the Irish; FitzGerald to Bewley, 30 Nov. 1922, ibid. Bewley was appointed on behalf of the 'Irish Government,' although the Free State Government did not officially function until 6 Dec. 1922.
80 Bank Statements of Chartres 1922-5, NA, DE 3/10/7; Chartres to Accnt. Gen., 13 and 15 Jan. 1923, NA, DE 5/27/3 for details of expenditure and the date of leaving Berlin.

81 Bewley to DEA, 4 Dec. 1922, NA, D/T S1917; Pokorny to DEA, 18 Jan. 1923, ibid.; Cabinet minutes, 9 Dec. 1922 and 27 Jan. 1923, NA, G 2/1 for this matter.

82 Bewley to DEA, 10 Feb. 1923, NA, DFA Berlin 1922-4.

83 Bewley, *Memoirs*, p. 88.

84 'Cousin' (Ryan) to McGarrity, 21 Sept. 1922, NLI, McGarrity, 17486(1).

85 Murphy, *Patrick Pearse*, p. 140; 'Cousin' (Ryan) to McGarrity, 13 Nov. 1922, ibid.; McGarrity to Stack, 23 Nov. 1922, ibid., 17640. See Troy Davis, 'The Irish Civil War and the 'International Proposition' of 1922-3', *Eire-Ireland*, Summer 1994, p. 98.

86 Lynch to McGarrity, 21 Dec. 1921, in Cronin, *McGarrity*, p. 132; Moylan to Liam (Lynch or Deasy), 28 Dec. 1922, UCDA, FitzGerald, P80/385(7); Michael Hopkinson, *Green against Green. The Irish Civil War* (Dublin, 1988) pp. 236, 237.

87 Davis, 'The Irish Civil War,' p. 99.

88 Statement by J.T. Ryan, 21 Feb. 1923, NLI, McGarrity 17486(1); Davis, 'The Irish Civil War,' p. 103.

89 Ibid.; Sister M.V. Tarpey, *The Role of Joseph McGarrity in the Struggle for Irish Independence* (Unpub. Thesis, Ann Arbor Univy., Michigan, 1970) p. 200; Gen. O'Hegarty to Col. Carter, 3 April 1923, UCDA, FitzGerald, P80/385(45).

90 Armstrong (British Consul General, NY) to FO, 12 Jan. 1923 and 18 Jan. 1923, PROE, FO 371/8488 and UCDA, FitzGerald, P80/385(14/1) for a copy of 12 Jan. 1923 letter, and NA, D/T S1976 for a copy of 18 Jan. 1923 letter.

91 Ibid.; O'Hegarty to Carter, 3 April 1923, UCDA, FitzGerald, P80/385(45); see John P. Duggan, *A History of the Irish Army* (Dublin, 1991) p. 100 for more on the structure of the Army.

92 Ibid.

93 Ryan to McGarrity, 14 May 1923, NLI, McGarrity, 17486(2); Davis, 'The Irish Civil War', p. 108.

94 Ryan to McGarrity, 4 June 1923, ibid.; Davis, 'The Irish Civil War', p. 110.

95 McGarrity to Ryan, 25 July 1923, ibid., 17486(3); Finerty to Ryan, 16 Dec. 1923, ibid., 17486(2).

96 *Irish Times*, 3 Jan. 1924; and NA, D/T S2305 for correspondence on the matter.

CHAPTER 12: *The Last Days of Chartres*

1 O'Driscoll, *Irish-German Diplomatic Relations*, p. 139; p. 151; p. 195; Keogh, *Ireland and Europe*, pp. 54-7.

2 Official to Cosgrave, 15 Jan. 1924, NA, D/T S2305.

3 Keatinge, *Irish Foreign Policy*, pp. 228 f. for some short and long term effects of the Civil War on Irish foreign policy.

4 O'Driscoll, *Irish-German Diplomatic Relations*, p. 64.

5 *Dáil Éireann, Parliamentary Debates*, 25 June 1923, vol. 3, col. 2394; See D.W. Harkness, *The Restless Dominion. The Irish Free State and the British Commonwealth of Nations 1921-'31* (Dublin, 1969) Chps. 1-4 for an excellent account of these events, although his opinion that Gavan Duffy's 'policy survived' (p. 32) requires some qualification in the light of the rejection of his plans for Europe.

6 Accnt. Gen. to Walshe, 24 Jan. 1923, NA, DE 5/27/3.

7 Chartres to Accnt. Gen., 8 Feb. 1925, Ibid.; Secy. Finance to Walshe, 8 April 1925, ibid.

8 Chartres to FitzGerald, 6 Jan. 1923, NA, DFA Berlin 1922-4; Walshe to Chartres, 9 and 19 Jan. 1923, ibid.

9 Nancy Power Statement, p. 13; *Irish Independent*, 4 Nov. 1935.

10 *The Nation*, 26 March 1927.

11 Ibid., 21 May 1927.

12 Power to ed. of *The Nation*, 21 May 1927, published on 28 May 1927.

13 *Clonmel Nationalist*, 11 Aug. 1923.

14 Ibid.

15 Barton to Duffy, 30 July 1924, Gavan Duffy family private papers.

16 Jones, *Whitehall Diary*, p. 184.

17 Nancy Power Statement, pp. 12, 13.

18 Chartres to Mulcahy, 5 Feb. 1924, UCDA, Mulcahy, P35b/137; Mansergh, *The Unresolved Question*, pp. 219–23 for the Boundary issue; Geoffrey J. Hand (introd. by), *Report of the Irish Boundary Commission in 1925* (Shannon, 1969)

19 Ibid.

20 *The Nation*, 26 March 1927.

21 Ibid.

22 Ibid., 2 April 1927.

23 Ibid.

24 Ibid., 28 May 1927.

25 *Irish Independent*, 16 May 1927 for death notice; 17 May for short tribute; 18 May for details of funeral; *Irish Times*, 16 May 1927 for death notice; 17 May for short tribute; *The Times*, 18 May 1927 for obituary.

26 Entry of Grant and Estate Duty Affidavit, John Smith Chartres, NA.

27 Correspondence with Michel Fuchs, University of Nice. I have no official record of her death.

28 Correspondence with George Chartres the family genealogist.

29 *Irish Times* and *Irish Independent*, 28 Dec. 1963; Robins, *Custom House People*, pp. 107, 108.

30. Keogh, *Ireland and Europe*, pp. 38, 39.

31 *Irish Times*, 30 May 1969; Briscoe, *For the Life of Me*, p. 315.

32 *Irish Times*, 3 Feb. 1969; Bewley, *Memoirs*, chps. 9–11.

33 Gerard Harrington, 'The Adventures of C.P.O. Charlie McGuinness', *Cork Holly Bough*, 1992.

34 Cronin, *McGarrity*, pp. 167–74.

35 Entry of Grant and Estate Duty Affidavit, John Smith Chartres, NA.

36 Jones, *Whitehall Diary*, p. 19; Julian Putkowski, 'Jack Byrnes, A2 and the IRA', *Lobster— Journal of Parapolitics*, No. 28, 1994.

37 Ibid., p. 175.

38 *Irish Independent*, 23 Oct. 1935.

Bibliography

Summary of Abbreviations for reference purposes

DE   Dáil Éireann
DFA   Department of Foreign Affairs
D/T   Department of Taoiseach
KDV   Killiney Archive—de Valera Papers
KGD   Killliney Archive—Gavan Duffy Papers
NA   National Archive
NLI   National Library of Ireland
PROE   Public Records Office, England
TCDM   Trinity College Dublin Manuscripts
UCDA   University College Dublin Archives

INSTITUTIONAL ARCHIVES AND PUBLIC RECORDS

House of Lords Records Office
Lloyd George Papers

Killiney Archives (Franciscan Fathers, Dún Mhuire)
Eamon de Valera Papers (KDV). Of special value were items 109, Dáil Éireann papers 1919; 141, Cabinet and Ministry notes 1921; 148, reports by Minister of Defence 1921; 151, correspondence with Michael Collins, 1921; 1375, correspondence with Gavan Duffy; 1471, correspondence with Sean T. O'Kelly; 1473, diary of Kathleen O'Connell.
Gavan Duffy Papers (KGD)

National Archives Ireland (NA)
Barton Papers
Dáil Éireann Cabinet and Ministry Minutes; Provisional Government Minutes; Irish Free State Cabinet Minutes.
Dáil Éireann Files (NA, DE) Of special value were 2/269, Foreign Affairs, 1919–1922; 2/270, Foreign Affairs and Germany, 1920–2; 2/304, Treaty negotiations, 1921; 3/10 and 3/12 series on Foreign Affairs accounts; 5/26 representation in Paris 1919–23; 5/27 representation and accounts, Berlin 1921–5.
Department of Foreign Affairs Files (NA, DFA)—Paris/France 1919–20, 1922–3.
Department of Foreign Affairs Files (NA, DFA)—Berlin 1921–2, 1922–4.
Department of Foreign Affairs (NA, DFA)—London 1922–3
Department of Taoiseach Files (NA, D/T) Of special value were S1393, resignation of Gavan Duffy; S2305, closure of the Berlin office 1922–4.

Gavan Duffy Papers 1125
Grant and Estate Duty Affidavit of John Smith Chartres
Lynch, Fionan, Papers DE 4/5/21

Note: All the above papers are in the National Archives at Bishop Street except the Barton
          Papers which are at the Four Courts.

National Library of Ireland (NLI)
John Devoy Papers 18094
George Gavan Duffy Papers 15439
Joseph McGarrity Papers 17458, 17486, 17640

Military Archives, Cathal Brugha Barracks

Public Records Office England (PROE)
Foreign Office Files
Ministry of Munitions Files
Sturgis Diary

Trinity College Dublin Manuscripts (TCDM)
Erskine Childers Papers

University College Dublin Archives (UCDA)
Desmond FitzGerald Papers
Hugh Kennedy Papers
Mary MacSwiney Papers
Richard Mulcahy Papers

Private Papers
Statement of Nancy Wyse Power to the Bureau of Military History

OFFICIAL PUBLICATIONS

Dáil Éireann, Minutes of Proceedings 1919–1921 (Dublin, nd.)
Dáil Éireann, Official Report (16–26 Aug. 1921 and 28 Feb.–8 June 1922) (Dublin, nd.)
Dáil Éireann, Parliamentary Debates, Official Record.
Documents Relative to the Sinn Féin Movement (London, 1921)
Intercourse between Bolshevism and Sinn Féin (London, 1921)
Official Report, Debates on the Treaty between Great Britain and Ireland (Dublin, nd.)

JOURNALS AND NEWSPAPERS

An Phoblacht
Capuchin Annual
Clonmel Nationalist
Collectanea Hibernica
Freeman's Journal
Irish Historical Studies
Irish Independent

Irish Press
Irish Press (Philadelphia)
Irish Times
Nationality
The Nation
The Times

REFERENCE BOOKS AND ARCHIVAL SOURCES

Burke's Irish Family Records (1976)
Burtchaell, G. and Sadlier, T. (ed.), *Alumni Dublinenses 1593–1860* (Dublin, 1935)
Drew Rolls, Army Medical Service
Imperial Calendar
Instituto della Enciclopedia Italiana, Fondata Da Giovanni Treccani (1950)
Land Owners in Ireland c.1876 (Baltimore, 1988)
Manager's Letter Files, News International
Peterkin, A. and Johnston, W. (eds) *Commissioned Officers in the Medical Service of the British Army 1660–1960* (London, 1968)
Register of Admissions, Middle Temple, London
Register of Licentiates, Royal College of Surgeons, Ireland
Royal College of Surgeons, Ireland, *The Medical Register* (1861)
Thom's Irish Almanac and Official Directory
University of London, General Register
Wellington College Register

PUBLISHED SOURCES: BOOKS AND ARTICLES

Barton, R., *The Truth about the Treaty and Document Number 2* (Dublin, 1922)
Bewley, C., *Memoirs of a Wild Goose* (Dublin, 1989)
Birkenhead, Earl of, *The Life of F.E. Smith, First Earl of Birkenhead* (London, 1959)
Boyle, A., *The Riddle of Erskine Childers* (London, 1977)
Brennan, R., *Allegiance* (Dublin, 1950)
Briscoe, R. (with Hatch, A.), *For the Life of Me* (London, 1958)
Campbell, P., *Thirty Five Years on the Job* (London, 1976)
Carroll, F.M., *American Opinion and the Irish Question 1910–1923* (Dublin, 1978)
Chartres, J.['Edward Seaton'], 'The Bloody English', *Irish Press* (Philadelphia) 7 Jan. – 15 April 1922.
Chartres, J. ['Fear Faire], 'The English Peril', *The Nation*, 26 March, 2 and 9 April, 1927.
Coogan, T.P., *Michael Collins* (London, 1990)
Cronin, S., *The McGarrity Papers* (Tralee, 1972)
Curran, J.M., *The Birth of the Irish Free State 1921–1923* (Alabama, 1980)
Davis, T., 'The Irish Civil War and the "International Proposition" of 1922–1923', *Eire–Ireland*, Summer 1994.
Duggan, J.P., *A History of the Irish Army* (Dublin, 1991)
Dwyer, T.R., *Michael Collins and the Treaty. His Differences with de Valera* (Cork and Dublin, 1981)
Gaffney, St. John, *Breaking the Silence. England, Ireland, Wilson and the War* (New York, 1930)
Gallagher, F. (ed. O'Neill, T.P.), *The Anglo-Irish Treaty* (London, 1965)
Gaughan, J.A., *Austin Stack: Portrait of a Separatist* (Dublin, 1977)
—— *Alfred O'Rahilly, vol.11, Public Figure* (Dublin, 1989)
Golding, G.M., *George Gavan Duffy 1882–1951* (Dublin, 1982)
Greaves, C.D., *Liam Mellows and the Irish Revolution* (London, 1971)
Hand, G.J. (introd.), *Report of the Irish Boundary Commission 1925* (Shannon, 1969)
Harkness, D.W., *The Restless Dominion. The Irish Free State and the British Commonwealth of Nations* (Dublin, 1969)
Harrington, G., 'The Adventures of C.P.O. Charlie McGuinness', *Cork Holly Bough*, 1992.
Hiden, J., *Germany and Europe 1919–1939* (London, 1993; first edition, 1977)
Hopkinson, M., *Green Against Green. The Irish Civil War* (Dublin, 1988)
Jones, T. (ed. Middlemas, K.), *Whitehall Diary vol. III. Ireland 1918–1925* (London, 1971)
Keatinge, P., *The Formulation of Irish Foreign Policy* (Dublin, 1973)
Keogh, D., *The Vatican, the Bishops and Irish Politics 1919–1939* (Cambridge, 1986)

—— 'The Treaty Split and the Paris-Irish Race Convention', *Etudes Irlandaises*, No. 12, Dec. 1987.

—— *Ireland and Europe 1919–1989* (Cork and Dublin, 1990)

Kotsonouris, M., *Retreat form Revolution* (Dublin, 1994)

Lawlor, S., *Britain and Ireland 1914–1923* (Dublin, 1983)

Longford, Earl of, and O'Neill, T.P., *Eamon de Valera* (Dublin, 1970)

MacEoin, U., *Survivors* (Dublin, 1980)

McGuinness, C.J., *Nomad* (London, 1934)

McKenna, K.N., 'In London with the Treaty Delegates', *Capuchin Annual* (1971)

Mansergh, N., *The Unresolved Question. The Anglo-Irish Settlement and its Undoing 1912–1972* (New Haven and London, 1991)

Mitchell, A. and Ó Snodaigh, P., *Irish Political Documents 1916–1949* (Dublin, 1985)

Murphy, B.P., *Patrick Pearse and the Lost Republican Ideal* (Dublin, 1991)

O Beirne-Ranelagh, J., 'The IRB from the Treaty to 1924', *Irish Historical Studies*, vol.xx, no.77, March 1976.

Ó Broin, L., *Revolutionary Underground* (Dublin, 1976)

—— *Michael Collins* (Dublin, 1980)

O'Cruadhlaoich, D., *Step by Step. From the Republic Back into the Empire* (No place or date of publication)

Ó Cuinneagáin, M., *On the Arm of Time, Ireland 1916–1922* (Donegal, 1992)

O'Driscoll, M., 'Irish-German Diplomatic Relations 1922–1939' (Unpublished MA Thesis, UCC, 1992)

Ó Fiannachta, P. (ed.), *Sean T.* (vol. II) (Dublin, 1972)

Ó Luing, S., *Kuno Meyer 1858–1919. A Biography* (Dublin, 1991)

O'Neill, M., *From Parnell to de Valera. A Biography of Jennie Wyse Power, 1858–1941* (Dublin, 1991)

Pakenham. F., *Peace by Ordeal* (London, 1935)

Peukert, D.J.K., *The Weimar Republic* (London, 1993; first edition, 1987)

Putkowski, J., 'Jack Byrnes, A2 and the IRA', *Lobster – Journal of Parapolitics*, No. 28, 1994.

Robins, J., *Custom House People* (Dublin, 1993)

Ryan, J.T., 'The Origin of the *Aud* Expedition', *An Phoblacht*, 25 April 1931.

Sexton, Brendan, *Ireland and the Crown 1922–1936. The Governor Generalship of the Irish Free State* (Dublin, 1989)

Tarpey, Sr M.V., 'The Role of Joseph McGarrity in the Struggle for Irish Independence' (unpublished thesis, Ann Arbor University, 1970)

Taylor, R., *Michael Collins* (London, 1958)

Tierney, M., 'Calendar of Irlande, vols.1, 2, 3 in the collection of Europe, 1918–1929, in the Archives Diplomatiques, Paris', *Collectanea Hibernica* (1979–80)

Valiulis, M.G., *Portrait of a Revolutionary. General Richard Mulcahy and the Founding of the Irish Free State* (Dublin, 1992)

Index